RAILWAYS IN VICTORIAN LONDON

RAILWAYS IN VICTORIAN LONDON

HOW RAILWAY DEVELOPMENT CHANGED LONDON

DAVID BRANDON

PEN & SWORD
TRANSPORT

AN IMPRINT OF PEN & SWORD BOOKS LTD.
YORKSHIRE - PHILADELPHIA

First published in Great Britain in 2025 by
Pen and Sword Transport
An imprint of
Pen & Sword Books Ltd.
Yorkshire - Philadelphia

ISBN 978 1 39905 112 5

Typeset in 11/14 Palatino by SJmagic DESIGN SERVICES, India.

Printed and bound in India by Replika Press Pvt. Ltd.

Pen & Sword Books Ltd. incorporates the imprints of Pen & Sword Books: After the Battle, Archaeology, Atlas, Aviation, Battleground, Discovery, Family History, History, Maritime, Military, Politics, Select, Transport, True Crime, Fiction, Frontline Books, Leo Cooper, Praetorian Press, Seaforth Publishing, Wharncliffe and White Owl.

For a complete list of Pen & Sword titles please contact

PEN & SWORD BOOKS LIMITED
George House, Beevor Street, Off Pontefract Road, Hoyle Mill, Barnsley,
South Yorkshire, England, S71 1HN.
E-mail: enquiries@pen-and-sword.co.uk
Website: www.pen-and-sword.co.uk

or

PEN AND SWORD BOOKS
1950 Lawrence Rd, Havertown, PA 19083, USA
E-mail: uspen-and-sword@casematepublishers.com
Website: www.penandswordbooks.com

CONTENTS

INTRODUCTION

For many years I have been interested in the history of London and the history of railways and have written several books on both subjects. Here I consider aspects of the impact and influence of the railways on London from the 1830s to the early part of the twentieth century. After a brief introduction, the book consists of essays or pieces on selected elements of this very diverse subject. Reference to some subjects may be found in two or more places. A comprehensive history of London's railways during the period under review would necessarily require a much larger volume. A short bibliography may help those wanting to read more widely.

Railways revolutionised the world, totally changing previous concepts of time, distance and speed. They initiated the communications revolution which continues in ever more complex forms to this day. They created a unified nation from the disparate parts composing the British Isles. They contributed greatly to consolidating the domination of London over so many aspects of British life. In the nineteenth century, London became the commercial and financial centre of the world, literally the world's leading city. It was also the capital of the British Empire, the largest empire the world had witnessed. Railways contributed greatly to this process.

Even before it gained railways, London's population far outstripped Britain's other cities. In the nineteenth century, its population grew by over 3.5 million. Its economic growth and outward physical expansion were greatly assisted by the development of a highly complex network of surface and underground railways. London housed many of the richest and most powerful people in Britain while, by contrast, possessing some of Britain's worst slums, scenes of poverty, deprivation and despair. Such juxtapositions were more evident in London than elsewhere. Henry Mayhew and J. Binny very effectively captured this contradictory character in the Introduction to *The Criminal Prisons of London* published in book form in 1862:

Viewing the Great Metropolis as an absolute world, Belgravia and Bethnal Green become the opposite poles of the London sphere – the frigid zones, as it were, of the Capital; the one icy cold from its exceeding fashion, form and ceremony; and the other wrapt in a perpetual winter of withering poverty.

In the last decades of the nineteenth century London was still growing rapidly but there were signs that its, and Britain's, world pre-eminence was under threat. The expense of running and policing the Empire was outstripping its economic and political benefits. Other European powers were engaging in their own imperial adventures. More ominously, they were also rapidly industrialising without experiencing the difficult trial and error experience that its pioneering role in the process had enforced on Britain. German unification had placed a major economic, naval and military threat right on Britain's doorstep. Other leading nations had noted Britain's poor showing in the Boer War (1899-1902). Large numbers of young, mostly working-class, men were rejected for active service as unfit on medical grounds, highlighting the inadequacy of Britain's social priorities and policies. Troubled labour relations, the seemingly insoluble 'Irish problem' and the growing tensions around the issue of women's political rights were all evidence of severe political and social stresses. Britain's seemingly unassailable earlier optimism and confidence concerning her role in the world was painfully eroding.

London is a living organism undergoing continuing and continuous change. Even the meaning of the word 'London' was shifting in the nineteenth century. Once, 'London' had primarily referred to the historic 'City' but now it included Westminster, the West End and the other closely built-up suburbs which were insidiously penetrating Surrey, Kent, Middlesex and Essex, and each other. London supported substantial numbers of rich people who, for centuries, had migrated from its filth, clamour, overcrowding and underlying menace to outlying settlements such as Uxbridge, Harrow, Chiswick, Dulwich, Enfield and Epping. They became increasingly dependent on their proximity to London. Enclaves of affluence remained in central London, continuing to emphasise the gap between London's rich and poor.

The railways reinforced the process whereby London's boundaries extended. They made an important contribution to London's growth. For railways to be built connecting suburbs to the centre, there had to be work opportunities in central London as well as other attractions for potential passengers. The jobs had to be sufficiently well-paid to enable employees to afford the train fares and the rent for their new suburban homes. Speculative builders were taking risks building homes on green field sites as were railway companies in hoping that housing development would follow the opening of lines and stations. Any understanding of London's extraordinary spatial and economic growth in the nineteenth century must take account of the contribution made by the railways.

The drive to promote and finance railways especially in the mid-century and the prodigious amounts of capital required for this purpose contributed greatly to the reinvention of the City of London as a specialised financial and commercial district having little need of a resident population. The City enjoyed a boom in an expanding

A well-known drawing by Gustav Doré looking up Ludgate Hill to St. Paul's and showing the extent of road traffic chaos in the 1870s. Note the steam train of the London, Chatham and Dover Railway crossing the controversial bridge connecting lines north and south of the Thames.

mid-Victorian economy which required new banks, insurance companies and various other institutions dealing in financial instruments such as stocks and shares. The drive of the railways to raise large amounts of capital greatly encouraged the growth of the financial and commercial sectors of the economy. Employment in the City increased exponentially simultaneously with its resident population emptying out. Intentionally imposing and prestigious office buildings sprang up, sometimes displacing ancient churches on the same sites and encapsulating the triumph of the material over the spiritual. The old coaching inns, which were so redolent of the golden age of the stagecoach, closed, were converted for other uses or were demolished. They had no place in the age of the railway. Instead of long-distance coaches converging on the City, it was now commuters. In 1854, about 624,000 entered the City on every working day. While most came from the inner suburbs and walked, 54,000 used trains.

Railways had an enormous impact on the everyday life of Victorian and Edwardian London and as late as the 1920s, most of the haulage of coal and general merchandise around central London was still performed by horses. Huge numbers were employed by the railway companies for collection and distribution. On the move, they produced an absolute cacophony on streets now largely paved with setts. Horse droppings and the undesirable creatures these attracted were the bane of the streets and urban life. In dry weather the droppings turned to dust which blew around covering all surfaces, getting into clothing, human orifices and open windows and doors. In wet weather the streets were awash with pools of ordure and other filth.

In the 1870s the French artist Gustav Doré produced a vivid visual impression of traffic congestion in Ludgate Hill looking towards St Paul's. There are dozens of horses and their attendant conveyances as well as large numbers of pedestrians milling about in a depiction of total chaos and traffic gridlock. The confusion is compounded by someone trying to drive a flock of sheep through the city streets. This is a reminder that while London was by far the largest centre of population in Britain, even then the countryside was still not far away.

In 1862, *Building News* informed its readers, 'We, who are constantly in the presence of the wondrous results produced by the locomotive and the rail, are apt to pass them by unnoticed, or at least without comment.' In warning readers against this tendency, it continued:

The invasion of the Metropolis by the 'Steam Horse' has, during the last quarter of a century, produced changes, not only in the physical features, but also in the manners, customs, modes of living, and even in the thoughts of its inhabitants, which are almost incredible. For a century previous to the year 1834, stagnation was the order of the day; but then came the locomotive into London, and all was changed.

One of several schemes for elevated railways to relieve gridlock on London's roads. This, the 'London Grand Junction Railway' would have run from the Clerkenwell district to Camden but it was never built.

The *Builder* in 1870 asked 'What would London now do without a railway? What would become of the immense holiday crowds who are regularly whirled over the country, fifty miles and back, in a single day…if the railways were suddenly to shut up shop?'

The *Builder,* aimed at readers many of whom would have had at least some involvement with railway construction, was understandably given to being very upbeat about their impact. Inevitably perhaps, this enthusiasm was not universal. The *New Quarterly* was positively curmudgeonly in an article in 1854:

Cast your eye for a moment on yonder train about to start and answer conscientiously whether it is possible to conceive anything much more clumsy or more thoroughly frightful than the boxes into which some 200 passengers are being stowed, unless it be the snorting and shrieking machine they are about to pursue.

The Thames Tunnel was a long time in the building. Work started in the 1800s, but it was not completed until 1843. What was supposed to be a two-carriageway road under the Thames ended up as a foot tunnel because money was not available to complete the ramps needed for vehicular traffic. The tunnel became a tourist attraction and was later notorious for the activities of thieves and prostitutes. In the 1860s it was converted into a railway tunnel. It remains a vital part of London's railway infrastructure.

In briefly considering various aspects of the changes brought about by railways in the London area, the period being covered is from the earliest days to the Grouping of the railway companies in 1923. This date was chosen because the rolling stock, the installations and the fittings of the railways, their working practices and their ethos were still then predominantly Victorian.

Chapter 1

SOME ASPECTS OF THE IMPACT OF THE RAILWAYS ON LONDON

GEOGRAPHIC AND DEMOGRAPHIC FACTORS

Any consideration of the impact of railways on London needs to examine the geomorphology of its location. London lies in a basin with the Chilterns to the north and the North Downs to the south. Low hills extend from the Chilterns and form the 'Northern Heights' around Hampstead, Highgate and Alexandra Palace. To the south, outriders of the North Downs are to be found at places like Streatham, Dulwich and Forest Hill. Through the basin flows the River Thames in a generally west to east direction. Many tributaries join the Thames in Greater London and flow in valleys which had a bearing on the alignment followed by some of London's railways. One of these valleys is clearly visible where the Fleet River flows below ground from the King's Cross district through Clerkenwell and Holborn to join the Thames just north of Fleet Street. Significantly, the Metropolitan, London's first underground railway, used this valley to reach its eastern terminus at Farringdon. The far more recent Docklands Light Railway follows the valley of the Ravensbourne after passing through Greenwich and heading for Lewisham.

London lies on an uneven bed of gravel, clay, sand and chalk greatly influenced by a period of glaciation around 500,000 years ago. Where it passes through London, the Thames has created a low-lying alluvial flood plain usually around two or three miles wide. These natural features have had a major bearing on the patterns of settlement around London. Before modern drainage systems became available, the subsoil largely dictated which areas would be used for building. A subsoil mostly of gravel drains freely whereas clay is impervious and was very difficult to work until modern means of tunnelling and excavation came into use in the nineteenth century. This meant that it was largely in the areas where gravel was predominant that building development had taken place. They therefore had the population to attract the interest of some early railway companies wanting to develop the potential traffic they offered.

In 1801, the population of London was just over one million. In 1822, William Cobbett, who lived in Kensington, set out to ride to Lewes in Sussex. His journey took him across the Thames to Kennington Common, Stockwell, well-heeled parts of Brixton and onwards to Croydon. He complained bitterly about what he saw: 'London and Croydon is [sic] as ugly a bit of country as any in England'. Warming to his theme, he likened London to a great festering sore, an 'infernal Wen' which he thought was sucking the strength and goodness out of the rest of England. He complains that houses cover half the nine miles to Croydon from Southwark and is particularly scathing about 'two entire miles of stock-jobbers' houses'.

London was spreading, accumulating suburbs which surrounded the ancient nucleus which had been relatively compact.

There was already a considerable network of short-stage coaches serving London. In 1825 there were about 600 such coaches providing around 1,800 journeys a day connecting the City and Westminster to such districts as Paddington, Camberwell and Clapham. Communication by road was vital to London and several new turnpike roads were built early in the nineteenth century. These included New North Road, Archway Road, Caledonian Road and the roads from St George's Circus in Southwark to the new bridges across the Thames which were improving access to the City and Westminster. However, a crisis point was soon going to be reached where the capacity of London's road system was unable to keep up with the increasing traffic resulting from the growth in its trade, business activity and population. Central London was in danger of strangulation!

We can be sure that Cobbett would have resorted to expletives had he done the same journey in 1911. By this time, London covered a vastly greater area and its population had risen to over seven million. New forms of public transport had been an essential factor in expediting that growth. Although these transport conduits largely converged on central London and had made movement around the capital quicker and easier, they also had a divisive effect. The ability to use them depended on the ability to pay. This led to a growing residential segregation of the various layers of society based on their levels of income. In medieval London rich and poor had frequently lived cheek-by-jowl. In the later seventeenth and the eighteenth centuries, pockets of concentrated affluence began to appear with elegant residential streets and squares mostly to the west of the area regarded as the traditional City, much of which had been immolated in the Great Fire of 1666. The tendency throughout the period under review and greatly encouraged especially by surface and underground railways was for the well-to-do and even the moderately better-off to move out of the City, either to desirable areas of the West End or somewhat further afield away from the noise, dirt and overcrowding of London's central districts. The poor mostly needed to remain living in inner areas within walking distance of their employment. Cheap workmen's railway fares introduced in the 1860s and becoming widely available in the 1880s, plus the later appearance of electric trams allowed many of those in regular work in central London to move home from the centre to new inner suburbs initially of an almost entirely working-class character. The large numbers of workers employed on a casual basis for example in the building trades, in the docks and in markets had little choice but to remain living close to where work might, or might not, be available. Another layer of working people was the lower middle class, often in clerical employment. They frequently saw themselves as a cut above what later became known as 'blue-collar' workers. Anxious to ape the middle classes, Mr Pooter, in that minor literary classic of 1892, George and Weedon Grossmith's *The Diary of a Nobody,* is the archetype of the aspirant to higher social status. He feels he has 'arrived' when, with his darling wife Carrie, he takes up residence in his new abode in Holloway, The Laurels, Brickfield Terrace. He describes it as 'a nice six-roomed residence, not counting basement, with a front breakfast-parlour. We have a little front garden; and there is a flight of ten steps up to the front door… We have a nice little back garden which runs down to the railway…' The Pooters of this world wanted to live with others of their ilk. Holloway was a 'cut above'. They and others who were better-off wanted to emphasise their relative status by retreating into what were largely one-class residential areas. Public transport helped them to do this and therefore both united and divided London.

The flight to the suburbs was very real for those wanting greater space and privacy. And then sometimes a further flight. In 1871, for instance, John Ruskin gave up his villa in Denmark Hill because new building development was encroaching on this leafy quarter and he moved further out. Each flight out of Central London left behind it an area already in decline into which the poor soon moved. Ironically, in the sixteenth and seventeenth centuries, much of the worst housing had been on the outskirts of the built-up area but now it was increasingly concentrated in several notorious pockets of poverty frequently referred to as 'rookeries'. Such districts, and St Giles and Seven Dials were among the worst, housed seething populations who gained a frugal living largely from begging and crime. Strangers penetrated such districts at their peril. The inhabitants had little use for public transport. Charles Booth was a social researcher who calculated that in the 1890s over thirty per cent of Londoners lived in poverty, two-thirds of which was caused by what he described as 'irregular employment'. Periods of illness or inability to work such as old age were dreaded. They would largely have been unable to afford to use London's growing public transport infrastructure.

By 1900, the more-or-less continuously built-up area of London extended as far as Kentish Town, Kilburn and Hammersmith in the west; Fulham, Wandsworth and Tooting in the south-west; Streatham and Sydenham in the south; Lewisham and Woolwich in the south-east; Millwall, Bow and Hackney in the east and Highbury and Highgate in the north.

The population of London and the county in which it was located was 1,114,000 in 1801. In 1861 this had grown to 3,223,000 and to 7,251,000 by 1911. This was headlong growth by any standards and the creation of the railway network was a vital factor in enabling this development to take place.

THE RAILWAYS COME TO LONDON

England's road system, extensively upgraded by the 1830s, had London as its hub. The earliest railways were largely built to serve the needs of the coal mining, quarrying and iron industries. They covered short distances and were usually designed to carry the bulky and heavy materials associated with those industries to the nearest navigable waterway. The areas they operated in tended to be distant from London and so, despite the capital's predominant position in the country's economy, railways appeared comparatively late in London. The first line, the Surrey Iron Railway, was sanctioned in 1801. It was a simple plateway with horse traction and it linked industrial enclaves around Croydon and the Wandle Valley with the Thames at Wandsworth. In that sense, it replicated the early railways in the industrial and coal-mining districts of the provinces. Many consider the Surrey Iron Railway to be the world's first public railway.

The first major railway in the metropolis is generally regarded as being the London & Greenwich (L&GR) which opened in stages between 1836 and 1838. The

Part of the viaduct on which the London and Greenwich Railway was built. Note the dwellings in the arches. Noise and vibration made these uninhabitable.

L&GR, about four miles long, was promoted largely to serve commuters from the Greenwich area into central London. It was not markedly successful in that venture, although it proved popular for 'leisure' travel, Londoners traditionally enjoying the delights of Greenwich on summer evenings and at weekends. Beer was quaffed and vast numbers of whitebait suppers were consumed. It became the custom to use river steamers in one direction and the railway in the other. This line used a legal procedure established for the building of the canals. This involved the compulsory purchase of land and often the demolition of large numbers of buildings along the route. Inevitably this process aroused controversy and had its victims. The land acquired for this line, however, was comparatively cheap and caused little disruption because much of it ran across largely unused terrain. Slum streets in Southwark that disappeared in a heap of rubble under the advance of this line included the delightfully named but less than delightful Frying Pan Alley, Foot's Folley, Oatmeal Yard and Crucifix Lane.

The line to Greenwich was built entirely on a viaduct consisting of no less than 878 arches. Viaducts were to become a feature of the railways approaching London across the flat terrain south of the Thames. The structures used on the approaches

An old coach of the Eastern Counties Railway. Its derivation from earlier stagecoaches is obvious.

to London varied with the nature of the local terrain. Cuttings and tunnels were characteristic of the lines threading the hilly districts on their way into King's Cross, St Pancras, Marylebone and Euston Stations. Liverpool Street managed to combine viaducts and cuttings. The L&GR had hoped to let its arches for residential purposes but failed to attract much interest. The Lord Mayor of London graced the opening ceremony and rather pompously declared that the railway would contribute 'to the happiness by promoting the wealth and the domestic comfort of that large class of the citizens of London whose villas adorned the picturesque scenes which abounded in the neighbourhood…' He was not referring to the woebegone inhabitants of Frying Pan Alley.

The London & Birmingham Railway (L&BR), completed in 1838, was unquestionably one of the largest public works ever undertaken anywhere in the world. Such projects demanded coal, timber, iron and bricks on an unprecedented scale and these requirements could only be met by greatly expanding the productive capacity of the relevant industries. Railway building therefore stimulated industrial growth and economic expansion. Coal, iron and steam power came together to

King's Cross Metropolitan Railway Station showing trains on mixed-gauge track shared with the Great Western Railway.

The early signals at London Bridge give an idea of the skills needed by engine drivers to ensure the safe movement of their trains.

provide huge numbers of new industrial jobs which in turn helped a mass-migration of country-dwellers to towns in search of economic betterment.

London's railway age had begun. By the end of 1852, trains of the London, Brighton and South Coast (LB&SCR) and South Eastern Railways (SER) were running into London Bridge, Waterloo was served by the London & South Western Railway (L&SWR), Fenchurch Street mainly by the London & Blackwall, Bishopsgate by the Eastern Counties and King's Cross by the Great Northern Railway (GNR). Euston hosted what had now become the London & North Western Railway (L&NWR) and Paddington the Great Western (GWR). A pattern had already been established whereby none of these terminus stations penetrated the most central parts of London. The capital was now connected with Birmingham, the Midlands and the North, East Anglia, Yorkshire and the East Midlands, the principal towns of the South Coast, Bristol and Holyhead and South Wales via Swindon and Gloucester.

Other surface lines followed. The first underground railway, the Metropolitan, opened in 1863, constructed on a shallow cut-and-cover basis. It ran from Paddington to Farringdon Street in the City. Its success in relieving road congestion quickly led to similar lines being opened. London's – and indeed the world's – pioneer deep-level tube electric railway was the City & South London, the first part of which ran from King William Street in the City under the Thames to Stockwell, opened in 1890. More deep-level tube lines followed but as far as public transport was concerned, the horse bus and horse tram were pre-eminent right into the 1890s. The first electric trams ran in 1901. An intensive network of electric tramways developed. Their cheapness, frequency and the convenience offered by their many stops meant that they came to provide robust competition for local stopping trains, particularly in the inner suburbs. Indeed, some inner suburban stations closed permanently during the First World War, ostensibly because of staff shortages but really because they had become unviable. Their passengers had largely switched to the electric trams. These vehicles were, however, banned from entering most of central London.

Some of the railway companies at first displayed little interest in providing services for those wanting short journeys within the metropolis. The L&BR when it opened had its first intermediate station as far out as Harrow, the GWR its first at Ealing. The interest of both companies was to develop long-distance travel

A District Railway station in 1897.

An early locomotive of the London & Birmingham Railway emerging from the engine house at Camden built to serve trains at Euston Station.

to and from the capital. They reasoned, at least initially, that the development of suburban traffic would create congestion and obstruct the movement of the long-distance traffic which they wanted to encourage as potentially more lucrative. Other later companies, such as that which became the Great Eastern Railway (GER), however, were eager to act as agents of demographic change and build lines which substantially contributed to the development of suburbs with a predominantly lower middle-class and skilled working-class character. Just how quickly some of these places developed is shown by the growth of West Ham. Its population rose from 6,500 to 267,400 between the 1801 and 1901 censuses. This sort of growth was not exclusively caused by the railway but was unquestionably greatly facilitated by it.

Railways were the product of the received economic and political wisdoms of the Victorian era – individualism and laissez-faire. The highly complex network of lines which came to serve London was never a system in any real sense; there was no underlying rationale. Instead, it was the rather haphazard

George Cruikshank was a prolific caricaturist and illustrator, greatly opposed to railways and the evils associated with drink. He portrays railways as a malevolent threat to the lives of ordinary people.

outcome of a desire of some investors in railway shares to get rich quickly and of others to find a safe and steady lodging place for their savings. It was also the product of virtually unbridled competition. Insofar as parliament intervened in railway affairs in the supposed 'public interest', it was with reluctance and a light touch.

A hitherto unexpected market had been unearthed. London's railways were on their way. So much was to follow. As the *Building News* said in 1862:

> The invasion of the Metropolis by the 'Steam Horse' has, during the last quarter of a century, produced changes, not only in the physical features of the metropolis, but also in the manners, customs, mode of living, and even in the thoughts of its inhabitants, which are almost incredible. For a century previous to the year 1834, stagnation was the order of the day; but then came the locomotive into London, and all was changed.

Cruikshank again with the same theme.

Even more extravagant was the claim made by *Building News* in 1870:

What would London do now without a railway? What would become of the immense holiday crowds who are regularly whirled over the country, fifty miles and back, in a single day with eight hours at the seaside, if the railways were suddenly to shut up shop? Brighton and Southend became seaside extensions of the metropolis, while Birmingham and Bradford could appropriately be described as outposts of the City. Physical contiguity or even proximity ceased to be necessary prerequisites to the kinds of activities, whether involving business or pleasure, associated with cities. The network of interdependency linking the farthest corners of England with the metropolis that Defoe had celebrated with his 'Tour' reached its logical culmination with the creation of the Victorian railway and telegraph systems. It could be said that all England was a suburb of London, and each part of that real Greater London proceeded to specialise not only in its material but its aesthetic, intellectual, and emotional production; knowing that whatever it did not provide could be had a short railway away.

What later became Southwark Cathedral can be seen in the background as the railway was extended from London Bridge through the Borough and Bankside towards the Thames and Charing Cross.

The country end of Cannon Street Station. This was the South-Eastern Railway wanting to make a splash in the City of London.

The frenzied spate of railway speculation, investment and building known as the 'Railway Mania' in the years 1844-7 had burned itself out by 1850 and an era of consolidation began of which intensive, even cutthroat competition and amalgamations were marked features.

It will be noted that no subsurface underground railways were immediately built south of the Thames as a quick response to the evident success of the Metropolitan and Metropolitan District railways north of the river in the 1860s. There were geological factors which were unfavourable to the building of subsurface lines in this area, some of which was low-lying and poorly drained. However, parliament raised no general objections to the building of overground lines south of the river through the densely populated predominantly working-class residential districts to be found there. Initially, there were only two main-line termini on the fringe of central London, these being London Bridge and, in 1848, Waterloo. They were quite well situated for commuters to cross the river to their places of employment, many of which were in the City. Traffic at both these stations was growing vigorously in the early 1850s and the attention of the railway

A busy scene at Cannon Street dealing with long-distance passengers to or from locations in Kent.

companies involved was directed at increasing their capacity and then reducing congestion around them by extending lines across the river. The result was the building, between 1860 and 1866, of railway bridges leading to Victoria, Charing Cross, Farringdon Street and Cannon Street. The first two were handy for the West End and the latter for the City.

The original frontage of Euston Station of the London & Birmingham Railway. This was the first terminus in London of a long-distance trunk railway.

Nearing Euston Station by Spencer Frederick Gore shows a small locomotive perhaps occupied in moving empty rolling stock.

The following years witnessed bitter competition, barely short of open warfare, particularly between two of the four large companies whose lines approached London from the south. These were the SER and the London, Chatham & Dover Railway (LC&DR). Battle had originally been joined by these two over access to Dover and the potentially lucrative cross Channel ferry traffic. This particular contest was won

A **'Radial'** 4-4-2T of the London & South Western Railway arrives at Malden c.1895 to pick up a sizeable payload of commuters bound for Waterloo and jobs in central London. Hats were obligatory! (Courtesy of John Scott Morgan)

by the SER who got there first, but in 1861 the LC&DR opened a route between Dover and London that was 12 miles shorter. The SER retaliated by obtaining powers to build a line west from London Bridge to the site of the old Hungerford Market at Charing Cross. This station was very conveniently situated for many purposes and opened in 1864. Back came the LC&DR with a line through the Holborn area to join up with the Metropolitan at Farringdon Street, opened in 1866. The SER could not ignore this and in the same year opened a station at Cannon Street, very convenient for the City. The rivalry between the two companies was replicated and added to by the LB&SCR in an extremely complex network of lines in the southern approaches to London in Kent and Surrey as they vied for business in the growing commuter belt. It is a moot point whether this led to over-provision of railways in London's southern suburbs. The fourth company approaching London from this direction was the L&SWR. It too built up an impressive network of suburban and outer-suburban lines but tended to avoid direct competition with the other companies.

The feverish pace of the building of surface railways, perhaps inevitably, slackened off, assisted by the financial crisis following the collapse of the banking company of Overend and Gurney in 1866. The railways had brought Londoners an unprecedented mobility and they made the most of it. In the early 1890s they were making an estimated 150 million railway journeys between the various parts of London.

By 1875 London's surface railway network was basically complete although some infilling followed. Examples were the line to Bromley North in 1878, the direct line of the London, Tilbury & Southend (LT&SR) from Barking to Pitsea of 1888 and the Bexleyheath Line opened in 1895. The Circle Line was completed, the District Line was extended at both ends, there were extensions to the Metropolitan Railway and the Great Central Railway (GCR) arrived in town. In the Edwardian period the most significant development was that of deep-level tube railways. It is probably fair to say that London's railways reached their apogee just before the First World War. Hints of contraction were becoming evident by that time.

LONDON'S RAILWAY TERMINI

London's first railway terminus was London Bridge, opened in 1836. Located near the southern end of the bridge itself, it was quite convenient for the City but distant from other parts of London north of the Thames. A glance at a map of London quickly reveals that none of the major stations is actually located in central London. Indeed, they are all, to a greater or lesser extent, peripheral to the centre of the metropolis. A major consideration was the cost of the land on which the stations and their associated installations were to be located. The sites chosen tended to be cheaper than if they had been more central. Even so, there was a price to pay. They were often sited inconveniently for the companies that owned them. They were certainly inconvenient for the travelling public.

At the height of the 'Railway Mania', proposals were presented to parliament for the approval for almost twenty lines into London, each of which would have had a terminus in Westminster or the City. The lines that were envisaged would have carved up central London, destroying its cohesiveness. It was obvious even at a time of laisser-faire that such developments could not be permitted. From the late 1830s there had also been calls for the building of one or two large terminus stations located more conveniently and closer to the centre of London. Such calls became persistent enough to warrant the establishment of a Royal Commission to consider the implications of these proposals. In 1846 this Commission recommended that major railway stations should not be allowed in a designated area of central London. The main reason given was that such a station or stations would generate vast amounts of road traffic which would only exacerbate the existing chaotic and chronic road congestion in much of London's central districts. Additionally, the disruption and necessary demolition that would be required in building their approaches and clearing the huge sites would be on a scale that simply could not be allowed. Concerns were also expressed about the resolution of possibly conflicting business interests among the partner railway companies using a central station. Could these be reconciled without possible state intervention? Although the Commission's recommendations did not actually have legal force, a principle was laid down for a 'box' or area of central London which main line surface railways would not be allowed to penetrate. This box was roughly contiguous with the limits of the continuously built-up area of London as it had been in 1800. This was Edgware Road and Park Lane in the west; the New Road (later Euston Road), City Road and Finsbury Square in the north; and Bishopsgate in the east. South of the Thames the exclusion zone was bounded by Borough High Street in the east, Vauxhall Bridge Road in the west and Kennington Lane in the south.

This exclusion of main line surface railways from central London became a principle of metropolitan town planning but it was never absolute. A project was broached by the L&NWR in 1863 for a station at Leicester Square and the SER produced a similar scheme ten years later. They never progressed beyond the proposal stage largely because of the understated but resolute opposition of several major landowners such as the Bedford, Portman and Portland Estates. These had enough power and influence where it mattered to ensure that such developments never took place. They were 'old wealth' and more than a match for what they saw as the vulgar, grasping 'new rich' commercial and industrial bourgeoisie who promoted railways. Few landowners were as adamant that the railways would not enter their domain as was the Duke of Bedford. He was determined to keep his Bloomsbury estate exclusive. The Duke was one man who could not be bought. This was all evidence of realpolitik, but it has already been said that the ban was not absolute. Central London never became a totally railway-free sanctum. Some terminus stations did penetrate its outer edges. These were Liverpool Street, Broad Street, Fenchurch Street, Cannon Street and Holborn Viaduct in the City and Charing Cross and Victoria elsewhere. A real anomaly was the opening in 1866 by the LC&DR of a link from its lines south of the Thames to the northern network in the King's Cross area. It crossed Ludgate Hill on a viaduct vilified at the time for obstructing the view of St Paul's and passed along the valley of the Fleet through Farringdon. What skulduggery was invoked so that it could gain parliamentary approval for this penetration of the exclusion zone?

There are fifteen stations in London that may be regarded as main line termini. They were built over a period of sixty-three years. From London Bridge in 1836 they followed through to 1899 with the opening of Marylebone. The number and the scale of some of these stations was evidence, if it was needed, that Britain's railways focussed on the country's capital. As well as London Bridge, Euston, Nine Elms, replaced by Waterloo in 1848, and the original Paddington date from the late 1830s. The 1840s saw the addition of Fenchurch Street and Bishopsgate which in 1874 moved to a more central position at Liverpool Street. King's Cross opened in 1852 and Victoria, Blackfriars, Ludgate Hill, Charing Cross, Cannon Street, Broad

The clock tower on the front of King's Cross Station. This was first seen at the Great Exhibition held in Hyde Park in 1851.

Street and St Pancras in the 1860s. Holborn Viaduct and Blackfriars followed in 1874 and 1880 respectively and Marylebone, as mentioned, in 1899.

The inconvenience caused by having so many stations scattered around the edge of central London has never been totally overcome. However, the building of underground lines such as the Metropolitan and Metropolitan District and eventually the creation of what became known as the Circle Line made inter-station transfers somewhat easier. Later, the various tube lines and the introduction of motor buses and taxis further expedited movement between stations. It remains a moot point whether one or more central stations would have been of more benefit to Londoners and the huge number of travellers passing through the capital.

Long-distance traffic was a feature of many of the termini we have mentioned. When stations like Waterloo, Victoria, Paddington, Euston, St Pancras and King's Cross came into use, they tended to stamp their character on their surroundings. This was, perhaps, not just the result of their imposing physical presence but also the expectations and behaviour of those who arrived and departed by train and the diverse cross-section of humanity that was attracted towards them but had no intention of travelling. As already stated, these stations were often built where the land was already relatively cheap. Much demolition of existing rundown property was often needed to clear a site for the railway's needs. Those older buildings that remained were frequently also rundown but often much of the new property erected because of the coming of the railway quickly became seedy. It is a sad reflection on human weakness that many adults, and here we are primarily talking about men, away from home constraints, succumb with some gusto to a variety of temptations. And temptations there were a-plenty in London. Prostitutes plied their trade around stations and brothels, yards and dark alleys were available close at hand. Cheap hotels witnessed clandestine assignations. Showy pubs on nearby street corners with their meretricious furnishings and fittings attracted new arrivals into London but housed members of the criminal fraternity eager to spot those marks who were easy game. Beggars, pickpockets, luggage thieves, pimps all hung around eager to extract tribute from the isolated and often confused and vulnerable individuals making their first encounter with London. Not least among this disreputable throng were those louche characters ready to 'befriend' the young, vulnerable arrivals, both female and male, then take them under their control and gradually introduce them to the world of prostitution and petty crime.

THE RAILWAY HOTELS OF LONDON

London has, of course, always drawn visitors needing to find accommodation but the concept of the hotel as we know it is a nineteenth-century invention, at least in Britain. In the eighteenth and nineteenth centuries, the very rich had houses in London where they might spend part of the year, particularly the 'season', if they wanted to be part of fashionable society. They might spend other parts of the year in their provincial estates or perhaps travelling abroad. At these times they might let part of their town houses to other well-heeled visitors. Boarding and lodging houses existed for poorer visitors. While the accommodation in some of these may have been tolerable, it is likely that most were Spartan or worse. Of course, expectations were lower at that time.

The unique role played by London in the nation's economy meant that it had large numbers of inns associated with the coaching industry. Examples were the George and Blue Boar, Holborn, and the Bull and Mouth, St Martins-le-Grand. The boom years of the coaching industry were probably from the mid-eighteenth century to the late 1830s. It is estimated that over two million people travelled by coach annually in the 1820s although coach travel was expensive, uncomfortable and frequently dangerous. Coaches simply could not compete with railways and the long-distance coaching industry quickly went into decline. The last mail coaches, the elite part of the industry, quickly surrendered their contracts to competing railways.

Although some new routes developed as short-distance feeders to the railways, the coaching era was effectively over. As a contemporary observer lamented, 'The great roads of former days are overgrown with weeds, the coaches broken up or perhaps turned into hen-roosts and the tea-kettle with its unmelodious whistle has taken full possession of everything and everybody.'

The existing types of accommodation were proving woefully inadequate given London's growing economic, political, commercial, social and cultural importance and its increasing number of visitors. Something more modern and radically better was needed. The word 'hotel' is of course French in origin but possibly its first recorded use in Britain was by a politician writing to his mother in 1780 on notepaper headed 'Nerot's Hotel' with a London address. 'Hotel' at first had genteel, even pretentious connotations, but came into more general use in the early nineteenth century to refer to establishments which had more luxurious accommodation and better facilities than most of the inns, but which were also, in some cases, quite raffish. Examples were Pulteney's, the Clarendon, and Long's, all of them being in Mayfair, a district even then characterised by the wealth and frequently by the dissipation of its inhabitants. Such hotels were often converted from the mansions of previous rich occupants. However, the origin of the large hotel lies with the railway companies of the nineteenth century in Britain.

The railway companies wanted hotels at their major stations in London because in the early days the punctuality of their trains could not be guaranteed and if passengers arrived in London late at night they might find themselves stranded. Equally, passengers wanting an early departure from London might prefer to stay overnight close to the station or, of course, if they lived close to but not in London and had to travel into town, they might not be able to reach the station in time for early departures. Also, the railway companies were in competition for certain traffic flows. They thought that having a well-appointed station hotel for the kind of affluent travellers they all wanted might give them a competitive edge over their rivals. The hotel was also a statement by the company owning the station. It frequently formed a façade to the street and was built to impress. Aesthetically, it was likely to provide a more pleasing sight that the vertical end of the train shed.

From more than 2 million coaching journeys being made in the 1820s, we arrive at the phenomenal figure of over 204 million railway journeys in 1863. This huge increase in travel boosted the demand for accommodation for long-distance travellers and encouraged both the railway companies and private entrepreneurs to invest in the provision of hospitality. However, the Acts of Parliament which authorised each individual railway company and line usually prevented them from using their funds for building and operating hotels. This can be seen in the case of the first railway hotel in London which served Euston Station of the L&BR. This was promoted through an associated 'London & Birmingham Railway Hotel and

Dormitories Co' which was then leased to a firm of foreign caterers. This pioneer hotel opened in 1839 and was curious in that it originally consisted of two separate buildings. That on the western side was called the Euston and provided somewhat superior accommodation to the adjacent Victoria. In 1914 a visitor commented, 'Comfort is studied rather than on display, and the fact that English waiters are employed ought to gladden the heart of every patriotic Englishman.'

The Great Northern Hotel was unusual because it stood adjacent to but was not part of the structure of King's Cross Station. Rather like the station itself, partly because the same engineer, Lewis Cubbitt, was involved, it was simple and unpretentious, a down-to-earth establishment designed to appeal to canny northerners visiting London for business or pleasure and who wanted solid value for money. It opened in 1854 and was rather odd because of its curved plan, necessitated by the alignment of the Old St Pancras Road.

The Midland Grand Hotel was, in effect, next door to the Great Northern but overawed it in every respect. It provided a grand façade for the Midland Railway (MR) which made a late arrival in London at its St Pancras Station. This hotel opened in 1873 although the building was not completed until some time later. It rears up in an almost intimidating fashion over Euston Road but had the original plans been adhered to, it would have had two more storeys. As it was, in its prime it had 500 bedrooms. The MR directors wanted to make an impact with their hotel, intending it to make an unequivocal statement that the Midland had arrived in town. Whatever else may be said about George Gilbert Scott's gothic tour de force, it certainly achieved this aim, and it has excited conflicting opinion throughout its history. Although Scott obviously won the competition to design a hotel at this spot, he went way over budget in doing so. It may have helped that he cleverly incorporated in the fabric many items of brick, slate and iron that were manufactured in the heartlands of the MR's territory. The Midland Grand was always at the cutting edge. It was among the very earliest buildings in London to install a revolving door, partly for swank and partly to inhibit draughts. Possibly even more avant garde was the provision of a ladies' smoking room in the 1890s. This was at a time when a woman smoking in public risked having her morals seriously called into question.

Good hotels were rare in the City, but the Great Eastern Hotel was opened in 1884 adjacent to Liverpool Street Station. It was the work of Charles Barry Jr, member of a notable family of architects. It was improved around the end of the nineteenth century when some imposing new facilities were added. The hotel served the needs of, among others, passengers to and from the Harwich ferries to the Continent.

The Great Western Hotel was, rather like the GWR itself, built to be noticed. Opened in June 1854, it was unashamedly flamboyant with a touch of French chateau styling. Its sumptuous furnishings and fittings set something of a precedent for others to follow. This was not surprising because the Great Western also considered itself a cut above the norm. It was the work of the well-known architect P.C. Hardwick. It is, however, easy to see the influence of I.K. Brunel in the fireproofing of staircases and passages, the elaborate bell system extending to virtually every room and the running of hot water pipes through the linen closets on each floor. The hotel was not initially owned and operated by the GWR and instead was leased to an associated company of which Brunel was the first chairman. The opening of the hotel was meant to be one in the eye for the L&NWR because the GWR had opened a line to Birmingham in competition with that company. The GWR took full ownership in 1896.

The Grosvenor Hotel did not reflect its railway associations in its name but rather the family name of the fabulously rich Westminster clan who owned much of the land in this south-west corner of central London. The hotel adjoined that part of Victoria Station that was operated by the LB&SCR, but it was not at first owned by that company. Opened in 1861, it was an impressive and opulent building which was intended to cater for the discerning clientele using the LB&SCR to travel to and from the Continent via Newhaven and Dieppe. The company that leased the hotel somewhat neglected it and relations between the companies were strained, eventually forcing the LB&SCR to buy the hotel and then let it to another company who greatly improved its services.

The Cannon Street Hotel formed the street frontage of the station with the impressive train shed behind it. By London standards it had limited bedroom accommodation but facilities which generated useful income in terms of what would now be described as excellent 'conference facilities', very useful for its location in the City. Ironically perhaps, given its location, this hotel witnessed the founding meeting of the Communist Party of Great Britain in 1920. Opened in 1867 it was initially run by a separate company but later bought by the SER.

Close by in the City was the Holborn Viaduct Hotel. This opened in 1877 for the LC&DR station of that name. This hotel was leased to Spiers & Pond who were establishing a considerable business in the provision of catering and hospitality facilities for railway companies. Like its near neighbour, it provided elegant and comfortable surroundings for business meetings and an intimate, almost club-like atmosphere for 'City Gents' who liked a cigar and brandy or two after an exhausting day in their counting houses before boarding their train into leafy rural Kent. It gradually fell on lean times and was requisitioned by the government in 1917, never returning to use as a hotel.

The Terminus could be described as a forgotten London railway hotel. It was opened in 1861 and operated independently of the LB&SCR although adjacent to its part of London Bridge Station. It was convenient for the City and for the dubious delights which Bankside and the Borough had traditionally offered. It was well-appointed but when the LB&SCR concentrated its long-distance traffic elsewhere, it lost trade and in 1893 had the unwelcome distinction of being the first of London's railway hotels to close.

The Charing Cross Hotel opened its doors in 1865 about a year after the station of the SER for which it provided a façade. As with the Cannon Street Hotel, E.M. Barry did the honours here. The hotel was imposing rather than elegant but was intended to provide particularly for the needs of cross-Channel travellers and enjoyed many years of prosperity. It was Barry who built the replica Eleanor Cross which stands to this day in the station forecourt. The SER had been accused of destroying several ancient buildings when it was clearing the sites for this station and for Cannon Street. The original cross had probably stood at the top of Whitehall where it commemorated the last resting place of Queen Eleanor's body before its burial in Westminster Abbey.

The Great Central Hotel otherwise known as the Hotel Great Central was the last to open of London's great railway hotels. It did so in 1899. It was built not by the railway company but by the prominent furnishing company of Maple's who

The imposing hotel which composed the street frontage of Charing Cross Station. Like Victoria, this station also catered for international travellers.

produced a superbly fitted out and comfortable hotel. Soon after it was completed, it was taken over by a new company called Frederick Hotels, associated with Maple's. As a somewhat elephantine structure containing no less than 700 bedrooms, it dwarfed or even browbeat the dainty little Marylebone terminus of the GCR which cowered close by. The GCR was a railway with grand aspirations and the hotel was intended to cater for well-to-do travellers from the north of England and the Midlands, some of whom might be heading for continental destinations. Unfortunately for the GCR, its trains could not compete for speed with those of other companies and the travellers did not turn up in the numbers hoped for. Nevertheless, it carved out a niche for itself as a luxurious place to stay and something of a reputation for housing the activities of those 'ladies of the night' who could afford to hire a room there as the base for the services they provided.

The railway hotels of London were unashamedly designed to cater for an affluent clientele. Although there were differences in the quality of the services offered, there is little doubt that they added considerably to the amenities of the metropolis and

Massive disruption being caused by the building of St Pancras Station in the 1860s. Railways tended to buy cheap land which frequently meant the displacement without compensation of large numbers of slum-dwellers.

A perhaps unexpected use for railway arches was as a roof above the head of some of London's homeless. There is nothing new about poverty and homelessness in London.

Railway arches were also used to provide work for unemployed men. They are breaking stones used for road building. More evidence of London's Victorian underbelly.

boosted its reputation as a place to be visited and enjoyed for leisure and pleasure purposes. Not least, they had a significant impact on the eating habits of those who used them. Previously it had been considered socially unacceptable for respectable women to dine alone or with others of the same sex in public eating places. Those restaurants that previously existed in London were mostly found in Soho and, as they were largely run by and frequented by foreigners, they were certainly not the place for refined ladies. It was a perhaps unintended function of the railway hotels to be at the forefront of providing places for genteel diners of both sexes. The hotels might provide rooms where food or other refreshments were available. Some might be for the exclusive use of either sex but increasingly the two sexes would mix in the opulent and decorous surroundings of the dining rooms that these hotels could provide. Many illicit liaisons were doubtless consummated elsewhere in these buildings. What a tale they could tell.

The railways played a major role in the development of the British hospitality industry and, as might be expected, it was in London that many of the largest and most opulent examples of this genre were to be found. They did, however, suffer for their pioneering role because they spawned not only imitators but other establishments which were larger and swankier, offering better facilities and services. Towards the end of the nineteenth century, some of them were looking outmoded and rundown. A number embarked on radical refurbishment and upgrading. The upper tier of London's hotels became extremely competitive and the Charing Cross Hotel, for example, found itself with five other newer and mostly grander hotels in the vicinity. It was fortunate that, for much of the time, the period up to 1914 was one in which there was an expanding demand for passenger travel by rail. The growth of London and of its attractions and facilities for visitors continued to provide not only a healthy market for travel to and from the capital but a rising demand for the services of its hospitality industry.

DISRUPTION CAUSED BY THE BUILDING OF LONDON'S RAILWAYS

During the nineteenth century, London developed into the hub of Britain's railway system with a network of great complexity the construction of which created enormous disruption especially in the densely built-up central areas. New railways in cuttings and tunnels had to be constructed through the existing complicated system of subterranean pipes, sewers, gas-mains, etc while roads frequently had to be reconstructed and large numbers of buildings had to be rebuilt or in many cases demolished. Inevitably, innumerable legal wrangles arose and provided a boom time for the legal profession. Emotive issues were raised where human remains in burial places needed to be disinterred and reburied elsewhere.

It was the host of legal, financial and other considerations in densely built-up parts of central London that encouraged the development of the 'cut-and-cover' system particularly for the early sub-surface underground lines. Where possible

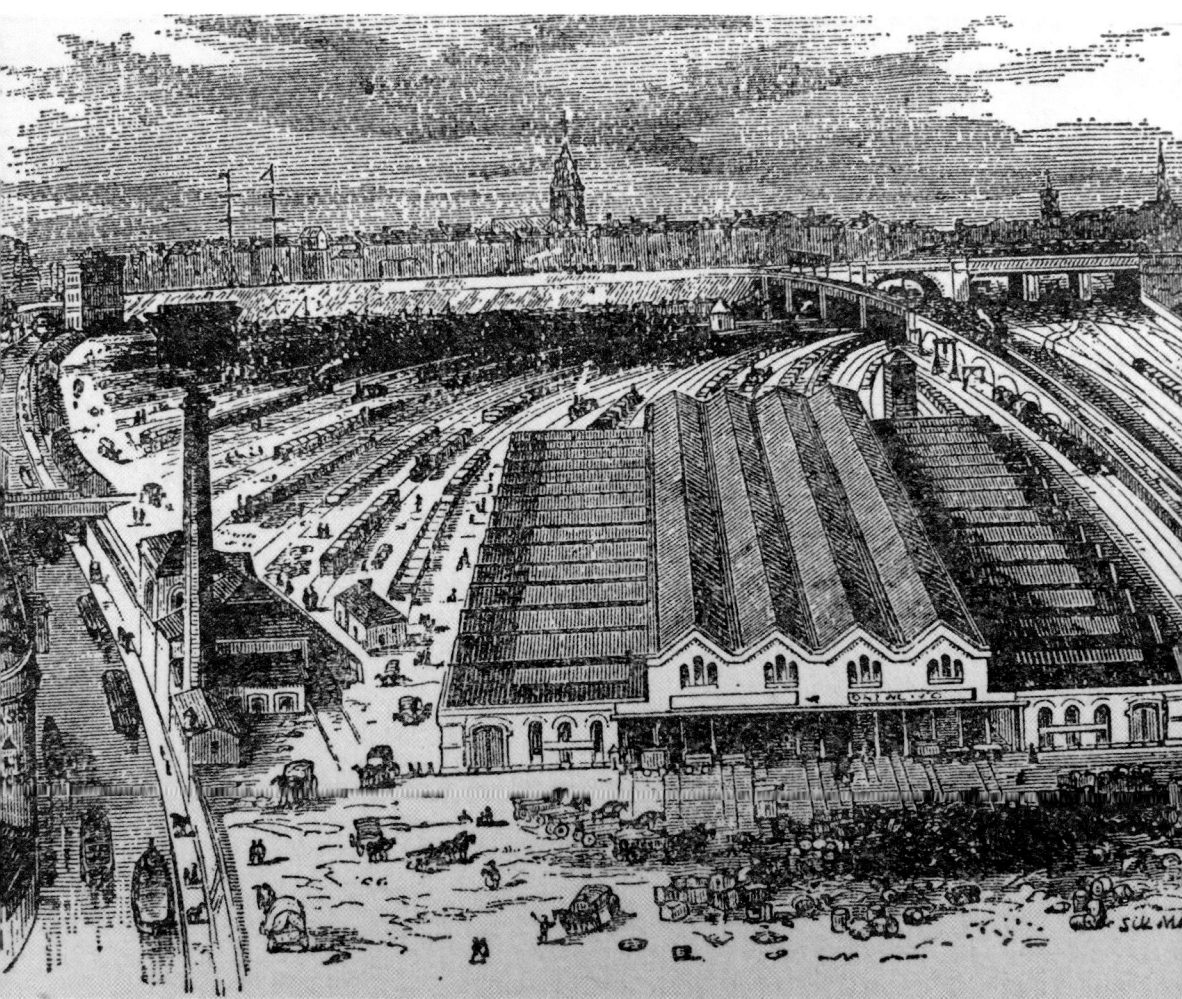

This shows the huge amount of land taken by the Midland Railway for the building of Somers Town Goods Depot, next to St Pancras Station. Some of the site is now occupied by the British Library on Euston Road.

lines might be aligned to follow the path but be built below existing main roads. This might minimise the amount of compulsory purchase of property needed or avoid expensive legal wrangles where damage to property was claimed. Sometimes new roads would be built in conjunction with railway construction in a form of social engineering whereby wide major roads were driven through some of London's most notorious slum enclaves or rookeries. This had had the effect of opening them up to closer public control.

Where possible, the railways tried to buy cheap land for their stations, sidings and other installations. Such land was frequently covered with substandard housing rented by people with little money, influence or bargaining power. An example was the extension made by the L&SWR from its original Nine Elms terminus to its replacement at Waterloo. This was reported as affecting 2,367 properties and the demolition of about 700 homes. When buying up such property, the railway companies acted as agents of slum clearance although not of course for public health or philanthropic reasons. Railway construction exacerbated the housing problems of the poor by demolishing dwellings while frequently involving no legal duty to re-house the former occupants. Usually, they were simply decanted into already overcrowded and crumbling housing nearby. As *The Times* stated, 'The poor are displaced but they are not removed. They are shovelled out of one side of the parish, only to render more overcrowded the stifling apartments in another part.' From 1874, however, the legislation sanctioning railway projects usually put some obligation on the railway company involved to re-house at least some of those being displaced. An example was the requirement imposed on the GCR in the late 1890s. It was seeking land for its proposed Marylebone Station and its associated railway installations. It gained the compulsory purchase powers it wanted but was required to build six blocks of tenements to re-house 2,690 of those living on the designated land. It is estimated that more than 3,000 other former occupants suffered displacement without any similar provision. It is likely that most of them simply spilt over into existing notoriously poor housing in the neighbouring Lisson Grove district.

Sometimes railway companies were required by law to make cheap workmen's fares available to and from central London and the inner-city districts to which at least some of the displaced residents had moved. It was only to be expected that the railway companies were less than enthusiastic about these requirements. However, they often managed to recoup the cost of these unremunerative fares by putting up the price of other tickets.

There is little doubt that, in the short-term at least, the coming of the railways did more harm than good for the housing of the less well-off. It has been estimated that railway-building in London in the second half of the nineteenth century involved the demolition of the homes of a minimum of 120,000 people. Most of these were victims of forces over which they had not the slightest element of control.

In 1853 the government required the promoters of private railway bills involving the demolition of thirty or more 'labourers' dwellings' in any one parish to provide a return of the number of occupants affected. These returns were known as 'demolition statements'. The accuracy of these returns has been regarded with some scepticism by historians. The figures may however be considered as indicative. The SER's extension from London Bridge to Charing Cross displaced 4,580 people and between 4,000 and 5,000 had to move when the North London Railway (NLR) built its extension from Dalston Junction to Broad Street.

In fairness, the displacement of around 1,300 largely poor residents had taken place when the early enclosed docks were being built in the first decade of the nineteenth century. No fewer than 5,750 people are thought to have lost their homes for the building of Regent Street some years later and uncounted numbers as the result of street improvements carried out by the City Corporation and the Commissioners of Woods and Forests in the 1830s and 1840s.

There was not just the disruption inflicted on the housing of the poor by the coming of the railways. The railways inevitably carved a swathe through much that was comfortably familiar although perhaps only appreciated once it was under threat or had been destroyed. Charles Dickens in *Dombey and Son*, published in 1848, exercises his descriptive skills to great effect when describing the impact made by the L&BR as it carved its way towards its Euston terminus:

> The first shock of a great earthquake had … rent the whole neighbourhood to its centre. Traces of its course were visible on every side. Houses were knocked down; streets broken through and stopped; deep pits and trenches dug in the ground; enormous heaps of earth and clay thrown up; buildings that are undermined and shaking, propped up by great beams of wood. Here, a chaos of carts, overthrown and jumbled together, lay topsy-turvy at the bottom of a steep, unnatural hill; there confused treasures of iron soaked and rusted in something that had accidentally become a pond. Everywhere were bridges that led nowhere; thoroughfares that were wholly impassable, Babel towers of chimneys, wanting half their height; temporary wooden houses and enclosures, in the most unlikely situations; carcases of ragged tenements, and fragments of unfinished walls and arches, and piles of scaffolding and wildernesses of bricks … There were a hundred thousand shapes and substances of incompleteness, wildly mingled out of their places, upside down, burrowing in the earth, aspiring in the earth, mouldering in the water, and unintelligible as any dream. Hot springs and fiery eruptions, the usual attendants upon earthquakes, lent their contributions of confusion to the scene. Boling water hissed and heaved within dilapidated walls, whence, also, the glare and roar of flames came issuing forth; and mounds of ashes blocked up rights of way, and wholly changed the law and customs of the neighbourhood. In short, the yet unfinished and unopened railway was in progress, and, from the very call of this dire disorder, trailed smoothly away upon its mighty course of civilisation and improvement.

The *Builder*, as usual, was enthusiastic about the progress of the iron road but, in 1860, we sense a slight element of concern:

> In all directions bands of workmen are as busy as moles burrowing the earth, each in his way, advancing the great drainage works; and now operations have

begun for making the underground of London available for railway purposes, and soon below the crowded streets the locomotive whistle will sound and trains roll rapidly along. The squares north of Hyde Park are blockaded, and poor ladies look out of their windows aghast, and postpone intended parties.

It was clear by the 1860s that the railways had become major agents in the transformation of land uses in London and of the increase in land values in its central parts. They consumed large amounts of land in gaining access to their major stations and for their stations, goods depots and warehouses, carriage sidings and other fixtures. The building of these frequently meant the displacement of many poorer residents. Even the better-off ones whose homes were not threatened by demolition often left the area because a large railway presence frequently created urban blight. Major stations like Paddington, Victoria, King's Cross and St Pancras saw the creation of an area of dependent cheap boarding-houses and small hotels which soon turned seedy.

'**Over London** by Railway'. This drawing by Gustav Doré shows a railway on a viaduct dominating a district of closely packed working class housing.

Where new railways penetrated already developed or developing suburbs, it was likely that a station would be built close to the existing centre, an example being Brixton. It was then probable that the area around the station would become an urban centre, the business and shopping focus for the surrounding residential district. Some, and Brixton is an example, developed large department stores and other retail outlets which meant that locals had no need to go 'up West' to shop if they did not want to. Despite the provision of a complex transport infrastructure in Greater London, it became a social phenomenon that many working-class Londoners rarely, if ever, went into Central London.

RAILWAY VIADUCTS

Many of the railways approaching London were carried on long viaducts often through areas which were already at least partly built-up. These viaducts could have an immensely disruptive impact locally. Their erection often involved considerable demolition of existing housing and areas often given over to small industrial premises. On a more human level, a viaduct could break up the social cohesion of a community by forcing its way through and thereby creating a physical division where none had existed before. For example, what became a greatly widened viaduct carrying the lines into London Bridge Station continues even to this day to constitute a dark, dingy and dangerous no man's land dividing parts of Southwark and Bermondsey from each other. A similar situation occurred with the approaches to Waterloo. It was widely recognised that this effectively closed off streets and destroyed the integrity of the districts through which it passed, often exacerbating their social decay.

Viaducts often provided a grandstand view of London's blighted districts. Charles Dickens had an acute awareness of social reality and particularly how it affected the less privileged. Once again in *Dombey and Son*, he writes of what he has seen from one of these viaducts:

Everything around is blackened. There are dark pools of water, muddy lanes, and miserable habitations far below. There are jagged walls and filthy houses close at hand, and through the battered roofs and broken windows, wretched rooms are seen, where want and fever hide themselves in many wretched shapes, while smoke and crowded gables, and distorted chimneys, and deformity of mind and body, choke the murky distance. As Mr Dombey looked out of his carriage window, it is never in his thoughts that the monster who brought him here has let the light of day in on those things: not made or caused them… it was so ruinous and dreary.

Dickens took this theme further when writing about Agar Town and Somers Town. These were established districts located between the L&NWR's Euston Station and that of the GNR at King's Cross. They consisted of some of London's worst slum housing interspersed with various small industrial premises, mostly engaged in noxious and polluting activity. His description is a vivid one:

> Every garden has its nuisance but every nuisance was of a distinct and peculiar character. In one a dung-heap, in the next a cinder-heap, in the third, which belonged to the cottage of a costermonger, was a pile of whelk and periwinkle shells, some rotten cabbages and a donkey: and the garden of another… had become a pond of thick green water.

He then described a mountain of refuse which acted as the centrepiece of this festering neighbourhood, and he mentioned a number of industrial premises. Among these were the sheds of rag collectors, knackers' yards and ramshackle buildings where soap was manufactured and bones boiled for glue. Also present were kilns for baking bricks and a small gas works. While the railways did not of themselves create slums, they certainly contributed strongly to urban blight and consequent human misery.

RAILWAYS AND LONDON'S INDUSTRIES

It is easy to think of Britain's coal-mining districts as the hub of the country's industrial capacity in the nineteenth century. However, in 1861 about fifteen per cent of jobs in manufacturing in England and Wales were in London. The size and cumulative spending power of the population and its commercial and financial pre-eminence created an enormous demand for an immensely diverse range of commodities. Compared, for example, to the massive mills of the Lancashire cotton industry, however, the manufactories of London were mostly of a much smaller scale and many were tiny. There were, however, some exceptions.

Two major industrial sites depended on the railways. One was the enormous plant covering 540 acres owned by the Gas Light & Coke Company at Beckton beyond the East End. Although much coal came by water, the plant, opened in 1870, was designed from the start to be served by rail. It was the largest gas works in Europe and its internal railway system amounted to 42 miles. On the south side of the Thames was the Royal Arsenal at Woolwich. This was Britain's largest and most important centre for manufacturing military equipment and munitions. This had an extensive narrow-gauge internal railway system and well-used connections with the South Eastern & Chatham's North Kent line.

The building and heavy repair of steam locomotives and other rolling stock is the kind of industry we would probably not associate with London, but five companies had works engaged in this activity. They were the L&SWR at Nine Elms; the Eastern Counties (later GER) at Stratford; the North London at Bow; LT&SR at Plaistow and the LC&DR at Longhedge, Battersea.

Stratford was probably the most impressive of these establishments. It was at the centre of a railway settlement originally called Hudson Town after George Hudson who had been the Company's chairman. Large numbers of country people from East Anglia resettled there, often having been displaced from agricultural work. Railway employment was steady, offered possibilities of promotion and was reasonably paid even if it involved a sharp break from the rustic way of life. It was therefore a tempting prospect especially for younger people from the East Anglian countryside. The works became very large. Like other sizeable companies, the GER attempted to be as self-sufficient as possible which meant that it was the centre of far wider activity than simply that of building and maintaining rolling stock. For example, it produced all the timetables and printed ephemera the Company needed. The Stratford district was one with a long history of industrial activity around the River Lea and it became a major industrial enclave.

Nine Elms was the first of London's railway engineering works, being opened in 1839. It expanded to the extent that it outgrew its site and its operations were removed to Eastleigh in Hampshire. This is interesting given its location in Battersea which predated the railways as a significant industrial district. It was the last heavy engineering factory so close to central London.

Several small private locomotive manufacturers could be found in London. They included Braithwaite & Ericcson who were early enough on the scene to enter their machine *Novelty* in the Rainhill Trials on the Liverpool & Manchester Railway in 1829. The largest of London's locomotive builders was George England's Hatcham works at New Cross which built about 250 locomotives between 1840 and 1872. When this works closed it was the end of private locomotive building in London and symptomatic at that time of the declining heavy industrial base of London. On a smaller scale was the well-known works of Saxby & Farmer at Kilburn which was a very successful supplier of signalling equipment.

London did have large factories, but it did not become a centre of heavy industry. A typical industrial workplace was on a workshop scale, probably too small to merit its own railway connections even where these might have been possible. In the period under review, it does not seem that railway connections were a major factor even when large-scale manufacturing facilities were being planned. Where the railways played a vital role in expediting London's industrial development was in bringing coal from distant mining areas, a traffic which grew to prodigious amounts. Some large factories were rail connected but many relied on deliveries by road haulage from railway yards. The resulting slow-moving horse-drawn wagons conveying coal were a considerable contributor to the traffic congestion that was a feature of many parts of London. Breweries, of which London had a very large number, were examples of processing plants which consumed large amounts of coal but few of them had direct railway connections. Before the development of efficient motorised road haulage in the 1920s, the products of many factories and workshops would have to be carted through the streets to railway goods depots before being dispatched to the provinces. Some of these goods depots were large enough and busy enough to generate a great deal of road traffic themselves.

Railways certainly contributed to the growth of London's industries in the Victorian and Edwardian period, but this was also the time in which London consolidated its position as one of the world's leading seaports and its docks handled quantities and a diversity of trade and commerce on a scale scarcely conceivable today.

RAILWAY EMPLOYMENT

London had several enclaves of concentrated railway activity. Five examples can be given: the Camden, Kentish Town, King's Cross and St Pancras area; Old Oak Common and Willesden Junction; Battersea and Clapham Junction; Bricklayers Arms and New Cross; Stratford, Bow and Plaistow. Engine sheds could be found in each of these areas, some of them extremely large establishments with huge workforces. The Stratford complex of the GER was by far the largest in London. The maintenance and operation of steam locomotives was very labour intensive, and these sheds provided large numbers of jobs. Some of these districts also had railway engineering workshops, goods depots, siding and marshalling complexes and carriage servicing facilities. These covered a huge acreage and shaped the topography of the districts involved. Frequently they were also the location of tangles of lines and junctions which used up large amounts of space and might create areas of underused and semi-derelict land unsuitable for any other purposes.

These areas were surrounded by districts of almost exclusively working-class housing which inevitably contained large numbers of railway employees and their families. Many more workers were required for station duties, track maintenance, as what are now called signallers, as shunters, looking after the vast numbers of railway horses as well as others in catering, security, clerical, administrative and management roles. Although statistical data exists to provide us with information about the numbers of those directly employed by the railway companies, there were large numbers of others whose income was wholly or partially derived from the presence of the railways. Some examples would be cabdrivers, plying their trade around the major stations, those employed in pubs and eating places adjacent to railway stations and workers engaged in the myriad industries whose business it was to supply the railways with the goods and services it did not itself provide. Many thousands were employed in cartage, much of which would have been to and from railway goods depots. Large numbers of tram and omnibus drivers and guards, at least in central London, worked routes which derived much of their patronage from serving railway stations. Another, perhaps more shifting, demographic was that of the navvies and labourers who were engaged in railway construction work, including that on the underground and later the tube railways.

Until the 1920s there was a prestige attached to railway employment in general, a perception of status that was real but did not pay the bills because remuneration was not overly generous. An almost militaristic disciplinary regime existed, and trade union activity was largely frowned upon. Hours of work could be long and what is now called 'antisocial'. Many working roles carried great responsibility and were inherently dangerous. Additionally, all railway workers were made very aware of their particular place in a delineated hierarchy of employment. On the other hand, a steady worker was likely to have a job for life with prospects of promotion for those with aspirations. Engine drivers saw themselves and were seen as the aristocrats of artisan railway employment. A stationmaster at one of the big London termini was a senior manager enjoying dignity and prestige. Such a man would parade in top hats and tails to supervise the departure of the main trains of the day. It was likely that he had started on the bottom rung of the ladder of railway employment. Nearly all railway employees and even members of their families enjoyed the privilege of reduced fares and some free passes.

LONDON SUBURBAN TRAINS ON SUNDAYS

Belief in the absolute sanctity of the so-called Lord's Day had considerable support in Victorian and Edwardian society, especially from those in a position to impose their views on others and who were often at the richer end of the social spectrum. For that growing section of society for whom overt religious observance in terms of regular attendance at a place of worship was unimportant, Sunday was treasured as the only day of the week for rest and/or the enjoyment of whatever forms of leisure activity were available and affordable.

Many of those who wanted to keep them for quiet devotion objected to the running of trains on Sundays. Some said that there should be no trains running and a few argued that only those that were absolutely necessary should run. Others thought that trains should certainly not run during the hours normally given over to church worship on Sundays, say between mid-morning and early afternoon. The board of directors of several railway companies thought it advisable to attempt to identify that proportion of income that was earned by those trains that ran during 'church hours' so that the shareholders who had voiced their antipathy to Sunday train working could forego the appropriate amount of company dividends. It would be interesting to know how many such people in practice gave priority to their avowed religious scruples over their financial interests.

Despite continuing condemnation from a vociferous section of the religious lobby, the demand for Sunday train services grew rapidly, especially those associated with travelling for pleasure. While it proved impossible to prevent pleasure-seeking people from using trains on Sundays, it became common practice over much of the Victorian and Edwardian period for suburban train services to be suspended during Sunday church hours. The practice only died out in the mid-1920s, but many Sunday timetables retained vestigial evidence of this earlier practice right into the 1950s and 1960s.

Until May 1839, Sunday and weekdays services on the pioneering L&GR had been the same but, in that month and as a result of pressure from the religious lobby, a revised Sunday timetable inaugurated a service suspended between 10.45am and 1.15pm. Over the following years it became common practice to suspend Sunday services, even those of long-distance services, for two or sometimes three hours in the middle of the day.

Such provision was general until the end of the nineteenth century when exceptions began to appear. The City & South London tube railway opened in 1890 and from 5 April 1891 started running trains from 1pm. In 1900 its trains started running at noon and this soon changed to 11am, a practice soon followed by the Great Northern & City Line. Both lines from 1 August began operating at about 8am. The Central London Railway opened on 30 July 1900 and from the start operated continuously on Sundays.

The first main line railway company to decide to run all day on Sundays was the L&SWR which did so from 6 October 1901. Several other companies had followed suit before the outbreak of the First World War. Most Metropolitan Line trains, for example, ran throughout Sundays from July 1903.

It was hard economics combined with increasing secularism that led railway companies increasingly to refuse to defer to the wishes of the Sabbatarian fraternity. The disposable income of large sections of the population rose through much of the period from 1850 to 1914 which helped to create a demand for what we would now call commercialised leisure facilities. Money was to be made by railway companies who provided transport for those bent on enjoying a healthy bout of hedonism on Sundays.

THEY WERE COMPLAINING EVEN THEN …

Railways have always aroused strong emotions. In the period from the mid-1830s to the early 1850s when the basis of Britain's comprehensive network of railways was being laid down, opposition to them was voiced from a wide range of sources and an even wider range of reasons. Some people such as the eccentric and irascible MP for Lincoln, Colonel Charles de Laet Waldo Sibthorp, wished all railways to hell as being 'private robberies and public frauds'. Many landowners were extremely vociferous in the protest they made against specific railway lines. Usually there was little principle involved and their blustering was a transparent cover for simple greed. Their landholdings would be affected by the alignment of a proposed line. They knew that the louder they opposed a scheme, the greater might be the financial compensation they would gain as a result of the compulsory purchase powers that railways received on gaining parliamentary authorisation. Landowners as a class, and some as individuals, had a great deal of political clout in mid-nineteenth century Britain. The concerns of others with less influence were frequently just ignored. The power of the landowning lobby and the amount of money they were able to screw out of the railway companies as compensation for the 'inconvenience' of being forced to sell their land, greatly inflated the cost of building Britain's railway network.

The initial tide of opposition from various quarters to individual railways or railways per se, slowly ebbed when it was becoming obvious that the railways were here to stay and that they tended to generate business and contribute to the growth of the economy and could be a source of enrichment, particularly to the already rich. Over time, however, they settled down to become a focus of criticism, largely, but not exclusively, from those who used them regularly. The 'chattering classes' have always been more numerous and vociferous around London and here we provide some examples of the issues on which they eagerly gorged in the period under review.

A hardy perennial of the complainants was timekeeping. Of course, the railways wriggled on the hook and tried to direct complaints elsewhere. There is nothing new about the blame culture even if it has reached unprecedented heights in recent years. Many services were operated by companies utilising legal running powers over the metals of other railway companies. It was perhaps only to be expected that the company owning the track would not give the same priority to the trains of other companies using its tracks that it gave to its own trains. Delays then often occurred and provided a rich source of grumbles. Sometimes the owning company and the one exercising running powers were at daggers drawn. The running powers issue was often used as a source of excuse or blame even though the average passenger probably had no real idea about this legal arrangement. In 1877, for example, we hear of the LC&DR blaming the GNR, the MR and the L&SWR, all of whom shared a stretch of line, for the constant lateness of its trains. Passengers, of course, were not interested in excuses. They just wanted trains to run on time.

A fruitful source of irritation was the apparent inability of railway companies to keep passengers informed about delays and other untoward events. Contemporary newspapers were full of grumpy outpourings from correspondents describing how their train had come to an unscheduled and prolonged halt for no apparent reason. One such writer vented his spleen because this stoppage had occurred on a line approaching London on a viaduct overlooking busy streets in which people were moving about freely. Some of them even waved as if mocking his predicament. At other times correspondents referred to prolonged waits at a junction while a seemingly endless procession of other trains was given precedence. Worse were the occasions on which trains made prolonged halts in tunnels and nervous passengers with overactive imaginations anticipated some appalling subterranean catastrophe.

Given that even as late as the 1890s most of the trains operating in the London area were composed of compartment stock, in fairness it was very difficult for operating staff to communicate with passengers on trains. Many letters inveighed against railway employees who resolutely refused to explain the reasons for delays or to provide information about how long the stoppage was likely to continue. Some, it was said, made dumb insolence into an art form. While most travellers would probably forgive the occasional out-of-course disruption if the reasons were explained, it must have been tiresome, for example, for the passengers whose 4 mile journey from Farringdon to Finsbury Park regularly took up to three-quarters of an hour simply because the lines traversed could not handle the volume of traffic. The reluctance or simple lack of resources of the GNR to provide the necessary infrastructure was not something the Company wanted its staff to explain to the travelling public.

The railways of London may have constituted a network, but they never amounted to a real system. Perverse delight seems to have been derived from ensuring that trains from different companies did not necessarily make convenient connections. There were many indignant correspondents who grumbled about how they had seen the train they wanted to connect with steaming off into the distance as their own train arrived in the station. They were further irked by what they saw as the scarcely concealed humour of the platform staff at the traveller's predicament.

By no means all delays and annoying events were the result of the railways' ineptitude. It took the travelling public some years to adjust to the unprecedented demands that were created by this revolutionary new form of transport. There were many cases of accidents or deaths and subsequent disruption and delay to services that resulted from passengers, for example, trying to alight from or enter trains in motion. In the early days it was not unknown for passengers, especially those in an advanced state of intoxication, to attempt to ride on carriage roofs. Others might be so befuddled that they decided to walk along the track and were then incapable of moving out of the way of approaching trains. The railway companies were not good at informing travellers about the cause of delays and so letters would go to the newspapers from irascible correspondents who blamed the railway when the problem lay with the stupidity of elements of the travelling public.

The carriages designed for short journeys in London and its immediate environs did not pretend to the rather plusher furnishings and fittings to be found in carriages intended for longer distance travel. Common sources of complaint were jerky braking and acceleration, springs ineffective against a variety of bumps and jolts, overcrowded compartments, dirty windows, and dusty, soiled and smelly seating. There were innumerable complaints about drunken or rude passengers, noisy and unruly infants and pets, about passengers who snored, others who held forth endlessly and boringly about issues they alone considered important to a captive audience within the compartment, and obese passengers whose girth required two seats when they had only paid for one. Others generating complaints were those burdened with parcels or luggage that they spread over the seats rather than placing them on the racks. Passengers who smoked malodorous pipes or whose breath smelt of garlic, for example, came in for opprobrium as did those accused of producing what were coyly referred to as 'windy emanations'. Uncongenial interactions with fellow passengers must have been greatly intensified in the close confines of the average railway compartment of the time.

Smoking was a constant source of complaint and controversy. The railway companies would probably have liked to abolish smoking on trains if only for the mess and the danger of fire that the habit created. However, in 1868 a parliamentary act required them to include smoking carriages in all trains conveying more than one class of passenger. Pipe-smoking was very widespread among working-class men and many working women and there were particularly strong mixtures of shag available which would have produced acrid fumes. Chewing tobacco, pipe-smoking and, to a lesser extent, cigarette smoking, were all often accompanied by the disgusting habit of spitting.

Despite the habit being prohibited, there were always people who insisted on smoking on underground trains. The Metropolitan Railway controversially employed men to see that the non-smoking rule was observed. They were regarded as 'spies', even by non-smokers and the practice was described by some as 'un-English'. Others happily puffed away in the accommodation in surface trains where smoking was banned and regarded it as an infringement of their personal liberty if anyone tried to stop them. There were even strange folk who were non-smokers who did not object to the most noxious of tobacco fumes because they at least partly neutralised other olfactory sensations such as the smell of fish well past its sell-by date which might emanate from the guard's van on a passenger train.

Women have an absolute right to travel on trains without fear of molestation. Early railway compartments were cramped and could be overcrowded. Some men with lascivious propensities took the opportunity to rub themselves against or otherwise touch female passengers in an unacceptable manner. There were always problems arising when women travelled alone and then found themselves being joined in their compartment by an unwelcome male passenger. Some men were intent on robbery while others made lewd suggestions or launched physical attacks of a sexual nature. The introduction of 'ladies only' compartments meant little to such miscreants who might go to great lengths to seek out women travelling alone. At the same time there were male passengers who were extremely wary of entering a compartment containing a single female traveller. It was not unknown for women passengers falsely to claim that they had been insulted or assaulted. A well-known case that went to court concerned a man who entered a compartment at Watford Junction on a train bound for Euston. The compartment contained a lone woman traveller who claimed that the man had indecently assaulted her. There were no witnesses to the alleged assault and if the woman had called out, unfortunately no one had heard her. Witnesses from nearby compartments, when questioned, described her appearance as entirely unruffled and not at all like someone who had just been subjected to an assault. In court, the woman mentioned indignantly that her fellow passenger had further insulted her by smoking a filthy pipe for the whole journey after she had politely asked him to desist. The case was dismissed. The magistrate ruled that a man making an attack of the sort claimed would not have been able to do so while also puffing away on his pipe.

Station staff came in for criticism. Booking clerks were often perceived as unpleasantly snobbish or condescending towards third-class passengers or insufficiently obsequious to those buying first-class tickets. Porters bore the brunt of many complaints often on the grounds of being insufficiently deferential or being downright rude. Some only grudgingly gave their assistance unless it was made clear that they would be tipped, and others were clearly disgruntled if they thought the tip was insufficient. Many of those who had the time and the inclination to write to the papers were precisely the kind of people most likely to be discourteous to railway employees because they considered them to be inferior beings.

The numerous irritations experienced by travellers and the various comedic situations created by the activities of the railways made for a rich seam of humour and social comment. *Punch* magazine, especially in its early more radical days, fully exploited this human tragic comedy.

Chapter 2

SOME MAJOR LONDON STATIONS

CASE STUDY – EUSTON

Euston was the first terminus of a trunk route in London. It was located at the bottom of a gradient of about 1 in 70. This was so steep that for the first seven years trains had to be hauled up to Camden attached to a continuous cable powered by stationary steam engines. Even when later locomotives were much more powerful, many trains out of Euston were still banked by a locomotive at the rear assisting the locomotive at the front and shoving the train up the gradient to Camden. While this made for an impressive sight and sound it was an operating nightmare.

The station opened on 20 July 1837. Euston Station, which stood on land once owned by the Fitzroys whose family seat was Euston Hall in Suffolk, was of great historical significance for being at the London end of the world's first trunk railway. It served the L&BR, but its pioneering role may have had less impact because at first its departures only went as far as Boxmoor in Hertfordshire. The line beyond to Birmingham Great Curzon Street was opened later.

Euston was not the original choice of the L&BR as the site for its terminus. Other locations considered were Islington, Tyburn, Maiden Lane near King's Cross and Camden Town. Just to the west of the Euston site, land was set aside for what was originally intended to be the GWR's London terminus. A joint station offered the attractive possibility of economies for both companies. However, negotiations fell through which is probably just as well as the companies later found themselves directly competing for passengers travelling to Birmingham, Wolverhampton, Chester and Merseyside. The two companies would never have been affable partners.

The original station was simple, with arrivals and departures platform under an overall roof or train shed. A far more imposing statement was Hardwick's symbolic Doric propylaeum or portico. Generally known as the 'Doric Arch', this grandiloquent statement in stone cost £35,000 and was a piece of brash triumphalism superfluous to the company's business of running trains and making a profit for its shareholders. The latter were outraged when they heard how much it had cost. Later development hid the Doric Arch from the Euston Road, thereby adding fuel to the resentment of those who thought it should never have been built. It gained its supporters much later. Sir John Betjeman was one and he described the Euston Arch as 'a gateway from England's capital and heart, London, to her stomach and toyshop, Birmingham'.

A two-storey building contained amenities such as toilets and waiting rooms. First class passengers had the best facilities, those reserved for second class passengers were distinctly second best but a lot better than the provision for third-class passengers which was initially non-existent! Some wealthy first-class passengers arrived at the station in their private carriages. By prior arrangement, these could then be loaded on to flat wagons and the horses placed in horse boxes. These passengers could then remain in their carriages during the journey if they wished. In the arrogant manner of the idle rich, they often arrived only minutes before the train was due to leave and then complained when the train left late having been delayed by the last-minute, time-consuming job of attaching their carriages and horsebox to the rest of the train.

At its opening, Euston boasted only three arrivals and departures each day and these served Harrow, Watford and Boxmoor. On 17 September 1838 the line was completed to Birmingham Curzon Street with a service of nine trains in each direction taking nearly six hours for the journey. A year later, two railway hotels were opened at Euston. The Victoria was a humble establishment while the Euston catered for first-class passengers and was much better appointed. It had 141 bedrooms and only closed in 1963 when the whole of the station was rebuilt for the imminent inauguration of electric services.

Although GWR trains never graced Euston, the Midland Counties (later Midland Railway) obtained running powers over L&BR metals from Rugby for its trains from the East and North Midlands and Yorkshire. These started operating in 1840 and ran until the Midland made other arrangements. Right up to the last days of the old Euston, Platform 9 was still known as the 'York', an example of unwitting historical evidence.

As traffic developed, the station inevitably expanded. Like Topsy, it just grew. It became a haphazard, complicated and unprepossessing jumble of buildings of different ages. It may have been the first major railway terminal in the world but Euston, over the years, proved to be increasingly inconvenient and inefficient for handling growing numbers of passengers and the trains in which they travelled. This was ironic because what became the central core of the station was the magnificent Great Hall opened in 1849. This was a combined concourse and waiting room providing a grandiose focus for the station which increasingly contrasted with the rather ramshackle nature of much of the complex. The architectural features of the Great Hall have often been described and no attempt will be made to do so here with one exception. The ceiling of the Great Hall was decorated with plaster bas-reliefs. These apparently symbolised places served by the trains of the L&NWR which became the station's owner. They were in pairs and were an impressive size, being 10ft long. I remember picking them out as a child. What caught my juvenile interest were the female figures. They were bare-breasted and very generously proportioned. I returned to the Great Hall time and time again for another eyeful and was often reluctant to tear myself away for my ostensible purpose at Euston which was trainspotting. The bas-reliefs represented London, Liverpool, Manchester, Birmingham, Carlisle, Chester, Lancaster and Northampton.

Things happened at the old Euston. On 29 May 1856, Herbert Spencer the philosopher was mugged by footpads and had his watch stolen in the station environs. In 1860 the band of the St Pancras Volunteers was given permission to use the crypt below the station for their practice, conditional on the noise they made not frightening the passengers. In 1864, the Queen's Waiting Room which was rarely used but which had been superbly furnished and fitted out, suffered the indignity of being converted into a parcels office. Soon afterwards the refreshment counter in the Great Hall was closed on Sundays because it had 'become a public resort for loungers and others' during the hours in which the nearby pubs were closed.

The L&NWR was not pleased when the MR built its own independent route to London and arrived with such an overbearing presence just along the Euston Road at St Pancras. This station opened in 1868 and its arrival forced the L&NWR to make various improvements at Euston which was looking distinctly old and tired by comparison. The ground in front of the station was cleared and two small entrance lodges erected which remain to this day. On the quoins of these lodges are incised gilded letters giving the names of principle destinations that could be reached by the company's trains. Even at this time, some of these places were far more conveniently served by the trains of competing companies.

Disparaging comments about Euston led to a further enlargement in 1892 which gave the station extra platforms and expedited improvements particularly to train operation. Despite these developments, the opprobrious comments about Euston continued. In 1900 the L&NWR board of directors obtained legal powers to embark on a much more thoroughgoing reconstruction of the station. The economic problems associated with the Boer War intervened and the plans were put on hold. In the event, reconstruction of Euston was postponed until the 1960s. The rebuilt Euston that emerged, while it may have been easier and more efficient to operate, quickly became one of Britain's most disliked large railway stations, aping although not quite achieving the extraordinary utilitarian repulsiveness of its near-contemporary, the rebuilt Birmingham New Street.

Euston came to be dominated by long-distance services to the West Midlands, to North Wales, Merseyside, Lancashire, the Lake District and Scotland and never had the intensive short-haul suburban provision that was a feature of so many other major London termini. The L&NWR was not at first particularly interested in serving the inner suburbs that were developing in the second half of the century but stations at Chalk Farm and Kilburn High Road opened in 1851, at Willesden Junction in 1866 and at South Hampstead and Queens Park in 1879. The nearest thing in the nineteenth century to a suburban service out of Euston was that to Watford which grew in intensity as the areas around the stations along the line developed residential and other functions.

The coming of the railways allowed people to travel round the country for pleasure, visiting places and buildings of historical, architectural and other interest. While such expeditions were not cheap, they attracted enough people of middling income to create a demand for guidebooks and other items containing material of a chatty, topographical nature. One such publication was *Rides on Railways* by Samuel Sidney. This takes the reader on a rail-borne perambulation over the lines of the L&NWR out of Euston. It is breezily informative and very redolent of the culture of the 1850s when it was published. Sidney makes some interesting comments on Euston. He describes the Arch:

> … as very imposing and rather out of place … Euston, to be viewed to advantage, should be visited by the grey light of a summer or spring morning, about a quarter to six o'clock…At the hour mentioned, the Railway passenger-yard is vacant, silent, and as spotlessly clean as a Dutchman's kitchen; nothing to be seen but a tall soldier-like policeman in green, on watch under the wooden shed, and a few sparrows industriously yet vainly trying to get breakfast from between the closely-packed paving-stones. How different from the fat debauched-looking sparrows who throve upon the dirt and waste of the old coach yards! Presently, hurrying on foot, a few passengers arrive: a servant-maid carrying a big box, with the assistance of a little girl; a neat punctual-looking man, probably a banker's clerk on furlough; and a couple of young fellows in shaggy coats, smoking, who seem by their red eyes and dirty hands, to have made sure of being up early by not going to bed. A rattle announces the first omnibus, with a pile of luggage outside and five inside passengers, two commercial travellers, two who may be curates or schoolmasters, and a brown man with a large sea chest.

He continues for several more pages, bringing the Euston of the 1850s to life.

ST PANCRAS

The Midland Railway was produced by the amalgamation of three existing companies in 1844. It was based in Derby where lines of the three companies met. Although it had outposts elsewhere, for example in places as diverse as Morecambe and Swansea, it was essentially a railway of the Midlands, and it became very aware that it lacked its own route to London. In its early days it was dependent on a company with which it had many rivalries for access to London. From Derby and Leicester its trains travelled over its own metals to Rugby from where London-bound trains used running powers over the L&NWR to Euston. This was far from ideal, and the issue was not really solved when the MR extended a route from Leicester on to Bedford and Hitchin whereupon from 1858 its trains then used running powers over the GNR's route into King's Cross. There was little love lost between these two companies was far from ideal. The GNR obviously required a toll for allowing Midland trains over its metals and, perhaps understandably, was disinclined to give them priority over their own trains. Additionally, the line from Hitchin to King's Cross soon became very congested. The MR did not want to be simply a provincial railway company dependent on others for access to London and it decided to create its own route from Bedford into London and not just for passengers. The company already carried large quantities of coal, especially from the Derbyshire and Nottinghamshire mining districts to the huge industrial and domestic market represented by London. An independent approach to London would be highly advantageous for the expansion and better handling of this traffic.

A GWR express for the West of England about to leave Paddington headed by a Dean 2-4-0. Longer distance traffic predominated at this grand terminus.

The MR may have made something of a belated arrival in the capital but when it finally got there in 1868, it did so with some panache. It built a spectacular terminus at St Pancras, announcing its arrival in uncompromising terms. A passenger station was built which totally overawed the King's Cross terminus of the GNR 'next door'. King's Cross, designed on dignified, simple and functional lines by Lewis Cubitt, was completed in 1852. The other station, a little further away, was Euston of the L&NWR. Apart from its magnificent gateway and the splendid Great Hall and Shareholders' Room, it was a piecemeal and squalid place for passengers and staff alike. The Midland was totally determined that St Pancras would outdo both stations.

The extensive site chosen for the station was far from ideal. It fronted onto the New Road (now Euston Road) which was desirable, but it also contained a canal, a gas works, an ancient church with a large and grossly overcrowded burial ground, an area of atrocious slum housing (Agar Town and Somers Town) and the watercourse of the Fleet River. The St Pancras district was one of London's seediest neighbourhoods. The wretched inhabitants of these rookeries were simply ejected without compensation when the landlords of the hovels in which they dwelt sold out to the Midland. Estimates of the number of those displaced by the building vary from around 30,000 to over 50,000. Another problem that had to be overcome was the presence of the Regent's Canal. The L&NWR in approaching Euston crossed the canal and then dropped down sharply into the station. The Great Northern went below the canal to reach King's Cross. The MR took a different approach. It crossed the canal and then remained on a high level which meant that the gargantuan trainshed and its equally gargantuan hotel rear up almost intimidatingly over Euston Road and King's Cross station.

Millions of words have been used to describe the architecture of St Pancras and only a brief account will be given here. The contract for the design of the station was awarded to W.H. Barlow and he and his associates produced a building strongly influenced by the latest technical advances. A huge train shed was built involving what was then the widest cast-iron span in the world. The structure undoubtedly gained some inspiration from the Crystal Palace which had housed the Great Exhibition of 1851 and showed the constructional use to which glass and cast iron could be put. The roof epitomised the confidence that the best engineers of the time had in these 'new' materials and their ability to construct outstanding buildings with them. The passenger accommodation was in effect built in mid-air within the arched structure because below it at ground level was a huge undercroft, the prime purpose of which was to house beer brought in bulk by the MR from the breweries of Burton-on-Trent.

Prodigious though this train shed might be, the Directors were not finished in their efforts to stamp the distinctive mark of the Midland on the capital. They decided to add a façade to the front of the train shed in the form of an enormous, imposing and extremely luxurious hotel. A competition was held and was won by one of the country's leading architects, George Gilbert Scott. He threw away the stated rules of the competition to come up with a florid creation in a loosely Victorian Gothic style totally dominating its surroundings with its cluster of towers and pinnacles perhaps seen best when looking down Pentonville Road. This was completed in 1876 as the Midland Grand Hotel and it immediately became one of London's premier hotels. It was one of the first to have lifts. These were then rather quaintly called 'ascending rooms'. The MR prided itself on the relative luxury of its trains and it unashamedly aimed the best facilities of the hotel at rich travellers. The Midland entertained hopes of developing a route to Scotland in conjunction with the North British and Glasgow & South Western Railways and the hotel was designed to appeal to the well-heeled Anglo-Scottish travellers it wanted to attract. The station and its hotel were a piece of deliberate showmanship. Ironically, the hotel was never quite the success the MR wanted it to be, and it went out of use as a hotel in 1935 but not before a rich American tourist had famously mistaken it for a church.

The station and the hotel have always excited comment not all of which has been favourable. Perhaps the most vehement criticism was voiced in an article in the *Quarterly Review* of 1872. These excerpts provide a flavour:

The Great Northern Terminus is not graceful but it is simple, characteristic and true. No one would mistake its nature and use. The Midland front is inconsistent in style, and meretricious in detail; a piece of common 'art manufacture' that makes the Great Northern front appear by contrast positively charming. There is no relief or quiet in any part of the work. The eye is constantly troubled and tormented, and the mechanical patterns follow one another with such rapidity and perseverance, that the mind becomes irritated where it ought to be gratified, and goaded to criticism where it should be led calmly to approve…An elaboration that might be suitable for a Chapter-house, or a cathedral choir, is used as an 'advertising medium' for bagmen's bedrooms and the costly discomforts of a terminus hotel, and the architect is thus a more expensive rival of the company's head cook, in catering for the low enjoyments of the great travelling crowd. To be consistent, the directors should not confine their expression of artistic feeling to these great buildings only. Their porters might be dressed as javelin men, their guards as beefeaters, and their station-masters don the picturesque attire of Garter-King-at-Arms…

The author of this venomous philippic hid behind a veil of anonymity and although various names were mentioned, Scott never ascertained the perpetrator with certainty. He could not but have been offended but there were plenty of other commentators who wrote admiringly of his efforts. One such, as succinct as the other was verbose, writing in *The Times* in 1878 said, 'Scott certainly produced in the Midland station at St Pancras the most beautiful terminus in London, remarkable alike for its convenience and its inspiring effect.'

In making their approach to the station, the engineers were forced to take an alignment through the large and very crowded burial ground of Old St Pancras. Reservations were voiced about desecration of the mortal remains interred in the burial ground and it quickly became clear that these were not necessarily being treated with due respect by the contractor and his men on the site. Bodily remains were scattered almost at random and with little sense of order. The public was rather ghoulishly attracted to the site and at first it was possible for them to view the work in progress. Much was made of the report by one such voyeur that he had seen a partially crushed coffin from which a bright and luxuriant tress of hair was visible, presumably from a recent interment. The architect in charge of the reburial was A.W. Blomfield and he instructed one of his assistants to ensure that the work was being carried out in a respectful and proper fashion. The first time he and this assistant visited the site they found a coffin containing two skulls such was the unseemly chaos they witnessed. The assistant was Thomas Hardy, then an architectural apprentice and the horrors that he saw made a lasting impression on him. He later put some of his thought into poetry in *The Levelled Churchyard* (1882) and here are some verses:

O Passenger, pray list and catch
Our sighs and piteous groans,
Half stifled in this jumbled patch
Of wrenched memorial stones!

We late-lamented, resting here,
Are mixed to human jam,
And each to each exclaims in fear,
'I know not what I am!'

The wicked people have annexed
The verses of the good;
A roaring drunkard sports the text
Teetotal Tommy should!

There's not a modest maiden elf
But dreads the final Trumpet,
Lest half of her should raise herself,
And half some local strumpet!

Few people who use St Pancras ever give any thought to exactly who St Pancras was. He seems to have been a boy, a native of Phrygia, who was converted to Christianity and then martyred for his beliefs by the Romans in the early fourth century.

St Pancras Station in the period under review did not handle the volume of traffic to be found at certain other London termini from which intensive suburban services operated. It did, however, provide direct services to a wide variety of provincial towns and cities. These included Glasgow, Edinburgh, Carlisle, Leeds, Bradford, Manchester, Sheffield, Nottingham, Derby and Leicester. In the 1950s, an argument was put forward that London had at least one major station too many and that St Pancras should be closed, and its services diverted to other stations nearby. St Pancras survived to undergo an extraordinary renaissance in the twenty-first century which saw it become London's rail gateway to the Continent.

PADDINGTON

The London & Bristol Railway, progenitor of the Great Western Railway, required a site for a London terminus. Consideration was given to locations at Pimlico near Vauxhall Bridge and at Victoria and legal powers were obtained for the GWR to make a junction with the L&BR in the Wormwood Scrubs area and then have joint use of its station at Euston Square. This proposal must have irked their engineer, Isambard Kingdom Brunel, whose grand vision for the Great Western would certainly not have included sharing a London terminus with a railway with what he regarded as a 'coal-cart' gauge, that is, not the broad gauge. When negotiations with the L&BR broke down, parliamentary powers were obtained for a line to a terminus at what is now Bishop's Bridge Road, slightly west of the future Paddington Station and on the site of what became the GWR's massive Paddington Goods Depot. The GWR's first London station opened on 4 June 1838, trains running only as far as Maidenhead. Through services to Bristol started on 30 June 1841. This station then expanded as traffic developed but it was an unimpressive terminus for a route that contained prodigies of civil engineering such as Wharncliffe Viaduct, Maidenhead Bridge and Box Tunnel. The site contained an engine shed designed by Daniel Gooch which was probably the first railway locomotive roundhouse. The location of this first Paddington Station was still semi-rural, and the parish authorities concerned were confused by the sudden explosion of traffic and human business and activity on their patch once the station was operational. One of the activities which understandably aroused concern was that of male travellers urinating over the bridge into the nearby Regent's Canal. Some did so quite ostentatiously, arousing the ire or even possibly the unspoken envy of some members of the parish council. At that stage the GWR provided no toilets at the station.

Every dog has its day, so the saying goes. This rather mean structure had its day when Queen Victoria arrived on 13 June 1842. She had been staying at Windsor

The vast undercroft at St Pancras has had many uses, one of which was to act as a bonded warehouse for beer brought down from by train from Burton-upon-Trent. The Midland Railway built up a lucrative business selling Burton's distinctive beers to thirsty Londoners despite the capital possessing many large breweries of its own.

Castle and took the train to London from Slough, the nearest railhead. Daniel Gooch, the GWR's Locomotive Superintendent, had driven the locomotive. Perhaps he felt the need to impress because he whirled the train to London at an average speed of no less than 44 mph. This was the young Queen's first journey by rail. She arrived in London sufficiently flustered by the experience for husband Albert discreetly to request that any future journeys on the GWR should be undertaken less speedily (and by implication less hazardously).

In February 1853, the directors of the GWR decided to build a permanent and grander terminus. Brunel masterminded the design of the station but collaborated with the eminent architect Matthew Digby Wyatt particularly on the roof and its supporting columns. Wyatt was also responsible for the delightful oriel windows in the trainshed. The roof with its extensive use of iron and glass drew on the example of the Crystal Palace, designed by Joseph Paxton, which had recently housed the Great

Exhibition in Hyde Park. Brunel had sat on the Committee which chose from several submissions the design they thought most suitable for housing the Exhibition. There was something of the Gothic cathedral in the new Paddington. It had a nave with aisles and even transepts, all under a towering roof of iron and glass and the effect was light and airy. Although not quite complete, the station opened to the public on 16 January 1854. Enlarged with the addition of extra platforms, today's Paddington would still be instantly recognisable to Brunel and Wyatt.

A few months after the station opened, the Great Western Hotel, designed by Philip Hardwick, began operating. This hotel provided the station's frontage onto Conduit Street (later Praed Street) but had not been part of Brunel's grand scheme for Paddington Station. It was a large and architecturally eclectic building, the first of the major railway hotels built in conjunction with London's large railway termini and by general agreement, it provided the best facilities among London's hotels at that time. It was, for a while, the largest hotel in Britain. The GWR had its eyes on what it hoped would be the lucrative and prestigious traffic in well-to-do passengers travelling to the far west of England, to Ireland via ports in the west of Wales and, if Brunel had had his way, also embarking in those ports on steamships designed by himself heading across the Atlantic to the USA. Only the best hotel accommodation would do for such people. By contrast, large numbers of rather insalubrious small hotels appeared in the shadow of Paddington, this becoming a characteristic feature of the streets adjacent to many of London's large terminal stations.

When originally opened, Paddington was almost on the edge of the continuously built-up mass of the metropolis. The GWR needed to minimise the inconvenience caused by the relative isolation of Paddington and it therefore played a major part in the negotiations that eventually led to the opening of the Metropolitan Railway. The first section of this line ran from nearby Bishop's Road to Farringdon on the western fringe of the City. Services started in January 1863. The GWR's participation meant that the line had to be built with mixed gauge track as the Great Western's trains were composed of Brunel's broad gauge rolling stock. Broad gauge trains ceased operating in March 1869. In 1865, trains began running on the Hammersmith & City line operating through Paddington. This line diverged from the GWR main line at Westbourne Park.

When the main line into Paddington opened, it passed through districts which were still rural. Acton and Ealing, for example, were just villages. The GWR showed little interest in serving such places and the first station out of London was West Drayton, over 13 miles away. As mentioned elsewhere (railways and suburban growth), the opening of a station at Ealing led to rapid building development in the vicinity. Even despite continuing suburban growth, the GWR in the nineteenth century gave the impression of being far more interested in long-haul passenger

The glory of the broad-gauge. An immaculate 4-2-2 of the type which hauled the Great Western Railway's front line expresses into and out of Paddington in the 1880s. Who wouldn't be proud to drive such a machine? (Courtesy of John Scott Morgan)

traffic. Paddington was always served by more long-distance trains than any of the other London termini.

The broad gauge (7ft 0¼in) was a typically grandiloquent gesture on the part of Brunel. He argued vehemently for its superiority in terms of speed, safety and carrying capacity and loftily disparaged the standard gauge lines. There are those who have always argued that Brunel was right, and it was the others that were mistaken. A broad-gauge network would, for example, certainly have been able to handle large modern containers more effectively. However, the fact is that with the rest of Britain's major railways going for the standard gauge (4ft 8½in), it became increasingly unrealistic for the GWR to think that all the other companies would eventually come round to its way of thinking. The inevitable had to be recognized, no matter how reluctantly. So it was that trains running over mixed gauge tracks arrived in Paddington in the second half of 1861. Brunel was long in his grave in

Kensal Green Cemetery before the GWR directors took the decision to abandon the broad gauge completely. Even then, with so much investment in broad gauge rolling stock and infrastructure, it was not until 21 May 1892 that the last broad gauge express train left Paddington for Penzance. This departed Paddington at 10.15am and was appropriately headed by the locomotive proudly named *Great Western*. This was a superb 4-2-2 designed by William Dean which had only entered service in 1888.

Some of the atmosphere of Paddington was neatly captured by Sir John Betjeman in *London's Historic Railway Stations*:

> The undergraduates of Oxford used Paddington; and so did Public Schools at Eton, Radley, Marlborough, Shrewsbury, Malvern…hunting people got out at Badminton; carpet manufacturers at Kidderminster; coal owners at Cardiff; jewellers at Birmingham; valetudinarians at Torquay, Leamington, Cheltenham, Tenbury Wells and Tenby; sailors at Plymouth, Devonport and Falmouth; organists used it for the Three Choirs Festival at Worcester, Hereford and Gloucester. The Welsh who seemed so often to be in trains, use it all the time.

Although Betjeman was writing in the twentieth century, what he said could equally well apply to Paddington in Victorian times. The station did always have an indefinable air that its trains served the cathedral cities of the West, the mellow limestone settlements of the Cotswolds, the dreaming spires of Oxford, the gorgeous red cliffs of Teignmouth and Dawlish, the balmy littoral of the Cornish 'Riviera' and mysterious far-flung places in West Wales beyond Swansea and Llanelli. For many, it was always the most romantic of London's big stations.

Chapter 3

UNDERGROUND RAILWAYS COME TO LONDON

L ondon in the 1850s was booming but in danger of sclerosis. It was a victim of its own success with increasing overall wealth and population, more visitors, more trade and commerce. The road system was already at saturation point and beyond. A radical solution to road traffic gridlock was urgently required. In 1855 it was said that it was quicker to travel from Brighton to London by train than to pass through the streets from London Bridge to Paddington. A grand central railway terminus did not seem a real possibility. No railway link between the major termini could possibly be built either at surface level or on viaducts through central London. Opinion moved first in favour of building sub-surface and then later to deep-level tube underground railways which, even if they could not actually solve the problem of road congestion, might at least help to keep it within certain bounds.

THE METROPOLITAN RAILWAY

London can claim many international firsts. One of the most notable of these is the world's first underground railway. This was the Metropolitan Railway. It had its origin in the Bayswater, Paddington and Holborn Bridge Railway and was initially planned to run over a route nearly four miles long from Bishops Road at Paddington to Farringdon Street on the western edge of the City. Not only would it tackle chronic road congestion, but it would allow passengers from the West, the Midlands and elsewhere to move easily from Paddington, Euston and King's Cross to the City. It opened for public use to great acclaim on 10 January 1863 and was soon carrying over 25,000 people daily. The previous day there had been a special train for the directors and selected guests who tucked into a sumptuous banquet at Farringdon. One guest who turned down the invitation was the aged prime minister, Lord Palmerston. Although not generally renowned for his levity, he made a rare quip when he excused himself from this event on the grounds that at his age he would rather remain above ground, knowing that it would not be long before he would be underground permanently.

It quickly became clear that the Metropolitan was going to be successful in terms of passengers carried and some easing of street traffic congestion. It proved that underground railways could be viable financially and could also generate the travel habit, meaning that people who previously might have stayed at home might now make journeys simply because a means of transport was now available.

Among factors put forward for the building of a high-speed transport link between the developing suburbs along the New Road (now the Marylebone and Euston Roads) and the City was the establishment from the late 1830s of important railway termini at Paddington, Euston and King's Cross and the stated intention of the Midland Railway to open one on the same axis, at St Pancras. These stations urgently needed improved transport links with other parts of the metropolis, not least with the City. Horse buses plied between Paddington and the City but became ensnared in traffic congestion. The road system was reaching saturation point.

Various schemes for underground railways had been put forward from the 1830s only to come to nothing but in 1854 parliamentary approval was given for a 'Metropolitan Railway: Paddington and the Great Western Railway, the General Post Office, the London & North Western Railway, and the Great Northern Railway'. However, the railway speculation 'bubble' had burst in the 1840s, the costs of the Crimean War had to be defrayed and little finance was immediately available, meaning that there was a delay before construction work began.

The City & South London Railway was the world's first successful underground 'tube' railway, and it used electric traction from the start. It opened in 1890 and ran for just over three miles from the City and then under the Thames to Stockwell. Trains were initially hauled by curious little locomotives hauling even more curious coaches with minute windows. They were claustrophobic and soon became known as 'padded cells'. Despite this, the line was a success. This scene depicts Stockwell Depot c.1895. (Courtesy of John Scott Morgan)

The line was built on the then novel 'cut-and-cover' principle with a deep trench or subway being excavated along which the tracks were laid, and which was then partially roofed over. Roads or buildings could then be erected over the path of the line. As far as possible to minimise the expense of compulsory purchase of buildings along the route or of tunnelling under other buildings which could be damaged and for which compensation might have to be paid, the line ran under existing roads. In many places the tracks were open to the sky to allow the smoke to disperse. Obviously while the construction work was going on, great disruption was caused to road traffic. It also involved the diversion of the complex system of pipes for the various utilities that runs unseen below the surface. The covered way resulting from these efforts was built sufficiently wide to house the broad-gauge track required by trains of the GWR. It had been agreed that their trains and those of the GNR would have access to the metals of the Metropolitan so mixed gauge track had to be provided. At Farringdon Street, the initial eastern terminus, a spur was built to the new Central Meat Market at Smithfield which was completed in 1868. The Metropolitan and the GWR, the two companies involved, clearly had their eyes on the business opportunities the new market offered.

Given the massive scale of the civil engineering works involved, the building of the Metropolitan was completed remarkably easily. The only major incident occurred in June 1862 when the Fleet River, the valley of which was followed by the railway between King's Cross and Farringdon, burst through retaining walls and flooded the workings. The Fleet was effectively a sewer, and the resulting mess does not bear thinking about. On 1 November 1860, the boiler of a locomotive exploded near King's Cross. The driver and fireman were killed as was an unlucky passing cabman when the locomotive's chimney landed on his head.

From the start there had been concerns about the smuts and smoke that would be produced by the steam locomotives hauling the trains. People living close to the line complained that their garden shrubs were being killed by the toxic sulphurous fumes created by the trains. Stations like Baker Street which were entirely subterranean were characterised by a poisonous and almost impenetrable fug which caused travellers to cough, splutter, expectorate and complain vehemently but largely impotently. The sooty miasma proved to be a boon for pickpockets. The carriages were poorly lit by oil lamps which emitted a foul smell and dripped on passengers. The dim light produced flickered capriciously. Regular travellers who wanted to read often stuck candles on to the inside of the carriage near where they were sitting. Early underground travel was not for the faint-hearted. Complaints poured in to the Company and not only from the travelling public. Those employed on operating the line asked for permission to grow beards and moustaches to provide a protection against the sulphurous fumes. Their requests were granted.

The Times had been highly sceptical regarding the likely success of the proposed line. An article told readers:

A subterranean railway under London was awfully suggestive of dark, noisome tunnels, buried many fathoms deep beyond the reach of light or life; passages inhabited by rats, soaked with sewer droppings, and poisoned by the escape of gas mains. It seemed an insult to common sense to suppose that people who could travel as cheaply to the city on the outside of a Paddington 'bus would ever prefer as a merely quick medium, to be driven amid palpable darkness through the foul subsoil of London.

In anticipation of the problems caused by operating steam locomotives below ground, an attempt was made to produce a locomotive described as 'smokeless'. The intention was for a white-hot firebrick to heat the water in the locomotive's boiler and produce the steam needed for propulsion without creating smoke while the locomotive was operating on the underground parts of the line. Robert Stephenson designed and built an experimental locomotive in 1861. Without doubt a great and resourceful engineer, the resulting locomotive was not one of his greater successes. True, the machine produced very little smoke, but it also produced very little steam and it was all it could do to pull itself around, let alone haul a train. Although an impressive-looking machine, its looks belied its performance and it quickly disappeared from public view, not, however, before having gained the derisive nickname 'Fowler's Ghost' because no one was sure that it actually existed. Fowler, later Sir John Fowler, was the engineer in overall charge of the Metropolitan project at this point. Daniel Gooch, the locomotive superintendent of the GWR, designed a class of powerful 2-4-0Ts for use on the Metropolitan. These had open cabs and life must have been grim for their drivers and firemen. Relations between the GWR and the Metropolitan became fraught, and the latter company introduced its own 4-4-0 tank engines built by Beyer-Peacock which proved to be highly successful. They had apparatus which allowed them to condense much of their steam. At least that was the theory.

Despite apocalyptic predictions that the building of underground railways would disturb the Devil, who would then proceed to wreak his revenge in many horrible ways, and equally dire warnings that tunnels and cuttings would collapse, crushing those brazen and stupid enough to travel on it, the line from Paddington to Farringdon was an almost total success. This was not before a disgruntled traveller had put pen to paper and written to *The Times:*

I was almost suffocated and was obliged to be assisted from the train at an intermediate station. On reaching the open air I requested to be taken to a chemist close at hand. Without a moment's hesitation he said, 'Oh I see, Metropolitan

Railway' and at once poured out a wine glass of what I conclude he designated Metropolitan Mixture. I was induced to ask him whether he often had such cases, to which he rejoined, 'Why bless you, Sir, we often have twenty cases a day.'

A journey on the steam-hauled underground was not for those of a delicate constitution. A traveller in 1887 described a journey from Baker Street to Moorgate as his 'first experience of Hades'. He continued:

The compartment in which I sat was filled with passengers who were smoking pipes as is the British habit, and as the smoke and sulphur from the engine filled the tunnel, all the windows have to be closed. The atmosphere was a mixture of sulphur, coal dust and foul fumes from the oil lamp above: so that by the time we reached Moorgate Street I was nearly dead of asphyxiation and heat. I should think these underground trains must soon be discontinued because they are a menace to health.

The Metropolitan was generally a success except for Sarah Dobner, a 56-year-old woman who had a bronchial condition greatly exacerbated, it was believed, by what the coroner's court described in 1867 as 'the suffocating atmosphere of the Underground Railway'. There certainly was an acrid fug for much of the time on the stations and the issue of adequate ventilation continued to excite controversy and was only finally ended with the electrification of the sub-surface lines. The Metropolitan claimed that the sulphurous conditions were beneficial to those with asthmatic and bronchial conditions. Fug apart, the Metropolitan Railway proved to be a safe and quick form of transport. Interestingly, when the line opened, the company refused to allow smoking on its trains, but pressure built up over the years and smoking coaches were introduced in 1874.

The construction of the line caused the kind of disruption which has become only too familiar to later generations of London right through into the twenty-first century. Official figures stated that just 307 people were displaced by the building of the Paddington to Farringdon line, but some contemporaries estimated a figure nearer 12,000 including some notorious slums in the Clerkenwell area.

The success of the Metropolitan Railway concentrated minds and was followed by the opening of the Hammersmith & City line in June 1864. This was built by a nominally independent company with the support of the GWR and the Metropolitan and was designed as a feeder to the Metropolitan. The track was mixed gauge and it connected Hammersmith with the Metropolitan at Paddington, thereby giving districts in West London direct access to the fringe of the City. One of the quirks of London's railway history resulted from the building of this line was that it spawned a branch which linked up with the West London and the West London Extension

THE TWOPENNY TUBE

"Hi, guv'nor, there ain't no station named on this ticket!"
"No; all our tickets are alike."
"Then, 'ow do I know where I'm going?"

The flat fare of twopence on the Central Line in its early days was a radical idea but also the butt of some humour as this slightly heavy-handed *Punch* cartoon shows.

Railways. With a connecting link to Victoria, this meant that trains of the LB&SCR appeared in Paddington and Great Western broad-gauge trains in turn graced Victoria, a piquant thought for today's railway enthusiasts.

The Hammersmith & City ran through some largely rural districts and where stations were opened in these areas, examples being Latimer Road and Goldhawk Road, it established the practice associated with the opening of underground railways whereby speculative builders frequently moved in soon afterwards and housing and other development quickly followed. Where the line had stations in existing built-up areas, it tended to have the effect of changing their social character. Ladbroke Grove was an example. The large and elegant terraces of this district were already degenerating into multi-occupancy. The opening of the line accelerated this process as well as leading to much infilling with smaller housing which came to be occupied by people from the lower-middle classes. The population of Hammersmith boomed as the result of the arrival of the Hammersmith & City and later the District Line.

The Metropolitan had become busier on 1 October 1863 when GNR trains began running to Farringdon Street. At the same time, broad gauge trains of the GWR commenced operating from Windsor to Farringdon. An extension had been

District Railway Beyer-Peacock 4-4-0T no 29 c.1903. Both the District and the Metropolitan Railways used very similar types of highly successful locomotives fitted with condensing apparatus and built by Beyer-Peacock of Manchester. (Courtesy of John Scott Morgan)

authorised eastwards to Moorgate Street in the City. To ease traffic flows it was decided that the line between King's Cross and Moorgate should be quadrupled and the result was the 'Widened Lines' as this stretch of line came to be known. Trains began running to Moorgate in 1865. GNR trains ran to places in Hertfordshire as far away as Hatfield and Hitchin.

An important development was a line running from just south of Farringdon Street through Snow Hill and Ludgate Hill. This line was operated by the LC&DR, and it opened to traffic in May 1869. It provided an important cross-London route which came to be used not just by the passenger trains of various companies but also by many freight trains. It was never part of the underground system although it traversed the Widened Lines north of Farringdon. It eventually became part of the Overground system and flourishes today. The LC&DR's line generated much controversy in its early years because it crossed Ludgate Hill on a bridge which spoiled the much-loved view up to St Paul's Cathedral. Yet more traffic began to flow on the Widened Lines from July 1868 when trains of the MR started running into Moorgate. In 1869 the GWR ceased to run broad gauge trains on the Metropolitan Railway.

The Metropolitan Railway was a pioneer when in 1864 it offered cheap tickets for workmen travelling early in the morning. These tickets proved immensely popular. From the start the company was happy to accommodate third class passengers and indeed over two-thirds of the accommodation on its early trains was for them.

Much has been made in recent years about the regenerative effect that an improved transport infrastructure can have on a stagnant or declining area. The Jubilee Line extension was an example. Proximity to the Metropolitan back in the 1860s became a major selling point in the advertisements of businesses close to its route, many of whom found that the railway brought them new customers. The Metropolitan soon became exceptionally busy. In 1865 over 350 trains left Farringdon between 5.15am and midnight.

THE DISTRICT AND INNER CIRCLE LINES

The Metropolitan Railway acted as a model for more similar lines. The most urgent need was for a line to link the various main line termini and hopefully reduce the road traffic they generated. An Act had been passed to build an embankment on the north side of the Thames intended to relieve traffic congestion along the Strand and to house a major sewer. This was the work of the great engineer Sir Joseph Bazalgette. It would economise on resources if such a line could run along this proposed embankment. The idea was that this line would extend the Metropolitan via the City, the Embankment, Westminster, Victoria and Kensington to Paddington. It was designed to be an inner circle railway link although it was, of course, not circular.

This proposal received parliamentary approval in July 1864. Once again, Sir Henry Fowler was the engineer. The section from Kensington to Tower Hill was called the Metropolitan District Railway. It initially had close links with the Metropolitan and it was intended that in due course the two concerns would amalgamate.

The line passed through some very affluent districts especially around Kensington and Notting Hill and met with considerable opposition from powerful landowners who were able to extract excessive compensation from the company. At Leinster Gardens, Bayswater, the line was in a particularly shallow cutting and the demolition of Nos. 23 and 24 could not be avoided. The company was legally required to maintain the appearance of the street and so wooden screens designed to replicate the facades of the two adjacent houses were erected and have become well-known among London's many visual oddities. Another curiosity which resulted from the building of the line can still be seen at Sloane Square Station. This is an iron conduit which crosses the station and contains the Westbourne, one of London's many hidden rivers. On rare quiet moments, a gurgling noise can be heard, usually after heavy rain.

The Metropolitan District, which we will now call the District Line, and the Metropolitan, fell out over various issues and the amalgamation never did take place. Worse than that, the acrimonious relationships between the two verged on the childish. In 1879, legislation authorised the two warring companies to work together and complete the circle as well as to build a link from Aldgate to connect with the East London Railway at Whitechapel. In 1884 the latter line was completed. No love was lost when the Metropolitan started running trains from Hammersmith via King's Cross and over the East London Railway to New Cross to connect with the SER. By way of an ill-tempered retort, the District then ran trains from Hammersmith via Temple and the East London Railway to New Cross Gate to link up with the LB&SCR.

The mutual antipathy of the Metropolitan and District descended to the level of farce. While final arrangements were being made for the opening of the Inner Circle, they were in dispute about access to a particular siding at South Kensington. The District asserted its territorial claim by running a locomotive and a short train into the siding and chaining it to the track to pre-empt any action by the Metropolitan. Before long, the Metropolitan came along with three of their locomotives, intent on removing the District Line's rolling stock from the siding. A tug-of-war then ensued with the Metropolitan literally trying to heave their hated rivals off the short piece of disputed track. The Metropolitan was unsuccessful in this venture.

Early extensions of the District Line took in Hammersmith in June 1877, Ealing 1879, Putney Bridge in 1880 and Wimbledon in 1889. The District and the LT&SR jointly owned a line connecting the District's Whitechapel terminus to the LT&SR at Bow. This opened in 1902. The District line benefited from serving South

Kensington, sometimes described as 'Albertopolis'. It became a focus of museums built partly with the profits from the Great Exhibition of 1851 of which Prince Albert had been a keen promoter. The District even built a pedestrian subway from South Kensington to Exhibition Road where the museums were housed, and it developed significant leisure traffic to these attractions. Another draw, access to which the District facilitated, was Earls Court with its exhibition halls and the Big Wheel, opened in 1895. This structure proved hugely popular during its working life of twelve years.

The Metropolitan Railway, for its part, came under the management of the bullish, even ruthless, Sir Edward Watkin. He had big ideas for it, wanting to develop it into a main line company and under his auspices it thrust north-westwards from Baker Street into Buckinghamshire. It opened to Harrow-on-the-Hill in 1880, Pinner in 1885, Chesham 1889, Rickmansworth in 1887 and Aylesbury 1892. The transport infrastructure for the 'Metroland' of the future was being built.

THE EAST LONDON RAILWAY

By the late eighteenth century, there was an urgent need for a better crossing of the Thames to the east of London Bridge, particularly between Rotherhithe and Wapping. There were docks and warehouses on both sides of the river and an effective means of linking them was required to avoid the long detour by road via London Bridge. A bridge was considered unsuitable so the idea of a tunnel at this point was advanced. No one had previously tunnelled such a distance under water and many people thought it simply could not be done. A company was set up to investigate the practicalities. A pilot tunnel was not far off completion in 1808 when the river broke in and the project was abandoned.

This shows that the Thames Tunnel eventually found a railway use. How the Brunels would have been amazed that this tunnel would eventually house a busy and crucial part of the railway network.

In 1818 Marc Brunel patented an ingenious tunnelling shield based on his knowledge of how the misnamed 'shipworm' or teredo, actually a mollusc, bored through wood lining a minute tunnel as it went. Confident that a machine had now been found to do the trick, the Thames Tunnel Company was established to build a tunnel, again from Rotherhithe to Wapping. Work started in March 1825. The tunnelling shield was the pioneer of all such devices including the immensely sophisticated tunnel drilling machines used today. The project proved extremely difficult and far more expensive than anticipated. Abandoned for a while, it eventually opened amid great celebration on 25 March 1843. It was designed for vehicular traffic with two carriageways, but it was never used for that purpose because there was no money available to build the ramps that would have provided access for wheeled vehicles. At first the tunnel attracted sightseers in large numbers, but the gimmick wore off and it became merely a rather grand underwater footpath decorated with many market stalls for a time. It later became notorious as a place where ladies of the night plied their trade and footpads lurked. The Thames Tunnel looked as if it was going to be a white elephant.

The carriageways were spacious, and it made sense for the tunnel to be used to house a railway running under the river. The East London Railway (ELR) was formed in 1865. It acquired the semi-derelict tunnel with a view to allowing railway companies to run their trains through it on payment of a toll. It was not intended that the ELR would operate trains itself. In 1866 the section opened from Wapping to New Cross (later renamed New Cross Gate) where it connected with the LB&SCR and the initial service through the tunnel was operated by that company. In 1876 the line was extended at the northern end enabling LB&SCR trains to run into the GER's Liverpool Street terminus. A short-lived through service between Liverpool Street and Brighton proved unsuccessful. The SER also had powers to operate through the tunnel and in 1880 it joined the fun with a service from Addiscombe Road to Liverpool Street through its own New Cross station. In 1884 these trains were diverted via the newly built Whitechapel Curve to St Mary's Junction on the joint line of the Metropolitan & District Railways. This provided access to the heart of the City of London, the West End and other parts of the metropolis and places further apart. On 6 October 1884 the Metropolitan began running services from its station at Hammersmith to New Cross and the District operated from its Hammersmith station to what was to become New Cross Gate. In 1886 the GER began running trains over the ELR to and from Liverpool Street.

Despite what might seem to have been a wide range of travel options offered by the East London Railway, passenger traffic levels proved disappointing. Income was low because so many passengers were carried at discounted workmen's fares. In August and December 1905, the Metropolitan and the District Railways respectively ceased to operate services through the Thames Tunnel. In 1911, LB&SCR trains from

Shoreditch to Peckham Rye were withdrawn and the surviving through trains south of New Cross and New Cross Gate were also withdrawn. A considerable amount of steam-hauled freight traffic passed over the East London Railway and there were occasional steam-hauled excursions from eastern parts of London to resorts on the South Coast. The East London Railway was a curious kind of backwater, and few would have predicted its reinvention with intensive services in the twenty-first century to a range of destinations previously undreamt of.

THE TOWER SUBWAY

The lines mentioned so far were sub-surface, employing cut-and-cover construction wherever possible. The Tower Subway was a pioneer of a different sort. It was the world's first tube railway, though others soon followed. It proved that tunnels could be constructed at a level deep enough to avoid the increasingly complicated network of sewers and pipes to be found under London. The underlying clays were relatively easy to bore through with the technology becoming available at that time.

Peter William Barlow was an engineer of many parts who wanted to see whether it was possible to build railways running underground in iron tubes. In 1864 his associate James Henry Greathead patented a circular adaptation of Marc Brunel's tunnelling shield. In 1868 the Tower Subway Company was formed to build a tube tunnel under the Thames from Tower Hill to Southwark. It was to be 445yd long and the Greathead device was to be used in its construction. The internal diameter of the tubes was less than 6ft 9in. The space between the tubes and the surrounding earth was filled with liquid cement, a process used in tunnelling ever since. At its deepest, the tunnel was 66ft below high-water level. Lifts were provided to and from the surface. A strange windowless and claustrophobic car with maximum seating for twelve ran along a track with a 2ft 6in gauge. Small stationary steam engines provided cable haulage and the official opening was on 2 August 1870. It was a remarkable piece of engineering, but the passenger car was too small to carry a viable payload of passengers. It was decided to cut losses and convert the venture into a foot tunnel from 24 December 1870. Pedestrians paid a one halfpenny toll to use it and in its new guise it was successful until Tower Bridge opened nearby in 1894. Passengers could walk across the bridge for free. Nobody wanted the subway then. The two little brick-built entrances to the tunnel can still be seen and the tunnel now carries water pipes. The northern entrance is at Tower Hill, the southern at Vine Street.

THE CITY & SOUTH LONDON RAILWAY

The Greathead tunnelling shield proved to be a great success and it was soon to be employed on a project of national, indeed international importance. This was the City & South London Railway (C&SLR) which was the first major underground railway in the world to operate in deep-level tube tunnels.

The City of London & Southwark Subway Company was incorporated in July 1884. Greathead was appointed engineer. The northern terminus in the City was to be at King William Street near the Monument and, having travelled under the Thames, the line would then pass under Borough High Street and Newington Causeway to terminate at Elephant & Castle. Work began in February 1886 and in 1887 legislative approval was given to the line being extended to Stockwell, giving it a total length of just over three miles. Steam-powered trains were bad enough on the subsurface lines but inconceivable on a tube railway. At first the intention was that the line should be cable-powered but the idea of electric traction had some appeal and so the decision was made to electrify it right from the start. Formal opening of the line took place on 4 November 1890 by which time the owners had changed its name to the City & South London Railway. Public services started on 18 December. The opening of this novel project generated great interest and over 10,000 passengers passed through the King William Street station barriers that day.

Small electric locomotives hauled passenger cars with seats for thirty-two. It is interesting that the early cars were not provided even with minute windows as the company argued that there was nothing for passengers to see. The cars which were noisy and claustrophobic, soon came to be known as 'padded cells'. *Punch* magazine, which enjoyed satirising new economic and social phenomena, referred to the line as the 'sardine box railway'. A flat fare of 2d was levied, passengers inserting their money in a turnstile. Although staff called out the names of stations, it is obvious that passengers preferred to have windows even if there was nothing to see and so later carriages were indeed equipped with them. All stations were provided with lifts from the start, necessary for a deep-level line. The line reduced the travel time between Stockwell and King William Street by more than half.

The C&SLR was successful, a total of 5,363,000 passengers being carried in the first full year, some undoubtedly riding just for the experience. It was extended to Moorgate in February 1900, the section from Borough to King William Street being abandoned. The new piece of line had a station near King William Street at Bank. It was an awkward site, and the booking hall was fashioned partly out of the crypt of St Mary Woolnoth church. This is a fifteenth-century church rebuilt by Wren after the Great Fire of London. It was later rebuilt by Hawksmoor but the use of its lower quarters cost the C&SLR £170,000 in compensation. While it may have been an ingenious piece of engineering, it was also an expensive one. In June 1900 a second extension to Clapham Common came into use and in 1901 another extension, to Angel, was opened. Moorgate was on this part of the line and there was an interchange there with the Metropolitan Railway, the first example of an arrangement which became a familiar feature of the underground and indeed a necessary one, for it allowed what was basically an unplanned collection of lines to be welded into something approaching a coordinated system. A northern extension to Euston was completed in 1907. The line was now a vital link between South London, Southwark, the City and the main line stations for the North. The line was incorporated into the London Underground Group on 1 January 1913.

In August 1893, the Charing Cross, Euston & Hampstead Railway received parliamentary approval. This was intended to run from a point near the Strand to the High Street at Hampstead with a branch to Euston. As with many other schemes in the 1890s, this one made little initial progress because of lack of money but work began in earnest in 1902. An extension was planned to rural Golders Green and a branch to the foot of Highgate at a point then called 'Highgate' but more familiar today as Archway. This project would be the first tube to include a branch and a junction, this being at Camden Town. Both lines were opened on 22 June 1907, and on that day, travel was free, over 120,000 taking advantage of an offer they could not refuse.

The Northern Line was unusual in having a station which could not be closed because it never opened. This was located at North End, Hampstead and was built in anticipation of housing development nearby which was slow in coming. Many parts of the station were built deep below but no building was ever erected at street level. This station was named informally as 'Bull and Bush' after the nearby pub immortalised in the music hall song.

THE WATERLOO & CITY

London's second tube railway was the Waterloo & City. This was a creature of the L&SWR which needed to make a quick connection from its Waterloo terminus to the City of London, the chosen destination of many of its passengers, particularly commuters. It had already given up the idea of a surface extension into the City or to London Bridge. These schemes would have been prohibitively expensive given all the existing buildings that would need to have been bought and demolished. Work on building a deep level tube began in 1894 and the destination was a spot near the Mansion House, the station being called 'City' for its first forty-three years. There were two separate tube tunnels, and electric multiple-unit traction was employed. Controversially, the initial rolling stock was ordered from an American company which was able to promise delivery earlier than the six British companies that tendered. There were grumbles about the lack of patriotism. The cars were completed at Eastleigh Works. The line opened on 11 July 1898. There were no intermediate stations. As an economy measure, no lifts were provided at either end of the line and passengers needed to be sound in wind and limb to make it to street level. The line quickly gained the nickname 'The Drain'. As the tube system grew in the years before 1914, there was never any attempt to subsume the Waterloo & City within the main underground system. Indeed, it was not until 1994 that it became part of London Underground.

Some unusual conditions were written into the Act authorising the Waterloo & City. Special care was required to safeguard the stability of the Mansion House, *The Times* office in Printing House Square, the viaducts of the SER and the LC&DR and the tunnels of the District Railway.

A curiosity of this line was that it has never had any physical connection with any other railway and when rolling stock needed extensive maintenance, it has always had to be raised by a hoist to a connection with the main surface lines at Waterloo. Because the line was used almost exclusively by commuters, it closed early in the evening and was not open at weekends.

THE CENTRAL LONDON RAILWAY

This major undertaking was London's third tube railway. 'Parliamentary approval was received in August 1891 for a line six miles long from Shepherd's Bush to 'Bank' in the City with the intention of a later extension to Liverpool Street. Work started on the building of the line in early 1896. Sir Benjamin Baker, Sir John Fowler and James Henry Greathead made a formidable trio to look after the engineering aspects of the project. Powerful electric locomotives were built in the USA and the coaches were more substantial than those used on earlier tube lines. Altogether, the 'Tuppenny Tube', as it was quickly dubbed because of its flat fare, seemed a more sophisticated railway than its predecessors.

The Prince of Wales, soon to be Edward VII, performed the formal opening ceremony. Grandiloquent speeches, copious toasting and sumptuous eating was the norm for the chosen few on these occasions. A gathering of the great and good and, doubtless, some of the not-so-good, was held at Shepherds Bush. Oddly, perhaps, Mark Twain was among the invited guests. The line opened to the public three days later, on 30 July 1900. Londoners (and others) thronged to enjoy an early ride. The line provided quick and easy access from residential districts in West London through the West End and into the heart of the financial and mercantile quarter. Its impact was immediately more evident than that of previous tube schemes. It was useful that the line ran the length of Oxford Street. This was developing as a retail hub and the Central Line is likely to have contributed to this process.

The Central Line was soon carrying heavy passenger traffic because its route enabled it to serve travellers for commuter, commercial and leisure purposes. However, no sooner had it started running than complaints poured in about the vibrations its trains were causing in buildings located above the line. The most vociferous complaints came from well-heeled and influential inhabitants of prestigious districts like Mayfair. Unlike the hoi polloi whose views could largely be ignored, the views of these complainants could not be lightly dismissed. A body of experts known as the 'Vibration Committee' investigated and concluded that the cause lay with the heavy and massive electric locomotives. In 1903, therefore, they were replaced by much lighter electric multiple-unit trains. Were these the first multiple-unit trains in Britain? Another issue which raised many complaints was the unpleasant aroma which permeated platforms and trains. Fans were unable to alleviate the problem and it was not until 1911 that a system was developed which washed and ionised the air and eliminated the smell. An ingenious innovation pioneered by the Central London Company was the placing of stations at the top of short, gentle gradients which meant that trains slowed down as they approached the stations and were then able to accelerate away more quickly. This gave appreciable savings in fuel costs.

The fact that the Central London Railway was a long time gestating was partly because of various engineering problems that were encountered but largely because of the difficulty in raising the necessary capital. The sub-surface and the C&SLR lines proved expensive to build but although they carried healthy numbers of passengers, they did not make much in the way of profits for their shareholders. Many other projects were able to attract smaller investors with the promise of surer and greater returns. The Central London was relatively lucky in that it managed to obtain much of its funding through a syndicate of prestigious financiers including several in the USA. Not the least of the engineering problems was persistent penetration of the workings by water from the Tyburn, a river which flows under Oxford Street not far from Marble Arch.

The Central London and indeed the other early underground lines made much in their advertising about their advantage in terms of speed over vehicular traffic on the streets above. The trains were smartly timed, but they often failed to keep exactly to their schedules because of the reluctance of passengers to embark on and alight from the trains quickly enough. One journal likened the customary speed at which passengers moved to the slow and dignified progress appropriate to mourners at a funeral. This issue was a question of education and so posters and publicity urged travellers to develop the sense of urgency that was essential if trains were to run on time. Their campaign was a successful one although it took a decade or more for it to become the norm.

In May 1908 a short extension was made from Shepherds Bush to Wood Lane to serve the White City. In July 1912 the eastern end of the line was extended to Liverpool Street to provide connections with main line trains to East Anglia and the intensive network of local trains running from that station. Legal authority was obtained to extend from Wood Lane to Ealing Broadway in 1913 but the war intervened, and this piece of line did not open until 3 August 1920. Two possible extensions which never happened and are scarcely remembered these days was one in 1902 which proposed to extend the line from Shepherds Bush to Hammersmith, Piccadilly, Strand and the City to form a 'Central London Circle'. The other was in 1913 when powers were obtained to make a connection from Shepherds Bush to the L&SWR at Gunnersbury which would have given the Central Line running powers to Richmond.

An unusual feature of the Central Line in its first two decades was the conveyance of parcels. Their delivery by cycle courier from a convenient station was included in the price.

THE PICCADILLY LINE

There was never a grand plan to build a line from Cockfosters near Enfield Chase in Hertfordshire, through central London, and on towards Hounslow. The modern Piccadilly Line has its origins in the Brompton & Piccadilly Circus Railway Company which was incorporated on 6 August 1897 and authorised to build a line, 2 miles in length, from Piccadilly to South Kensington. On the same day, the Metropolitan District Railway obtained powers to build a deep-level tube line under its existing sub-surface line between Earls Court and Mansion House with an intermediate station at Charing Cross. The Great Northern & Strand Railway received parliamentary sanction on 1 August 1899 to build a line about 6 miles long from Wood Green under the Great Northern Railway's main line to Finsbury Park and King's Cross and then on to a terminus in the Strand.

It was about this time that the transport scene in London was hit by a whirlwind in the shape of one Charles Tyson Yerkes. Ruthless entrepreneur or enterprising businessman depending on one's point of view, he was an American looking for promising outlets for spare US capital. Backed by a syndicate of other American financiers, in 1900 he gained control of what became the original section of the Northern Line and in 1901 did likewise with the District Railway. In 1901 he established the Metropolitan District Electric Traction Company which absorbed the District, the proposed Hampstead Line and various other companies that had been authorised to build tube lines, but which had not yet commenced construction work. These included the Brompton & Piccadilly Circus (B&P) and the Great Northern & Strand (GN&S). In 1902 the Metropolitan District Electric Traction Company changed its name to the Underground Electric Railways Company of London Ltd. The B&P and the GN&S were merged with the latter project being abandoned north of Finsbury Park and being extended from Piccadilly Circus to Hammersmith in an agreement with the District Railway.

There now followed a feeding frenzy of tube railway promotion and in 1902 twenty-six Bills came before parliament seeking legal authorisation. The London United Tramways was proposing a tube line from Charing Cross to Hammersmith via Hyde Park Corner while a rival American financier, J. Pierpont Morgan, appeared on the scene and announced in May 1902 his intention of promoting 40 miles of tube line which would include one from Tottenham and Southgate to Hammersmith. In the event, Yerkes totally outmanoeuvred this, and other schemes promulgated by Morgan who withdrew wounded from involvement with London's proposed tube railways. The London United Tramways was also subsumed within the Yerkes group.

We seem now to arrive in an age not only of feverish tube-line projection but also of verbose tube line nomenclature. In late 1902 the GN&S and the B&P projects were basically brought together as the Great Northern, Piccadilly & Brompton Railway. The proposed section north of Finsbury Park was formally abandoned while a link from Piccadilly to Holborn was to be built to bring the two projects together. The section from South Kensington applied the earlier powers granted for a tube line below the District's own line and then a surface line to run to Hammersmith alongside the District. The proposal for a line to Aldwych now became one just for a short branch from Holborn.

Yerkes may have bullied and browbeaten his way round the capital's emerging underground railway system but he even he showed that he was not immortal, and he died back in the USA on 29 December 1905 without seeing any of his schemes come to fruition.

What was now generally called the Piccadilly Line from Finsbury Park to Hammersmith was opened throughout on 15 December 1906. The Aldwych branch was opened on 30 November 1907. The terminus station of the branch was originally called 'Strand' and became 'Aldwych' on 9 May 1915. The area around the present-day Kingsway and Aldwych constituted a notorious slum and the building of the line was one way of opening the area up for new development.

In October 1911, the platforms of the Piccadilly and District Lines at Earl's Court were linked by an escalator, the first in London. The travelling public were cautious of this device and so 'Bumper Harris', a man with a wooden leg, was allegedly employed to travel all day up and down this escalator. The assumption presumably was that if it was safe for a man with a peg leg, it was safe for everyone else. It must have worked because escalators soon proved they were here to stay. The story may be apocryphal.

THE BAKERLOO LINE

In the 1860s it began to be seen as desirable for a railway link to be made between Charing Cross and the increasingly important terminus of the L&SWR at Waterloo. Such a link would expedite travel between the Surrey shore and the governmental and administrative hub around Whitehall and Westminster and the leisure and retail facilities of the West End. Early attempts to open a link met with little success. The first was the Waterloo and Whitehall Railway proposal of 1865 which intended to use pneumatic propulsion. Nothing came of this scheme. In 1882, the Charing Cross & Waterloo Electric Railway was legally incorporated to build an electric line under the Thames. It seems that work was started but shortage of money caused construction to cease, never to be resumed.

The idea did not disappear, however. In March 1893 the Baker Street and Waterloo Railway was incorporated by law. Money again prevented progress but in 1896 a

A District Railway train arriving at Putney Bridge hauled by one of the ubiquitous and capable 4-4-0Ts. Circa 1900.

business consortium of venture capitalists obtained parliamentary sanction for a line from the projected terminus of what would later be the Great Central Railway in the Marylebone district to Waterloo. Work began in August 1898. In 1900, powers were obtained to make extensions to Elephant & Castle and to Paddington. The consortium, known as London & Globe, failed in 1901 and work ground to a halt. The man behind London & Globe was a crook who enjoyed a short time as a fat cat before investigation revealed his business empire was built on a quicksand of creative accounting. His name was Whitaker Wright and when the balloon went up, he had a sudden urgent desire to travel overseas. He was extradited in 1903 but committed suicide with cyanide while undergoing trial. A saviour, although no fairy godmother, appeared in the shape of Charles Tyson Yerkes then busy gaining control of as much as of London's nascent deep-level tube system as possible. He bought the London & Globe interests in the Bakerloo in March 1902. His Underground Electric Railways Co. of London Limited undertook to restart work on the Bakerloo.

A corporate image was emerging for the new company. The passenger station buildings and the interior walls of the stations themselves were designed by Leslie W. Green and all had certain similarities and were intended to be immediately recognisable as tube stations belonging to the UERL. Green had undertaken his professional training when the decorative style known as Art Nouveau was emerging and his buildings show evidence of this general style. Green's stations had features in common, but which could be readily adapted to the demands of individual sites. The buildings were built around a load-bearing steel frame upon which brickwork and then ox-blood red glazed faience cladding was applied. It is this faience which is perhaps the most characteristic feature of Green's buildings. The contracts under which Green worked specifically laid down that he was responsible only for the surface buildings at street level. Many of these stations remain remarkably intact, perhaps a case of something looking right and therefore working right.

The first section of the Bakerloo was that from Baker Street to Lambeth North, then Kennington Road. The line was opened on 10 March 1906. Business was slow at first but developed encouragingly within the first few years.

It is worth mentioning that the name 'Bakerloo' was created by 'Quex', a journalist with the *Evening News.* Certain ultra-fastidious characters objected, *The Railway Magazine* calling Bakerloo a 'gutter' name, but the public soon warmed to it and the Company officially adopted 'Bakerloo Line' in July 1906.

THE GREAT NORTHERN & CITY RAILWAY

The Great Northern and City Railway (GN&CR) was a product of the rapid growth of the northern suburbs of London towards the end of the nineteenth century. The GNR was finding it hard to handle all the growing number of suburban trains at King's Cross. Even with the use of the Metropolitan 'Widened Lines' to Moorgate and the running of some NLR trains from Broad Street to the northern suburbs, it was common for serious delays to be experienced at King's Cross.

The outcome was the passing of the Great Northern & City Railway Act on 28 June 1892 which authorised the construction of a line from Finsbury Park to Moorgate in the City. Following the example of the City & London Railway, the line was to be built in twin deep-level tunnels bored with the assistance of a Greathead tunnelling shield, thereby avoiding the disruption which had occurred during the building of the Metropolitan and Metropolitan District sub-surface railways. A crucial difference, however, was that the GN&CR would be built large enough to allow the passage of main line rolling stock. Until Crossrail, later the Elizabeth Line, it was unique in being the only shield-driven underground railway in London that could accommodate such stock. The line was to be electrified from the start; steam locomotives being prohibited under the terms of the Company's Act. A close relationship with the GNR was enjoyed at first, two of its directors also being directors of that company.

Stubborn opposition was experienced from a tramcar company which put on extra cars along much of the projected route while the Company found it very difficult to raise the required capital. This caused a crisis at boardroom level, changes among the directors and it was August 1898 before the contractors were ready to proceed. The troubles were not over, however, because the GNR announced that it would not allow through trains from the GN&CR onto its own lines north of Finsbury Park although the latter company would have running powers over the GNR into Finsbury Park. Various other unforeseen entanglements provided discouragement but at last, on 14 February 1904, the line was open for traffic. There were three intermediate stations initially, at Old Street, Essex Road and Drayton Park and another was added in June 1904. This was Highbury, which proved to be the busiest of the intermediate stations. From the start, serious competition was experienced from electric street tramways and later from motor buses. In 1913 the GN&CR was acquired by the Metropolitan Railway partly in the hope that it would be able to make extensions to the line at the southern end, but which never took place.

THE UNDERGROUND AND THE GROWTH OF LONDON

The real growth of the Underground lay in the twentieth century, outside the immediate purview of this book. However, the system was extending its tentacles in the late nineteenth century and playing a role in the development of London's suburbia. What helped this process was an increase in the real income and spending power of substantial numbers of the middle classes. This section of society proliferated with the large-scale expansion of the professions, of administration, commerce and the tertiary sector of the economy in London. Many such people were eager to live in greener, quieter surroundings away from their places of employment in Central London, much of which was still squalid, dirty and noisy. The spread of the Underground system both helped to create this demand and to respond to it.

Central London's daytime population was increasing almost exponentially while the night-time resident population declined quite dramatically. The population of the City in 1871 was 74,987. In 1901 it was just 26,923. The populations of Westminster and Holborn which were 248,363 and 93,423 respectively in 1871 fell to 183,011 and 59,405 in 1901. The daytime population of the City rose from 170,000 in 1886 to 360,000 in 1901. This meant a steady increase in commuter traffic among reasonably affluent daily travellers who could afford the fares into the leafy suburbs. The underground and the suburban mainline services also benefited by the opening of substantial numbers of large department stores in Bayswater, Knightsbridge and around Oxford Street and quality specialist shops, in Bond Street, for example. These came to be patronised on a regular basis by reasonably well-heeled suburban wives for what some describe as 'retail therapy'. The railways in turn helped these retail outlets. Exhibitions, theatres, galleries and other leisure activities assisted in filling up seats on trains at off-peak times.

THE UNDERGROUND AND ROAD CONGESTION

The capital's underground railways grew out of the urgent need in the middle of the nineteenth century to reduce the level of road traffic and the congestion it caused in

Central London. The creation of an underground network – system seems to be the wrong word for it – was left to private enterprise without any overall strategy for London as a whole. Did it succeed in tackling traffic congestion?

The answer is almost certainly no. The period from the 1860s to 1900 was one of almost continuous growth – of the British economy as a whole and more specifically of London's economy, of its population and of its role in the life of the nation. More and more people in the capital simply meant increased numbers moving around London travelling to and from work and for business, pleasure and recreation. Visitors and tourists boosted the numbers on the move. Quantitative evidence is lacking. The linking of the main line termini via the emerging underground system almost certainly would have kept most travellers who arrived at one terminus and caught a train from another, off the streets. However, as has been pointed out, the main line stations generated large amounts of their own road traffic in terms of hackney carriages, cabs and carts and much of this would have been of a nature unsuited to the underground.

The major public transport medium above ground in Central London was the horse omnibus. A division of labour seems to have taken place. In situations where underground trains and horse buses served the same districts, their relative speed over longer distances gave the trains a considerable advantage. The buses, on the other hand, were much more suitable for short journeys and very convenient with their large number of picking-up and setting-down points. This meant that buses and the underground were largely catering for the needs of different kinds of travellers. Even in the late nineteenth century, there was a degree of stigma attached to bus travel and the railways astutely offered first class accommodation at premium fares for those who wouldn't have been seen dead on an omnibus. However, there were tracts of Central London which in 1900 were still not served by underground trains and where, therefore, their impact on traffic congestion was minimal.

Holborn Viaduct and Queen Victoria Street were completed in 1869 and 1871 respectively by the Corporation of London as major schemes tackling gridlock. That road congestion continued to be a bugbear of London life is evident from the radical programme of road-building launched by the London County Council in the 1890s. Among the products of this campaign were New Oxford Street, Shaftesbury Avenue, Charing Cross Road and Kingsway. They may have helped to tackle gridlock in the streets, but they were also designed to penetrate and disperse some of Central London's most notorious slum districts and criminal rookeries such as Seven Dials and St Giles. Visitors to London throughout the nineteenth century commented on its chronic street congestion and the slowness of getting around at street level. Without the railways and the Underground it would be even worse.

Chapter 4

RAILWAYS AND LONDON'S SUBURBAN GROWTH

Central London at the start of the Victorian age was still densely populated. Back in the eighteenth century there had been some outward migration of prosperous city merchants, senior government employees and others to peripheral districts but the lack of public transport into the suburbs confined this movement to the very affluent who possessed their own carriages. This exodus was in marked contrast to the huge and unprecedented growth of suburbs in the last two thirds of the nineteenth century. No significant working-class migration from the centre of the Metropolis had taken place before that time. In the 1830s and 1840s, London workers, be they moderately prosperous artisans or impoverished casual labourers, still lived within walking distance of their work which was likely to be within a two or three-mile radius of Temple Bar, hence the term 'walking suburbs'. Although London's population was growing rapidly, its industrial structure and the geographical distribution of its inhabitants had changed little from the mid-eighteenth century.

By 1900, Greater London had become an almost continuously built-up area covering over 15 miles in each direction with a population of over 6 million. Suburban development was not something new to London in the nineteenth century and suburbs were never static. Suburbs tended to start as appendages to the parent city but, as the parent grows, themselves to be absorbed by it and, in turn, to throw out their own appendages. Holborn, for example, was once a part of extramural London. It had ceased to be a suburb centuries before. Dulwich, Greenwich and Highgate were other villages peripheral to London. Even when there were green fields separating them from London, they increasingly came under its influence. London crept out and gradually engulfed them and, while retaining some of their previous character, they imperceptibly changed first into suburbs and then into part of the parent 'Greater London'. These prestigious villages retained much of their earlier character, but some other former villages were not so lucky and only vestigial evidence of their rural character remained.

By 1914 the whole physiognomy of central London had been transformed almost beyond recognition. Large and densely packed inner-urban residential areas had frequently given way to acres of workshops, warehouses, railway yards, offices and commercial premises interspersed with working-class housing. Wide streets had been cut through the menacing and largely criminalised slum rookeries such as that of St Giles. The central area of London was increasingly depopulated and around it had grown a new working-class London, almost encircling the centre and broken only by an aristocratic and upper middle-class enclave extending from Kensington and Paddington to Bloomsbury and Hanover Square.

During this period, central London had experienced a crisis. Until the coming of cheap mass travel to and from the developing suburbs in the 1870s and 1880s, London suffered from a marked contradiction between the growth of its commercial, administrative, financial and cultural functions, all of which required large reserves of labour, and its ability adequately to house the expanding workforce that those workaday activities required. London's population growth accelerated dramatically in the nineteenth century. Between 1821 and 1851 it almost doubled; by the end of the century, it almost doubled again. While the demand for labour continued to grow and cheap working-class transport remained very limited, the increased population having perforce to be concentrated in central London.

This great rise in the population was not accompanied by a proportionate addition to the housing stock. The economic development which spurred the increased job opportunities and population growth was the key factor in the long-term displacement of the working-class population from the central area. Two vital developments in the 1830s and 1840s greatly assisted London's economic and commercial expansion. The first was the removal of import duties, especially the repeal of the Corn Laws. One result of this was a large increase in trade through the Port of London. The second was the development of a national railway network centred on London which gave the capital a highly favoured position as a centre of concentration and distribution both in international and national trade. London became the greatest entrepot city in the world. A large cheap and ready supply of labour was crucial. The problem was how and where to house them.

By 1901 it was estimated that the residential population of the City was no more than a few thousand. The result was a vast increase in land values in the centre of London. Compared to commercial rent derived from business premises, the profits to be obtained from house property were usually insignificant. Between 1861 and 1881 the population of the City itself fell from 113,387 to 51,439 while the City's rateable value rose from over £1.3 million in 1861 to nearly £3.5 million in 1881 and £4.85 million in 1901. By 1901 it was estimated that the resident population of the City had fallen to less than 4,000.

What occurred was, in effect, the enforced eviction of a large percentage of London's workers from their homes close to their places of work. They went, not because there were better job opportunities outside central London, but because their homes were demolished, and the sites redeveloped for commercial and industrial purposes including railways and their installations. While the City's resident population fell drastically, the number of workers its businesses required rose significantly. The daytime working population of the City rose from 170,000 in 1866 to 301,400 in 1891 and much of this greatly enlarged workforce necessarily needed to travel to and from work and home.

The railways played a considerable part in this demographic movement. It has been estimated that at least 76,000 people were displaced from their housing by railway building work between 1853 and 1901. This process was at its most intensive between 1853 and 1885. The effect of clearances for railway purposes was almost always an increase in overcrowding in the area immediately surrounding that in which the clearances had taken place.

In the 1850s and early 1860s, the districts hardest hit by building clearance brought on by railway projects included Bankside and the Borough, Clerkenwell, the St Luke's area of Finsbury, Shoreditch, Bethnal Green and Whitechapel. These were densely populated areas and the various schemes between them involved the displacement of at least 23,000 local people. With cheap transport simply being unavailable, these demolitions meant overspill into and overcrowding in adjacent areas of equally poor-quality housing. In 1875 a further 13,176 persons were displaced by railway projects. Particularly hard-hit was Bethnal Green while the notorious district known as Agar Town, adjacent to what was to become St Pancras station, virtually ceased to exist, making way for extensive railway goods provision. Other factors added to the displacement particularly of poor and virtually powerless people from the central districts. In giving the metropolis its complex web of railway lines, there was a heavy price to pay in human misery. Official attitudes could resemble those of Thomas Gradgrind in *Hard Times* (1854) by Charles Dickens. He personified the utilitarian harshness and meanness of many successful wealthy Victorian businessmen. In 1882, a member of the Metropolitan Board of Works followed in Gradgrind's footsteps with this declaration. 'Hard as it may seem to turn out hundreds of poor families to make room for business premises, there is really little hardship in it to complain of, for due notice is given and compensation to a limited extent is afforded.'.

The building of the railways involved clearing some of London's worst housing. Low-paid and casual workers by necessity needed to live close to their places of employment but the railways, in displacing them, tended to exacerbate London's housing problem. They were usually decanted into already overcrowded accommodation nearby. With a shortage of accommodation and the general rise in land values created in the central area by the railways, rents rose and put the poor under greater and greater pressure. In 1874 new regulations were brought in which required the promoters of railway projects involving displacements to provide alternative accommodation. In practice, this requirement was frequently evaded. Even where new housing was built, it was not always available at the time of displacement and, when completed, ended up being taken by other families who could afford the higher rents that were a feature of such housing. The railway companies were unwilling housebuilders. It cost them money and they did not consider it to be their business.

Migration to the suburbs was not a simple, continuous process. There was a peak in the process in the 1860s only for it to be ended by the economic crisis created by the collapse of the prominent banking house of Overend and Gurney in 1866. Railway companies and speculative builders were among the hardest hit. There was little new suburban building or transport development until 1875. A boom between 1876 and 1880 which saw much speculative building around Camberwell, Battersea, Wandsworth and Fulham and which involved large numbers of lower middle-class and 'respectable' working-class people from the central districts migrating outwards, had much to do with street tramways establishing themselves as an instrument of mass travel to and from work, although railways also played their part.

The railways did much to mould the appearance of suburban London. Here an overbridge puts its stamp on a street in a district served by the Great Eastern Railway.

The process of suburbanisation and the existence of cheap transport by road or rail to support such development were never straightforward. In the early 1880s speculative builders had over-reached themselves and the Metropolitan Board of Works noted large numbers of dwellings intended for working people lying empty in Tottenham, Stamford Hill, Peckham, Battersea and Wandsworth. Across the whole of London, the proportion of empty houses rose from 4 per cent in 1882 to almost 8 per cent in late 1884.

While the suburbs were generally cleaner and often greener than the central parts of London and therefore seemingly more wholesome, the contrast between one and the other was not necessarily clear-cut. It was not unknown for people who had migrated in the 1870s being forced to return because of the perceived problems of suburban life and travel. Even small changes in the cost of living could affect decisions about moving out or even moving back. Rents were almost always cheaper in the suburbs but almost everything else was more expensive. There was often little work available for women in the suburbs and a lack of cheap markets. Workmen's cheap trains could be very inconveniently timed. Such trains might drop their users at their London terminus by, say, 7am, whereupon they could be faced

Doré's depiction of a workmen's train at Baker Street.

with an irritating wait of an hour or more before their workplaces opened. There might also be problems with the timing of the end of the working day and return trains. All this deterred some working people from moving out of the centre and forced others to return, forsaking the suburbs. This put further pressure on rents in central London and could make it more profitable to build property for rent there than invest in speculative building in the suburbs. This was a living, dynamic, ever-changing process.

In 1860 the LC&DR obtained parliamentary authority to extend lines in South London which required substantial demolition of residential property, and this provides an example of the conditions involved in such cases. The Company was required to put on two trains daily in each direction between Victoria and Ludgate Hill *via* Brixton, Camberwell and Walworth. The price of a weekly ticket between any two stations was one shilling. To ensure that such facilities were only used by 'artisans, mechanics and daily labourers, both male and female', those who bought the ticket were required to give the name and address of their employer. One train left each outer terminus at 04.55 and after stopping at every station reached the inner terminus just before 06.00. On Mondays to Fridays the evening trains left at

A scene during the frenzy of house building in the newly developing suburbs served by the Great Eastern Railway in north-east London. The houses may have been monotonous, but they were well built, and many have stood the test of time.

18.15, and on Saturdays at 14.30. By 1882-3 there were 110 workmen's trains running daily in London, being used by an estimated 25,600 passengers. By 1912 workmen's tickets represented about 40 per cent of all suburban journeys within six to eight miles of the centre of London.

'Commuting', a word seemingly American in origin, literally means travelling to and from work by public transport regularly enough to earn a 'commutation' on the fare in the form of a discounted season ticket. Commuting in the broadest sense if it simply means travelling a significant distance between home and work, pre-dates the railways and even horse buses. The City of London and the district of Westminster had long offered a rich variety of job opportunities and people living in outlying villages such as Islington and Camberwell would walk to and from their homes and their places of work in such places well before Victorian times. Walking for most people was just part of living in the pre-public transport and pre-motor car age and they thought little about regularly walking distances which would make most of

Palmers Green was a developing suburb of a somewhat superior character as indicated by these fine Victorian dwellings. Railways played a major role in urbanising districts like this on the fringe of London.

today's keep-fit devotees go weak at the knees. Other better-off 'commuters' might use short-haul coaches such as those operating in the mid-eighteenth century from Highgate to Covent Garden. The richest folk would travel in their own carriages. Of course, far more people lived in central London in the 1800s and, being close to their work, did not need to commute. This changed dramatically during the century with far-reaching consequences. The desire to put distance between the home and the workplace was strong among those Victorians who could afford it. It was an understandable aspiration. London was filthy, smelly and pestilential although becoming less so as the century progressed. It was overcrowded, noisy and sooty. It was also menacing, even highly dangerous in many parts, although that situation was also improving by the 1900s.

Before the pioneering L&GR opened in 1836, horse buses had appeared on London's streets in 1829 with a route from Paddington to the Bank of England. Not itself a huge success, its example did, however, spawn many further routes, some reaching out of the centre to link up with various outlying villages as well as connecting intermediate districts within central London. Competition was vigorous. While this helped to keep fares down, horse buses largely remained unaffordable to the mass of London's low-paid workers as, of course, did hackney cabs and other vehicles for hire.

The L&GR, as well as having its pioneering role, exhibited other characteristics of suburban lines. It linked London with a genuine suburb and at unsurpassed speeds. Journey times were cut from an hour to just twelve minutes. Horse buses could not compete, and steamboats were relegated to the provision of pleasure trips rather than everyday journeys. The line ran on a viaduct the building of which involved the demolition of much poor housing en route and it introduced a new element to the built environment of London – the railway arch. These were often let as small workshops, but they gained a degree of notoriety when untenanted ones quickly came to be used for immoral purposes and even for the disposal of the bodies of unwanted babies. They also provided an unofficial roof over the head of many of London's homeless and were greatly appreciated as such. So, London's first suburban railway was not simply a new and efficient form of public transport but something which had a varied impact on the cultural life and economic and social relationships of the metropolis.

The L&GR was quickly followed by two other short lines, the London & Blackwall and the London & Croydon specifically designed to link central London with the places mentioned. After that much of London's rapidly growing railway network consisted of longer lines even if they were not of the inter-city character of, say, the London & Birmingham or the London & Southampton. An example was the North Kent Railway opened in 1849 and running out via Lewisham, Blackheath and Woolwich to the Medway towns. Lewisham and Blackheath were already highly desirable residential villages with many large houses. Lewisham began to take on a much more working-class character after the railway was built. Blackheath continued to be fashionable although enclaves of working-class housing developed, some of their residents finding work locally, serving in the big houses for example, and others commuting the short distance to London Bridge. Horse buses appeared, feeding passengers onto the railway at Blackheath from neighbouring, still very rural, villages such as Eltham. This was the process of suburbanisation and the railways contributed greatly to this process.

Some of the early railway lines in London brought travellers to the fringe of the built-up area such as the initial terminus of what became the L&SWR at Nine Elms, Battersea. This was inconveniently located on the south side of the Thames and onward connections with central parts of London were made by steamboats. The L&GR terminated at London Bridge on the cheaper side of the river but located quite handily for the City. The companies wanting to establish convenient terminal stations soon discovered to their chagrin that it was difficult, almost impossible, to obtain parliamentary powers to build lines through or erect stations in wealthy areas of the Metropolis. The consequence was that those lines which did manage to penetrate what might loosely be described as central London did so on its periphery where somewhat cheaper land was available. Even in an age when more people were prepared to walk, these stations were inconveniently situated and a theme in London's transport history ever since has been efforts to improve communication across central London to serve the capital's major stations more effectively as well as to provide links through the built up area in between.

London Bridge Station was in the unfashionable and therefore relatively cheaper district of the Borough and Southwark. The Eastern Counties, later GER, had its first London terminus at Bishopsgate, in the unfashionable Shoreditch district where, again, land was cheap. Initially the City Corporation refused to allow railways to intrude into its ancient boundaries largely on the grounds that railway stations would exacerbate existing traffic congestion. That was the stated reason, but the City was also anxious to protect its interests in the Pool of London from possible serious competition from the East and West India Docks which were likely to be served directly by railways. However, it relented and allowed Fenchurch Street Station to be opened in August 1841 for the London & Blackwall Railway. This station was approached on a viaduct which had involved the displacement of over 3,000 people from festering slums just to the east of the Station.

In the 1870s a new form of public transport began to appear on London's streets. This was the horse tram. The use of rails enabled horses to pull a car with a bigger potential payload than a horse bus. Trams were the archetypal working-class form of transport. They charged much lower fares than the railways and, although they were slower, they had the convenience of running more frequently and calling at far more stops, sometimes providing a virtually door-to-door service. A network of routes run by different companies developed, mainly serving areas of close-packed working-class housing in the inner suburbs. They were largely excluded from central London, but the railways quickly found that the horse trams and especially their electric successors provided serious competition in the inner suburbs. Where the trams passed through undeveloped districts, housing soon followed and a senior official of one of the tramway companies was able to say in 1884 his trams had helped to relieve overcrowding in the centre of London by making it possible for working class people to live a few miles out and commute. A knock-on effect was that in some of the inner suburbs, the previous inhabitants who liked to think of themselves as genteel and a cut above, moved further out of London as more proletarian neighbours moved in. Former unfashionable districts became 'gentrified'. Formerly affluent areas slid down the social scale. London has never stood still.

The North London Railway had less than fourteen route miles of track but was far more important than this would suggest. It provided a vital link for freight traffic from northern and western parts of the country to London's docks. It also operated passenger services in the increasingly densely populated districts around north and north-west London and, with running powers, some services into Hertfordshire. Here an NLR train leaves an inner-suburban station, thought to be Dalston Junction. (Courtesy of John Scott Morgan)

The impressive frontage of Broad Street Station of the North London Railway next door to Liverpool Street Station. In its heyday, this was an extremely busy station catering particularly for commuter traffic.

Workers' trains at Liverpool Street during the Saturday mid-day rush hour. Five-and-a-half days was the lot of vast numbers of working people, and they were always keen to get home. The railways laid on trains to help them to do so.

Many of the railway companies had little initial interest in providing services aimed at the lower end of the market. The GWR staunchly refused to use the word 'suburban' in its timetables well into the 1860s. Such an attitude attracted public criticism. Events were to force the hand of many railway companies. The NLR was the first to be required by parliament to make some provision for those made homeless by the building of a new line. Much demolition of housing was involved when their Broad Street terminus was built in the middle of the 1860s. They were required to put on special workmen's trains with low fares for those displaced who now had to live further from their places of work. The GER paid the same price a few years later when planning its Liverpool Street terminus next door to Broad Street. In 1883 a Cheap Trains Act was passed which in many cases insisted that railway companies ran special trains with cheap fares for working people.

Not everyone was pleased with the workmen's fares. They had the same kind of effect on middle-class suburbs that the horse trams had. They brought the tone down! The middle-class residents of affluent suburbs were horrified when the serenity of their existence was threatened by proletarians taking up residence in their neighbourhood, attracted by cheap fares on the GER. The petit bourgeoisie moved on to pastures new. The social engineering carried out by the railways was given voice by a senior manager of the Great Eastern:

Wherever you locate the workmen in large numbers, you utterly destroy that neighbourhood for ordinary passenger traffic. Take, for instance, the neighbourhood of Stamford Hill, Tottenham and Edmonton. That used to be a very nice neighbourhood…but very soon after this obligation was put upon the Great Eastern Company…of issuing workmen's tickets…the district is given up entirely, I may say now, to the working man.

It would be too easy to say that all the railways did was to encourage a kind of decanting process as people tended to move out of central London and that each suburb took on a distinctive class character with the better-off constantly moving further out. The reality was far more complex. The population of Greater London grew rapidly but certain districts grew far faster than others, West Ham being an example. Newcomers did not necessarily want to live in central London. Their job prospects and earning expectations had a considerable bearing on what they could afford in the way of housing, and they might not be looking to live and work centrally.

As suburbs became established, they could take on an economic life of their own. Some became towns themselves, both urban and suburban, dependent on being near London but with a wide range of employment opportunities of their own. Wealthy suburbs needed hordes of domestic servants. They were not well-paid and tended to live not too far from their work. Most suburbs took on a mixed character.

A former village like Hampstead which was already fashionable before the railways arrived and continued to be fashionable, developed pockets of deprivation close to and contrasting with districts where conspicuous wealth was very evident.

As previously mentioned, the London & Southampton Railway (later to be the L&SWR) had its first London terminus inconveniently located at Nine Elms, Battersea. The line opened in 1838 and stations were provided in the westerly direction at Wandsworth, Wimbledon and 'Kingston'. The history of stations with anomalous names is a fascinating one and Kingston qualifies for inclusion. It was a short distance from the ancient and important town of Kingston-on-Thames. Kingston was obviously a convenient hook on which to hang a station name in the hope of attracting business. An affluent settlement developed around the station which came to be known in some quarters as 'Kingston-on-Railway'. This rather prosaic name displeased the well-to-do incomers and so, miraculously, 'Surbiton', an old name for the neighbourhood, was revived, dusted down and bestowed on what it was hoped would continue to be a socially exclusive neighbourhood graced by a railway which could carry the paterfamilias quickly and easily to and from his workplace in Westminster or the City. Surbiton proved to be a lusty infant, for generations succeeding in fighting off every attempt by its larger neighbour, Kingston-on-Thames, to subsume it. It has been described by that great railway and social historian, Jack Simmons, as 'the oldest suburb in Europe, perhaps in the world, that was called into being by a railway'.

Surbiton was very much a middle-class suburb, sharing that character with others such as Ealing and Sidcup. As the railways expedited housing development, so some such places developed similar characteristics. Most of the earliest new housing would be within easy walking distance of the station but those who could afford their own conveyances, the 'carriage folk', might well live in larger villas, further from the station, in substantial grounds and often on higher land where such existed. Adjacent to the station might be one or more parades of shops, often with accommodation for the proprietors above. There might be a pub and perhaps some humble cottages nearby, probably housing the families of the many workers required for domestic service locally. These suburbs were usually well laid-out and spacious, with earlier trees preserved where possible, and sizeable gardens. Even the more modest of middle-class inhabitants wanted privacy and seclusion. Such aspirations might be only partly satisfied unless the residents were first class season-ticket holders whose homes might well be hidden from the road by curved driveways through stands of fast-growing trees and shrubs. An enjoyable lifestyle could be had in such places and the railways played a major part in helping it to happen.

Descending the social scale was a lower middle class consisting of middling managers, supervisors and senior clerks. This was the social group satirised gently, affectionately and so perceptively in *The Diary of a Nobody*. The hero Charles Pooter

Further out from central London would be found less densely developed suburbs containing bijou detached villas in various somewhat eclectic styles. A railway station would not be too far away.

and his family have just moved into The Laurels, Brickfield Terrace, Holloway. This, the Diary tells us, is:

> … a nice six-roomed residence, not counting basement, with a front breakfast-parlour. We have a little front garden; and there is a flight of ten steps up to the front door, which, by-the-by, we keep locked with the chain up. Cummings, Gowing, and our other intimate friends always come to the little side entrance, which saves the servant the trouble of going up to the front door, thereby taking her from her work. We have a nice little back garden which runs down to the railway. We were rather afraid of the noise of the trains at first, but the landlord said we should not notice them after a bit and took £3 off the rent. He was certainly right; and beyond the cracking of the garden wall at the bottom, we have suffered no inconvenience.

Pooter sets much store by being a City clerk and by the respectability and status that the job and his address suggest. And there were thousands more like him, many of them living in Holloway. Charles Dickens in *Sketches by Boz* (1836-7) describes the behaviour of these denizens of the 'walking suburbs'. He writes, 'The early clerk population of Somers and Camden Towns, Islington and Pentonville, are fast pouring into the city…middle-aged men, whose salaries have by no means increased in the same proportion as their families, plod steadily along, apparently with no object in view but the counting house.'

Some neighbouring suburbs were very similar to Holloway. They were not 'created' by the railway, mostly being developments of much earlier hamlets and other small settlements originally a short distance from inner London. In their initial period of nineteenth-century expansion, the Pooters and others who moved into them would have walked or taken a horse bus to their places of employment in the City. However, their population growth encouraged companies like the GNR and the North London to provide stations and the railway came to play a major role in

Consciousness of class has always been a very strong feature of British society. The late eighteenth century saw a large increase in clerical and administrative jobs of a white-collar character. Such workers saw themselves as a 'cut above'. If they could do so, they left inner London for 'respectable suburbs' where they could mix with the 'right kind' of people but ideally be served by a convenient railway station.

assisting their growth. Hackney, Islington, Wood Green and Hornsey are similar locations owing much to the presence of local railways encouraging settlement in the years up to the First World War.

These suburbs were not unattractive and were a cut above others largely intended to house people further down the social scale. These were built to house lower middle-class families, shop workers, clerks and skilled working people in regular work. They included Tottenham, Edmonton, Clapton, Leyton and Walthamstow. Such districts developed very rapidly in the last quarter of the nineteenth century. Much adverse comment was voiced about how they were composed of standardised, long, unimaginative streets of terraced houses with minimal front and back gardens and a high density per square acre. These homes met the strictures of the Public Health Act of 1875. Monotonous they may have been, but they were solidly built, and many thousands are still in residential use in the twenty-first century, having in some cases become gentrified and therefore 'desirable residences'.

Clearly, in these suburbs housing was zoned along the lines of income and the less clear but related concept of class. These districts north and north-east of London were provided with large numbers of workmen's trains while, by contrast, beyond Walthamstow and Chingford, for example, the higher and healthier terrain attracted a more middle-class and affluent population with little desire to avail themselves of the greatly discounted workmen's fares and the down-at-heel passenger stock they utilised.

The tenets of laissez-faire did not allow any sympathy for slum-dwellers displaced when their homes were demolished, and their occupants were simply decanted into neighbouring and probably already overcrowded slum property close by. Attitudes and practices were changing, however. In 1862 the GER was looking for the site of a major terminus close to the City but the chosen location, the later Liverpool Street Station, contained much appalling slum housing. The Act in 1864 authorising the powers for compulsory acquisition of this land broke new ground by requiring the GER to operate a daily train from and to Walthamstow and Edmonton at the very low fare of 2d. This was intended to encourage those living in densely packed and low-quality housing around the City to move away but maintain their jobs by taking advantage of what quickly became known as 'workmen's fares'. We do not know how many of the impoverished denizens of the Liverpool Street site were able to take advantage of this offer, but the GER went on to operate workmen's trains in a major way and by 1900 about 6 million 2d return and 4 million half-fare passengers were being carried by the Company into Liverpool Street each year. They all travelled in trains arriving before 8am.

It should not be thought that the GER was wholly altruistic in running services the profits from which, at best, were marginal. They sought to concentrate the provision of these cheap services in part of their suburban territory while excluding the provision of such services to other areas which held out the prospects of yielding much more lucrative traffic from better-off passengers. For example, on the line to Loughton, workmen's tickets were not issued at stations beyond Leytonstone. Trains on this line provided an unusually high number of first-class seats at the expense of third-class accommodation. On its main line out towards Chelmsford and Colchester, workmen's tickets were not available at stations further out than Chadwell Heath. The London County Council was established in 1889 and it always tried to ensure that provision for workmen's trains was included in the legislation authorising new railways.

Much housing in London's central districts remained grossly overcrowded and substandard into the twentieth century, despite the admittedly rather lukewarm efforts of the main line railway companies to assist in the dispersal. The railways did not provide a comprehensive system of cheap and efficient local transport in London. The agents for this were to prove to be the underground railway system, electric overground railways, electric tramcars and, later, the motor bus and the more short-lived trolleybus of which London had the largest system in the world.

Croydon, with a population of about 12,500 in the 1830s, was a substantial town before the railways arrived. Its position on the trunk road from London to Brighton meant that it was busy with stagecoaches in which some affluent local people commuted to London. It became an important focal point for railways which contributed to its very rapid growth, especially from the 1860s. It came to enjoy fast and frequent services to London with no fewer than eight stations within its boundaries and it gained a character both urban, as a town in its own right, and suburban because it became the favoured dormitory home of very large numbers of commuters. It had pockets of real affluence in the nineteenth century but perhaps never quite the exclusivity that the inhabitants of Surbiton fought so vigorously to preserve. A large network of short-distance surface railways played a major role in opening access to the countryside of Kent and Surrey and contributed much to the extension of Greater London into those areas. 'Southern Electric' was to become a familiar slogan in the twentieth century and the railways had a formative influence on the growth and the demography of this area.

London north of the river is very different from those parts of the metropolis to the south of the Thames. Historically, it is undeniable that in terms of population and a host of other factors, the centre of gravity of ancient London was located north of the Thames around the City and Westminster. The railways north of the river were markedly different from those to the south. Four major companies, or five if you include the Great Central (GCR) with its belated arrival on the scene, ran out of London in a northern or westerly direction. They were the GWR, GCR, L&NWR, MR and GNR operating out of Paddington, Marylebone, Euston, St Pancras and King's Cross respectively. Leaving the GCR aside, the other four companies were interested mainly in long-distance traffic at least at first, and the few stations they opened in the early years within 20 miles of London generally had infrequent services.

The Great Western opened a station at Ealing in 1838. The village was small but an established and affluent one with many large houses and traffic was initially

A Metropolitan Railway train headed by another 4-4-0T forges through the north London suburbs on the tracks of the Great Northern Railway.

A 2-4-0 of the Great Northern Railway speeds through the 'Northern Heights' with an express to the north. An extraordinary array of trains connected London directly or indirectly with all parts of the British Isles, but travellers were always inconvenienced by the multiplicity of termini in the capital and the difficulty of getting from one to another. The underground railways developed partly to solve this problem but even today provide only a partial solution.

slow in building up. In conjunction with the Metropolitan Railway, a limited service of through carriages from Ealing was put on, running into the City. In the 1860s and 1870s, with large-scale residential development taking place, railway business at Ealing grew rapidly. From 1879 the GWR found itself competing with the District Railway whose avowed intention was to encourage house building along its line from central London via Hammersmith. It had some success. It seized much of the growing commuter traffic because its line provided access to a wider range of places in central London. In the 1890s, Ealing was sometimes referred to as the 'Queen of the Western Suburbs', having grown large relatively gracefully. What working-class housing existed was mostly tucked away in West Ealing and was certainly a feature of its nearby neighbour, Acton. Modern Ealing would not be what it is without the railway.

The L&NWR was not initially interested in local services out of Euston, and it was almost by chance that what became Willesden Junction developed into a major interchange with the NLR. Several long-distance expresses called there because the NLR provided handy connections with many parts of Greater London. Housing development took place around Willesden, but the fate of the surrounding area was largely dictated by the mass of lines that eventually converged at Willesden and around its near-neighbour, Old Oak Common. They became the centre of a tangle of engine sheds, carriage sidings, shunting yards and varied industrial development, much of the latter located where it was because of the railways. Local housing development was largely for the working class.

The MR also showed little early interest in local traffic into and out of St Pancras, except perhaps at Hendon but it did build the Tottenham and Hampstead Line, jointly with the GER, largely so it could gain access to the London Docks and keep other companies out. Although there were several stations along the line there is little evidence that its presence contributed to the residential development of the districts through which it passed. The GNR, by contrast, saw the possibilities for traffic in the Northern Heights and beyond and extruded a line from Finsbury Park north-westwards to the then rural fastnesses of High Barnet and Mill Hill with a branch from Highgate to Alexandra Palace. Another branch left the main line at Wood Green and headed for Enfield. These schemes were carried out partly for imperialistic reasons to pre-empt other companies moving in or to provide competition and give them a run for their money. Opened in the late 1860s and early 1870s, except for the 'Ally Pally' branch, they were mostly successful in attracting residential development and generating considerable passenger usage.

As London grew from the Middle Ages to the eighteenth century, what new building development occurred tended to be to the west of the City. A feature of the nineteenth century, however, was London's growth eastwards into Essex and the railways played an important role in this. Some well-to-do residents had large houses in such places as Hackney, Clapton and Enfield but tended to move away as working-class housing began to encroach, often as a result of tramways and railway building.

It is likely that the London & Blackwall Railway helped to stimulate the growth of places like Limehouse and Poplar, but the most obvious development was that stimulated by the Eastern Counties (from 1862 the GER) along its line towards Cambridge following the Lea Valley, opened in 1840. The ECR wanted short-haul passenger traffic and opened numerous stations on this route as far as Broxbourne and threw off branch lines to Enfield (1849) and to Loughton in 1856. The ECR was a standing joke for tardiness and inefficiency but was successful in assisting the urban development of the lower Lea Valley. Its successor, the GER, found landowners in the still rural areas to the north-east of London eager to sell their land for building development so long as it would be provided with the necessary transport infrastructure. The results of this opportunism were a line to Walthamstow opened in 1870, extended to Chingford in 1873 and another through Stoke Newington to Edmonton, opened in 1872.

The GER was a victim of its own success, generating so much traffic to and from the inner working-class suburbs that a severe strain was placed on running line capacity. It found itself operating what was said to be the most intensive steam-hauled local passenger services in the world and it performed miracles with the diminutive locomotives of the early years heaving heavy loads up Bethnal Green Bank out of Liverpool Street. Having both the pleasure and the pain resulting from its role in creating the working-class suburbs with their high levels of passenger usage, they refused to issue workmen's tickets from stations beyond Walthamstow and on the Loughton branch, thus effectively deterring builders from erecting homes for working class people. So, while Walthamstow's population developed from 5,000 in 1851 to nearly 100,000 in 1901, other small towns like Loughton, Chingford and Epping remained socially more exclusive and did not expand at anything like the same rate.

The General Manager of the GER, giving evidence to a Royal Commission in 1884, shed light on the social processes being initiated by the railway in London's north-eastern suburbs. Describing the impact of workmen's fares on Stamford Hill, Tottenham and Edmonton, he said:

That used to be a very nice district indeed, occupied by good families, with houses from £150 to £250 a year, with coach houses and stables, a garden and a few acres of land. But very soon after this obligation was put upon the Great Eastern to run workmen's trains … speculative builders went down into the neighbourhood and, as a consequence, each good house was one after another pulled down, and the district is given up entirely, I may say, now to the working man. I lived down there myself and I waited until most of my neighbours had gone; and then at last, I was obliged to go.

The London County Council, established in the late 1880s, did all it could to encourage cheap workmen's fares. Many people who could never be described as 'workmen' took advantage of the cheap fares which usually meant an extremely early journey into London and correspondingly late return. In many cases it also involved travelling in cramped and uncomfortable rolling stock on the basis, presumably, of the passengers getting what they paid for. The railway companies were evasive on the issue of whether they made profits on shifting the commuters travelling with such tickets. They certainly shifted them in huge quantities but in doing so incurred the wasteful expense of using rolling stock which might only make one inward and one outward passenger-carrying journey per day. The railway companies' real interest was in the much more lucrative business of serving the needs of first-and-second class passengers. They were very successful in making railway travel the accepted way in which the middle-class suburbanites not only went to and fro from work but used also them for socialising and other leisure purposes.

The LT&SR was opened in the 1850s primarily to serve what was thought would be a lucrative potential excursion traffic at Southend and later in the 1880s freight traffic to the developing docks at Tilbury. A second line further north through Upminster was opened in 1885. The western end of the line was soon carrying an intensive cheap suburban traffic from such places as Barking and Plaistow that developed very rapidly as working-class residential districts. The LT&SR proved to be the most prosperous of all the railways serving the inner suburbs and its growth was positively headlong. In 1870-4 the average number of passengers carried annually was 1,939,082. In the first decade of the twentieth century the figure reached over 3 million.

Where possible, speculative builders generally preferred to erect housing for middle-class occupants. They ideally wanted stations to have fast and frequent services up to Town and the stations to be located less than a mile from the housing developments. They wanted to buy land as cheaply as possible and in places which met the other criteria. This could be an elusive mix and some developers got their fingers badly burnt.

It was not just the builders who took a risk and sometimes came unstuck. A railway company might build a line through a rural and sparsely populated locality in London's hinterland in the confident expectation that the opening of stations would attract builders and rapid housing development. An oft-quoted example of such a line which was an almost total failure in this respect was the GER's Edmonton to Cheshunt Loop. This was opened in 1891 and was provided with three intermediate stations. There was, however, nothing inevitable about housing following the opening of a railway. It simply did not happen with this line which had the dubious distinction in 1909 of being one of the first in the Greater London area to close to passenger traffic. It was successfully reopened in 1960.

Electric tramways, the Underground and the 'B' Type bus were between them providing a complex and comprehensive transport infrastructure for the capital by the Edwardian period, reaching into parts the main line railways could not or did not want to serve and trams had for some time being providing stiff competition on short-haul services in the inner-city areas.

The main line companies did not take these challenges lying down. New lines and stations were opened largely serving districts some way from the centre. Some lines were electrified providing quicker and cleaner and more attractive services capable of taking on competition. As if accepting that some loss of inner-suburban traffic was inevitable, from the middle of the 1900s the railway companies mainly concentrated on building up middle-class commuter and other traffic to places between a dozen and thirty miles from central London. No serious competition was likely to be experienced over that kind of distance.

The companies put their publicity departments to work. The L&SWR railway extolled the virtues of residing at Epsom, only twenty-five minutes from Waterloo. The GWR encouraged people to move to settlements in the lush and historic Thames Valley such as Henley while the GNR promoted the health advantages of living in the 'Northern Heights' in places like Barnet and Finchley.

As ever, new lines and stations were no guarantee that significant housing development and consequent useful traffic would follow. Lines to Uxbridge for the GWR and Metropolitan and to Neasden for the GCR, for example, were not followed up by much new housing before 1914. By way of contrast, the electrification of the Metropolitan Railway in 1905 greatly encouraged expansion

Putney Station of the London & South Western Railway viewed from Upper Richmond Road c.1912. In this delightful period piece note the presence of motor buses although the day of the horse bus was not quite over. Electric trams and motor buses were to prove serious competitors with the railways for suburban passenger traffic. (Courtesy of John Scott Morgan)

of the existing settlement of Harrow and contributed largely to the beginning of housing development at Wembley and Ruislip. Harrow's population grew by 67 per cent to 17,074 in 1911 while nearby Wealdstone's growth in the same period was a remarkable 102 per cent. As late as 1901, the entire Wembley district had a population of only 4,519. However, it came to be served by six railway stations operated by four different companies. Marylebone could be reached in eleven minutes, the City in twenty-four. This facility encouraged a building boom so that by 1911 the population had grown by 137 per cent.

The GNR had built several lines into the 'Northern Heights' beyond Finsbury Park. This was commented on by Edward Walford, a London historian, in the 1890s. He described how the Great Northern had earlier been markedly unenthusiastic about penetrating this hilly area of countryside and villages partly because of the engineering problems involved and because it was sceptical about the business prospects such lines would offer. However, it built lines to Edgware, High Barnet, Finchley and Alexandra Palace which proved largely successful. Walford neatly encapsulates a sense of the impact of the coming of the railways to a particular part of London's hinterland:

> The Great Northern now has at least 4,000 season ticket holders, and trains call at Holloway and Finsbury Park continuously during the working hours of the day, and every train is crowded with passengers. Speculative builders have been very busy in the north of London, which was until lately regarded by them as a terra incognita … A fatal blow was dealt to this state of things by the connection of the Great Northern with the Underground Railway. All at once London discovered that there were no more salubrious breezes, no greener fields, no more picturesque landscapes, no more stately trees than could be shown in the district of country bounded by Highgate Hill on the one side and Barnet on the other. The green lane of Hornsey and Southgate ceased to be such…Ancient mansions…were pulled down; broad parks were cut up into building lots; and instead we have semi-detached villas – much better, as a rule, to look at than to live in – advertised as being in the most healthy of neighbourhoods, and in half an hour's ride of the City.

Summing up, the railways were a necessary but not of themselves a sufficient condition for the growth of many of London's inner and outer suburbs. Even today, for those who care to look, a journey on a local train out of many of London's termini can provide fascinating visual evidence of the layer cake nature of Victorian housing development and support for both the specific and the general points made in this chapter. It can also provide evidence that contradicts those points. It is this complexity which is just one aspect of the fascination of the history of railways and of London.

Chapter 5

RAILWAYS AND THE PURSUIT OF PLEASURE

GETTING OUT OF TOWN

Londoners worked hard and played hard. Some of the local nineteenth century attractions waiting for their halfpennies and pennies were commercial businesses like Cremorne Gardens, Chelsea; Vauxhall Gardens; Beulah Spa at Dulwich and Bagnigge Wells and Islington Spa at Finsbury. Changing tastes in the nineteenth century saw these going into decline. However, London has always benefitted from possessing numerous historic open spaces, many of them freely accessible for the public. These were added to by new gems such as Victoria Park in 1842. Many historic villages, woods and commons drew the masses on high days and holidays. Access to these places was usually free but they often acquired other attractions and amenities which could be enjoyed for a few pence. Trips up and down the Thames, increasingly during the nineteenth century on steamboats, were immensely popular. London's rising population and its growing aggregate spending power made the commercial provision of leisure sound financial sense.

It was inevitable that the railways would get involved. The L&GR was one of the earliest companies to respond to the potential demand and it started running an intensive service on Sundays at very cheap fares which allowed people to leave Greenwich to return to central London after midnight. The London & Brighton Railway, forerunner of the LB&SCR, took the idea up in the 1840s. It ran extremely cheap excursions from London to Brighton on Sundays and these proved exceptionally popular. On Whit Monday 1844, for example, the Company put on a special train of fifty-seven carriages drawn by six locomotives. The excursionists enjoyed a return trip for the price of a single fare. No sooner were the trippers pouring off this train at Brighton than they were joined by nearly 1,000 members of the Carpenters' Benevolent Society who had chartered a train of their own. The arrival of trainloads of chirpy, cheerful Cockneys added another facet to the many-sided character of Brighton. It was not long before claims were being made that increased crime in the town could be blamed on outsiders, especially trippers from London. The Metropolitan Police were content. They had quiet Sundays.

Railways provided a quick, easy and relatively cheap means whereby Londoners could enjoy a brief escape from the 'Smoke'. Tens of thousands headed for the seaside at places like Margate, Hastings and Brighton.

In 1891, 900 London stevedores visited Southend by cheap railway excursion. Many ignored the briny and instead spent the day drinking. By the time the return excursion was due to leave, many were hopelessly drunk. Sporadic fighting with the police broke out in the High Street. The publicans of Southend must have been glad to see their train steam away, although only, of course, after the stevedores had spent their money. This had become the pattern at many of the seaside places easily reached by train from London. An unofficial estimate on one Sunday in 1857 suggested that about 42,000 pleasure-seekers had left six London terminus stations on special trains with discounted fares.

The single-minded hedonism of the trippers and the avarice of the railway companies determined to make money out of this new market on Sundays incurred the wrath of the Sabbatarian movement and, particularly, of the Lord's Day Observance Society. They did not want the sanctity of the Sabbath to be profaned by levity and licentiousness. Instead, they thought that Sundays should be devoted to attendance at worship, to rest or quiet pursuits. They objected to the employment of workers to operate and service the trains on Sundays. Dire warnings were gleefully issued of the hellish fate awaiting those wicked enough to make such outings, but they fell on deaf ears. Most ordinary people had no truck with such arguments. Sunday was their one day off work and by hook or by crook, they were going to enjoy it. Their desire for pleasure, the commercial interests of the railway companies and business communities in the places the excursion trains visited ensured that Sunday specials had arrived and would stay. It needs to be said, however, that there were still large numbers of Londoners in low-paid, periodic or partial employment for whom the cost of such excursions was simply prohibitive.

Most people in trade and commerce worked on Saturdays. Pressure developed from the 1840s through organisations such as the Early Closing Association for Saturdays to be worked as a half-day. The Association was keen on the idea that workers and their families should get out into the countryside to commune with nature and fill their lungs with clean air. Perhaps they could learn to recognise a few wildflowers or the call of some songbirds. It was believed that they would benefit greatly from this form of 'rational recreation'. What better form of transport was there than the railway to carry them out to the babbling brooks, the meandering lanes and the ancient churches embowered in yews and rook-infested sturdy and ancient oaks?

One of the first substantial employers to give their workers Saturday afternoon off was Truman, Hanbury & Buxton, the brewers of Shoreditch. The growing move to close workplaces around midday was a slow process but had two results for the railways. The first was for extra trains to be put on to deal with the flow of homeward-bound workers after midday on Saturday. Second was the appearance of regular timetabled Saturdays-only half-day excursion trains to various destinations from London stations in the afternoon. The first of these was probably on the SER in 1857 and it enabled its users to enjoy the delights of Woolwich or Blackheath while not having to return from those places until as late as ten o'clock. By 1887, no fewer than 115 such Saturdays-only trains were leaving London in the warmer months.

The Victorian period was one of slowly rising living standards and expectations for a substantial section of the population. Especially with the price of some foodstuffs falling significantly towards the end of the century, large numbers of lower middle-class and skilled and semi-skilled workers in regular employment enjoyed rising real wages. More money to spend and some decline in working hours created a demand for packaged, commercialised leisure provision. Evidence of the heightened aspirations of some middle and working-class Londoners was the issuing of cheap tickets to a seaside or other destination for travel outward on Saturday with a return on Sunday or even Monday. This was the birth of the weekend holiday. The first such tickets were advertised in the 1840s and they clearly generated useful business because a few companies ran Mondays-only return trains from such seaside places as Felixstowe, Ramsgate and Bournemouth.

Travelling to and staying by the sea was simply not possible for the bulk of working-class Londoners who had to be content with something closer to home. London was well-placed in that respect with natural attractions and beauty spots in all directions. Epping Forest had long been a well-loved destination and became much easier to reach once the railway line to Chingford opened in 1873. A good warm sunny Sunday could see the Forest besieged by at least 50,000 Londoners, the bulk of them from the East End. Other favourite resorts were Blackheath, Greenwich, Hampstead, Kew Gardens, Richmond and Wimbledon, all of which were readily accessible by rail from 1870 or earlier. Other places easily accessible by rail if further away included Hampton Court, Windsor and the North Downs around Dorking. A couple of enterprising companies even put on anglers' tickets at a discounted rate while ramblers could have tickets which allowed them to travel out of London to a station on one line and return from a station on another. The railways helped people to escape the sounds and smells of London, even if only temporarily. This development must have had huge, although unquantifiable, benefits.

From early times, well-to-do commuters residing in places like Ramsgate, Broadstairs and Margate, left London to enjoy seaside living but travelled to London by train for work. Many Londoners in turn travelled to the Kent coast for leisure purposes. Here we see a South Eastern & Chatham 'E' Class 4-4-0 of a class introduced in 1905 heading out of London c. 1914 with an express (possibly a special) for towns on the Kent Coast. (Courtesy of John Scott Morgan)

As the excursion idea caught on, guidebooks appeared pointing out to their readers the sights and associations to be enjoyed, the means of getting there, where to obtain refreshments and other useful information. London provided a big market for such publications. One extolled the virtues of Walton and Weybridge in Surrey. These places, it was claimed, could be enjoyed at any time of the year but the best time to visit was late July and August when the heather was at its most attractive. 'A ride of three quarters of an hour takes the smoke-laden inhabitant of the Metropolis to a scene luxuriantly mantled with this lovely flower'.

It is likely that the purchaser of such a guide wanted to spend his or her leisure time in ways rather different from the excursionist to Margate or Brighton, who probably preferred boozy and bawdy delights. Another guidebook praised the delights of Cobham and told its readers that tickets from London to Cobham cost 1s 6d and there was a choice of twenty-four trains. Cobham Church should be visited to enjoy a spot of brass-rubbing and it helpfully pointed out that heel balls could be

Many working-class Londoners spent their limited annual holidays picking hops in the Kent countryside. They mostly went by train and special were laid on for them. The South Eastern Railway which handled many of these trains seemed to reserve their most run-down carriages for the purpose.

bought at most cobblers at the mere cost of a penny for two. No excursion to Cobham was complete without a visit to Cobham Hall to view works by such painters of eminence as Titian, Rubens, Holbein and Van Dyck.

The excursion train was seen as bringing cultural and social benefit. Charles Knight, one of the leading writers and publishers of guidebooks, pointed out that:

> The Excursion Train is one of our best public instructors. It is also one of the cheapest. At a rate for second and third-class passengers, varying from twenty-five miles for a shilling, or from little above a halfpenny to less than a farthing a mile, hundreds of thousands of travellers from London, during 1850, have been carried into the heart of our most beautiful inland scenery – to our Watering places – to our Ports – to our Universities – to our great Seats of Manufactures and Commerce. Upon the same principle, Excursion Trains from the Provinces have duly brought visitors to London. Nor is this all. From all the great manufacturing and commercial towns, Excursion Trains are constantly bearing the active and intelligent artisans, with their families, to some interesting locality, for a happy and rational holiday. The amount of pleasure and information thus derived, and of prejudice thus removed, cannot be estimated at too high a rate.

RAILWAYS AND SPORT

Railways were an important influence on the siting of several professional football grounds. Extremely rough and ready games with few rules and many injuries had been played since time immemorial. In the nineteenth century, such activities increasingly found themselves under critical scrutiny. Large gatherings of working people, especially young men, were boisterous, often drunken and regarded as a potential threat to law and order. The physical energy and passions that such games aroused needed to be channelled and controlled. The second half of the nineteenth century saw the emergence of national bodies that codified the game with rules and discipline at all levels including the novel concept that players would obey a referee – the impartial man in charge and the arbiter of disputes. The bigger clubs began to build enclosed stadiums and embraced commercialisation and professionalism. With serious amounts of money being invested in clubs, it was important to attract paying spectators in large numbers. The football grounds therefore had to be readily accessible. Railways were seen as an ideal way of shifting the large crowds making their way to and from the matches.

Tottenham Hotspur had their first enclosed ground at Northumberland Park in 1888 but it proved too small for the club's ambitions. They then built a new state-of-the-art stadium In Tottenham intentionally close to White Hart Lane station of the GER. Proximity to railways was a major factor in the siting of Chelsea's Stamford Bridge ground and Queen's Park Rangers even had a ground at Park Royal built for them by the GWR. The Den, the former ground of Millwall, was located close to three railway stations and one of Fulham's early grounds was near Parsons Green underground station. The Crystal Palace was the venue for several cup finals in the late 1890s and early 1900s. It was well-served by railways, the two stations catering for that popular venue being large and designed for the shifting of big crowds.

Just as anarchic violent football games attracted the opprobrium of the 'respectable' middle classes, so prize-fighting or pugilism also gained their disapproval. It was certainly barbaric, the contestants sometimes receiving appalling injuries which on occasions proved fatal; the crowd becoming frenzied because of the amount involved in the bets being laid on the outcome, while many fights broke out among the highly partisan and frequently drunk spectators. Huge crowds attended bouts between the best-known fighters. Roués from the aristocratic classes attended. Increasingly, magistrates banned such bouts, and they were driven 'underground'. Wherever possible, locations were found in natural hollows, preferably in remote spots near country railway stations. Ideally such locations were close to a county border so that in the event of a raid, all concerned could slip 'next door' into an area of different police jurisdiction. The railway companies had no scruples about organising special trains to these degrading events. The destinations were kept secret until the last minute and when the footplate crew and guard reported for duty, they usually had no idea where their destination would be that day although, of course, the crew had to have the route knowledge to 'sign the road'. Examples of excursion trains being put on for London devotees of pugilism were those to Sawbridgeworth in 1842 by the Northern & Eastern Railway, Wolverton in 1845 (the L&BR) and the L&SWR to Farnborough in Hampshire in 1860.

Samuel Smiles, the very model of mid-Victorian earnestness, would naturally be expected to have supported railway excursions to places of historical interest or natural beauty as part of pursuing the concept of 'rational recreation'. He was Secretary of the SER and in 1859 he had to appear before a hostile committee appointed by the Home Office to explain why his company persisted in running excursions to prize-fights. He was disarmingly candid. He told them that the demand, and the prospect of profit, made the running of these trains commercially irresistible.

Railways made a considerable contribution to the development of horse-racing, the so-called 'Sport of Kings'. Like football, horse-racing became codified and controlled in the nineteenth century and, similarly, the venues at which the sport took place became enclosed and the whole business far more commercialised. With large amounts of capital invested in the industry, it became essential to draw in the crowds. The railways and the horse-racing industry marched forward together, mutually supportive. The southern environs of London had several racecourses which were handily served by rail. The best-known was probably Epsom and this was served by what became the LB&SCR's Epsom Downs Station opened in 1865. This was then followed by the SE&CR with Tattenham Corner Station in 1901. Remarkably, these were the termini of lines purpose built to serve the racecourse and which saw minimal use other than on the few race days per annum. At their outer ends these lines both traversed what was then largely empty countryside but both stations were large, being designed to handle mass crowds. Further away were other racecourses such as Newmarket, Doncaster and Aintree, all of which were served by special trains from London. In 1905 a course was opened at Newbury. The GWR had a financial interest in this project and built a station, only open on race days, adjacent to its Reading to Taunton main line. Trains ran directly to this station from Paddington.

THE DISTRICT RAILWAY AND EXHIBITIONS

The Victorian era displayed a great belief in the infinite potential for progress of which humanity was capable. It was earnestly believed that the arts, science and technology should be harnessed in order to create a better world. There was a sense of awe and wonderment with the evidence that the planet was effectively shrinking with the development of new and faster forms of communications such as steamships, railways and the electric telegraph. There was a thirst for knowledge and self-improvement across society. It is hardly surprising therefore that the nineteenth century saw the staging of many major exhibitions, especially in London. Railways played a crucial part in making these events possible by providing the means of transport for visitors to get there and back.

The District Railway benefited by serving the area sometimes known as 'Albertopolis' or 'Museumland'. Prince Albert had invested much time and effort with others in the planning of the Great Exhibition of 1851. He was a very serious man and he earnestly, if somewhat naively, believed that the development of international trading links was a path to worldwide amity. He argued that this worthy objective would be encouraged by an exhibition that brought together the industrial and commercial products of the developed and developing nations and emphasised the intertwining of art, science and manufacture as means in the advancement of the human lot. The Great Exhibition was a marked success (even if it was distinctly nationalistic) and the profits from it partly went to the buying of land and the building of museums and educational establishments in what became the Exhibition Road area of South Kensington. The station at South Kensington which came to be served by trains of the District and Circle Lines was opened in 1868. It was ideally placed to bring visitors to the various attractions of this cultural quarter. A pedestrian tunnel 22 chains long opened in 1885 to allow underground passengers for free and non-railway users for a toll of 1d to walk under cover from South Kensington to the cluster of attractions around Exhibition Road. The first exhibition to was to be served by the District Railway was the International Inventions Exhibition in 1871.

Earl's Court as a venue for exhibitions opened in 1887 on a patch of derelict land between various railway lines and close to the District Line's West Brompton Station as well as Earl's Court Station itself. The District Line opened a covered pedestrian way from the station to Warwick Road and the entrance to the exhibition ground. Over the next few years, many successful exhibitions and other spectacles were staged at Earl's Court and the District did good business taking people to and fro. An excellent earner for the District was the Big Wheel which was a prominent feature of the West London skyline from 1895 to 1906, a forerunner of the London Eye.

The National Agricultural Hall was yet another exhibition centre in this district. It started business in 1884 and was renamed 'Olympia' in 1886. It came to be known for spectacular shows which combined education and entertainment. The exhibition centre was next to Addison Road Station (now Kensington Olympia) which, although it was not served directly by District Line trains, brought the company revenue from originating stations on its own lines.

In the ways mentioned and by many other means, railways played a critical role in the development of leisure for the teeming millions of London. In 1871 legislation introducing Bank Holidays was implemented and demand for trains to carry Londoners away from the squalor and grime of everyday London life expanded almost overnight. More business came the way of the railways.

Chapter 6

SUPPLYING LONDON'S NECESSITIES

BLACK GOLD

Traditionally, most of London's coal was brought down the east coast in tough, hard-working little collier ships from the rivers Tyne, Wear and Tees. The virtual monopoly enjoyed by the businesses involved in this trade was perceived as artificially inflating the price of coal and was a long-standing source of resentment. An additional irritant was the periodic disruption of the coasting trade by inclement weather. At its worst, this could stop the movement of the sea coal, as it was known, thereby causing shortages in the capital accompanied by sharp price rises. Hopes were soon expressed that the railways could break this monopoly and help to bring about a substantial fall in the price of London's coal. This possibility was recognised by the promoters of the Stockton & Darlington Railway who were moving coal from pits in County Durham down to the River Tees. From the Tees it could be shipped south along the coast to London. The shorter distance involved would hopefully allow it to undercut the price of coal from further north.

The railways proved to be rather slow to start transporting coal to London. Probably the first regular bulk consignments of coal by rail to London began in 1845, using a rather circuitous route from Derbyshire via Rugby, originating on the MR and running into London over the metals of the L&NWR. In 1850, just 55,000 tons of rail-borne coal arrived in London by contrast with the 3.5 million tons that arrived by sea. From then on, however, the railways became seriously interested in the money to be made from carrying coal to London to supply the immense and growing demand from its industrial and domestic consumers. The GNR was the first company to enter this business seriously and soon after its direct line from Doncaster via Grantham and Peterborough opened in 1852, it began shifting bulk trainloads of coal from South Yorkshire and the East Midlands. The L&NWR soon followed. In 1867, rail-borne coal exceeded that carried by sea for the first time. The coastal trade fought a rearguard action with bigger ships and better loading and unloading methods but could not effectively challenge the way the railways came to dominate the traffic. The MR later became a serious player after its own direct line to London was opened, competing most directly with the GNR. The GWR also supplied the London market with particularly high-quality types of coal from South Wales. The MR was to become the largest mover of coal to London.

A great deal of London's rail-borne coal arrived at yards in the north and west of the metropolis but there was of course considerable demand for coal from places south of the Thames. The trains of coal were sorted in large marshalling yards such as Brent (MR) and Ferme Park (GNR) in North London and then tripped around London via the West London/West London Extension Line or through Central London via the Metropolitan Railway and Snow Hill and over the line of the LC&DR through Ludgate Hill to depots in South London. The L&NWR for example had a coal depot at Tulse Hill and even a joint one with its hated rival, the MR, at Peckham Rye, opened in 1891. A sizeable marshalling yard was built at Hither Green in the 1890s, just to the south-east of Lewisham. This handled large quantities of coal brought in by the Midland and the Great Northern Companies. The trains involved had travelled over the Metropolitan, through Farringdon, Snow Hill, Metropolitan Junction then London Bridge and the SER. An example of business enterprise was the L&NWR's agreement with NLR which enabled it not only to have access to the London Docks but also to elevated coal depots at Broad Street and Haggerston and to sidings in such places as Kingsland, Hackney, Bow and Poplar and to various industries in the East End that needed large and regular supplies of coal.

The coal which arrived from the provinces in train loads was sorted into local pick-up goods trains which dropped off three or four loaded wagons here and half-a-dozen there. Almost every station in London's periphery eventually had two or three coal sidings with their characteristic storage bunkers made of old sleepers, their rows of carts, coal merchants' offices and weighbridges. The coal was then delivered to the domestic consumer by horse and cart, only later by lorry. Larger industrial premises might have their own coal sidings. The railway wagons themselves were primitive, being of small capacity, unbraked and wooden-bodied and were either owned by the colliery companies or by coal merchants. In either case, the names were prominently displayed on the sides. Where space in the yards was limited, coal drops were built so that coal could be discharged from wagons directly into bunkers below.

During the nineteenth century, the amount of sea-borne coal arriving in London continued to increase but the railways' share of the growing trade grew much more quickly to around 60 per cent in the 1880s. The railways played the major role in keeping the capital reliably supplied with coal at affordable prices. Coal was the source of Victorian London's lighting and heating and the fuel for its industrial production. The railways therefore performed a task which was vitally important to the capital's development.

BRINGING IN THE MEAT

Demand for meat was immense as London's population was expanding so rapidly. The railways established lucrative business from meeting that demand.

There were four wholesale meat markets in or close to the City. The major one was Smithfield and it was also the most contentious. It was established in 1638 by the City of London Corporation and soon attracted criticism because of the mess made in the streets by animals being driven there. The drovers were notorious for their drunken and offensive behaviour. The animals often got out of control and charged around the streets, causing mayhem and injury. The beasts were slaughtered at premises around the market and the sight and sound of this was becoming increasingly offensive and unacceptable by nineteenth-century standards. Blood and reeking heaps of gore piled up in the surrounding streets. In 1855 the market for live meat was transferred to a new site at Copenhagen Fields, north of King's Cross. The Metropolitan Cattle Market had no direct railway link but was close to the GNR. The old Smithfield was then rebuilt as the main London market for meat. It was adjacent to the Metropolitan Railway and the GWR opened a subterranean depot into which whole trains could be shunted. It was not as successful as had been hoped.

Passengers on Metropolitan Railway platforms might be surprised as a goods train shuffled past and might have been even more surprised to know that it contained carcasses destined for Smithfield.

The L&NWR and the GWR developed a sophisticated business moving imported cattle from Ireland, often slaughtered where the beasts came into England, for example at Birkenhead, and much of this was destined for the London market. Through the century, an increasing amount of meat came into Britain from overseas. In 1872 a Foreign Cattle Market opened at Deptford on the Thames, and it was served by a branch of the LB&SCR Railway. The development of refrigeration meant that large and fast ships crossed the world from countries like Argentina, Australia and New Zealand and were able to bring substantial supplies of cheap frozen meat into the London Docks. The capital took the lion's share of this meat but the railway companies with the GWR and the Midland most dominant, were at the forefront of developing refrigerated vans which then distributed meat around the country.

Much meat came into London through the docks some of which was then distributed through the country by rail. Handling the live animals and the meat provided many jobs for Londoners and useful business for the railways.

FISH FOR LONDON

The Revd W. Awdry had a 'Flying Kipper' express fish train in one of his entertaining railway stories for children. Kippers, being smoked and cured, did not need especially rapid transportation and along with dried, salted fish, had for centuries been sent by sea. Much of this trade came down the east coast and up the Thames to London. There were other sources, mostly along the south coast. Fish in this form formed a significant but probably not particularly popular part of the diet of Londoners, useful especially at times when meat was scarce or, at least in theory, when it was banned on certain days for religious reasons. For centuries, fresh fish had been caught off the coasts of Kent and Essex, brought up the Thames and landed for the London market at Queenhithe and Billingsgate. Fresh fish were also taken from the Thames itself and coarse fish from some of its tributaries in the London area and from ponds and other watercourses. However, Londoners had the reputation of not being particularly keen on eating such types of fish. Sprats, whitebait and jellied eels were exceptions to the rule and were eagerly consumed whenever possible.

This situation changed rapidly in the Victorian period as the railways developed an extensive business in carrying fresh fish. This was a highly perishable commodity which benefited by the speed the companies could offer in getting it in reasonable condition to the London market. An argument could be put forward to the effect that Grimsby, Lowestoft or Fleetwood, for example, were every bit as much railway towns as the better-known Crewe, Swindon or Eastleigh. The railways were the making of these fishing ports leading to the development of a large-scale, highly capitalised industry dependent on rail for whisking the precious and perishable cargo off to the urban markets, most especially London. This is not the place to participate in the sometimes-heated debates about whether fish was first fried with chipped potatoes in London or in any one of several disputed locations in the north of England. Wherever it was invented, with the aid of the railways it became a staple item of the diet of working-class Londoners. It was cheap, it was sustaining, and it was responsible for bringing about a very marked improvement in the diet and the health of the working class. The middle-class, however, affected to look down on fish and chips. That was their loss.

An impressive 'Claughton' Class 4-6-0 of the London & North Western Railway heading out of London with an express towards the West Midlands or the North c.1914. London became the hub of Britain's railway system despite being nowhere near the centre of the country. (Courtesy of John Scott Morgan)

FRUIT AND VEGETABLES

London, because of the size of its population, had for centuries exerted a strong demand on the agricultural and horticultural activities which took place in its rural hinterland. The rich soils of the Thames Valley attracted vast numbers of market gardens while large quantities of fruit were cultivated in Kent and vegetables were grown in Essex. Further out, vegetables, especially carrots, were grown in profusion around Biggleswade in Bedfordshire. Biggleswade carrots arrived in London by the wagonload, courtesy of the GNR. Ironically, the railways carried another kind of cargo out of London, this time to the growers. This was the euphemistically named 'nightsoil', the contents of closets, as well as scooped up horse-droppings. The horse was the prime mover of the London streets and hundreds of tons of dung were deposited on the streets every day. Both human and equine waste made excellent fertiliser. This was a fine example of recycling – nothing was wasted.

If there can be said to have been a general pattern, it was that land used as market gardens close to central London often quickly disappeared under bricks and mortar and so new market gardens areas opened on the periphery only in turn to be gradually pushed further away as London expanded outwards. The railways had something to do with this process since building development often followed the opening of stations, even those at first deeply rural. Sometimes marginal land was brought into use for market gardening, the Lea Valley around Broxbourne being an example, the GER being on hand to transport the produce.

The efforts of growers around London were not sufficient to feed London's burgeoning population in the Victorian period but the railways provided access to almost the whole country, creating in effect a national market. They never had a monopoly of transporting the products of agriculture and where the produce was the sort which did not deteriorate quickly, canals and coastal transport still had a large role to play right up to the end of the period under review.

Some railway companies diversified their operations to include the running of fruit and vegetable markets. The GER established two such markets, at Bishopsgate and Stratford. The first, though successful, had to close quickly owing to legal problems but Stratford went from strength to strength. In 1879, its first year, 5,000 tons of produce arrived by rail. In 1887 the figure had increased to 33,000 tons. The GNR had a potato market at King's Cross and the MR a similar market at nearby St Pancras.

MILK TRAFFIC

There was no more perishable foodstuff than milk. Vendors were still leading cows through the streets of London as late as the 1860s and milk could be bought, on tap as it were, straight from the udder. These cows might be grazed on any open land around the metropolis. Others were kept in dismal, overcrowded byres in the slum areas, adding their unique contribution to the heady mix of noxious odours emanating from such places. It is estimated that in the 1850s there were still around 20,000 of these woebegone beasts giving milk in London. It was not, of course, pasteurised at this time.

Before the coming of the railways, transport being slow meant that what milk Londoners consumed was produced locally. Supplies carried by rail began to arrive in London in the mid-1840s. The first company to enter this business was the GER, bringing milk in from Brentwood and Romford. This initially met with a somewhat hostile reception, perhaps understandably, because the containers used for this milk had no form of temperature control and it was not unknown for the milk to be off by the time it reached the consumer. Londoners liked to see their milk come out of the cow. Then they knew it was fresh.

An outbreak of cattle plague or rinderpest in the 1860s killed large numbers of animals and rendered cow-keeping much less desirable within London itself. In the 1870s, for the first time, rail-borne milk supplies exceeded those of local milk. In 1890 over 80 per cent of London's milk arrived by rail. As London's population rose rapidly, so did the demand for milk. The transport of milk became big business for several railway companies, most particularly those serving the wetter western side of the country where the lusher pastures tended to be found. The L&SWR, for example, established a sizeable depot at Semley in Wiltshire, collecting milk from large numbers of producers in the area. Operations were on a sufficient scale to justify six milk trains daily to London. Other companies moved smaller quantities. Milk trains were lucrative, were given priority and usually moved at express passenger train speeds.

Milk travelled long distances over the metals of the GWR from Devon, Cornwall and West Wales, for example, as well as from places nearer to the capital such as Berkshire. The GWR was quick to see that money could be made from the transport of milk and it went on to become the largest carrier of this product to London. The records show that in January 1884, 527,293 gallons of milk arrived at Paddington. Swindon (Wiltshire), Faringdon (Berks) and Devizes (Wiltshire) were among the major places despatching milk to the capital. As demand developed, milk was bought to London from more far-flung parts of the GWR's system. In the early days, milk was conveyed in a variety of metal containers which evolved into the later ubiquitous large iron churns which were heavy to move when full and not, to our eyes, a very hygienic method of transport. The use of sterilised, glass-lined tanks had to wait until the 1920s.

The availability of cheap, fresh supplies had a highly beneficial effect on the diet of Londoners. In 1850, it is estimated that Londoners each drank about six gallons of milk a year. Just before the First World War, the figure had risen to around 21 gallons. Given the enormous increase in London's population over this period, this was a remarkable development, and the railways should take the credit for much of it.

Chapter 7
RAILWAY CRIME

From their earliest days, railway stations have attracted all manner of human detritus, much of it being criminal in nature. London's termini might almost have been designed with society's drifters in mind. In most cases, the stations provided easy access to covered space twenty-four hours a day. For the homeless that offered the possibility of snatching some sleep and was often better and perhaps marginally warmer than dossing down elsewhere, possibly under the stars.

London's major termini provided a multiplicity of opportunities for a diverse range of people operating just inside or, in many cases, outside the law. Those offering freelance but illicit porterage services; female prostitutes, rent boys; procurers and procuresses; touts of all sorts; robbers; luggage thieves, cadgers; those bent on sexual assault eying up their potential victims – likewise those bent on robbery; cowboy horse-cab operators; conmen looking for gullible marks; card sharpers; rich men, poor men, beggarmen, thieves.

London has long attracted inward migration from the provinces. People came hoping, or believing, that London offered them a better future. The sheer size of London, the wealth generated and conspicuously displayed there, its anonymity and the opportunities it offered for criminal activity, have also attracted casual and career criminals, some of whom found rich pickings. London has also always drawn to it the vulnerable and the dysfunctional. They have included young people desperate to get away from physical and other types of abuse at home; the bored and disaffected; drug addicts, even in the nineteenth century; people trying to escape from something but not necessarily knowing what it was or unclear about what they wanted; those hoping that a move to London might kick-start a new and better phase in their dreary lives. Many of these drifters were not well-equipped to deal with the dangers and temptations offered by the metropolis. Many were lured into the sex trade. This hotchpotch of humanity has tended to arrive particularly at the London termini of services originating in the north of England and Scotland. Many were scared, callow, vulnerable. Some were no more than children. An informal reception committee of low-life characters would be waiting to 'befriend' them as soon as they got off the train.

Pickpockets found rich rewards for their efforts in densely crowded railway stations and carriages. In the enclosed compartment carriages, a common ploy was for a pickpocket with charm and plausibility to express concern for a wealthy-looking traveller and to offer to swap seats, away from a draught, for example. The thief would already have noted the disposition of likely valuables about the victim's person. In the minor melee created by changing seats in the crowded compartment, any useful items would be deftly removed. The skill required for removing the items without being detected, picking the right victim and obtaining agreement for the move while timing all this just before a station stop at which the thief alighted and vanished, should not be underestimated. A journalist interviewed a retired thief who still earned his crust by passing his skills on to rookies, declared with considerable pride that it was 'as much a fine art as pianoforte-playing or high-class conjuring'.

Another kind of villain was the luggage or baggage thief. One of the most spectacular hauls made by such operators occurred in the 1870s at Paddington Station. A member of the Countess of Dudley's entourage foolishly placed her employer's jewel-box on the floor for a few seconds while assisting a colleague. The box vanished in a trice. The contents consisting of diamonds worth £50,000 were never recovered.

ASSAULTS AND ROBBERIES ON TRAINS

Early passenger carriages contained enclosed compartments which could provide the scenario for any number of unpleasant experiences. These compartments brought travellers into very close proximity with their fellows. A crowded carriage could enforce undesirably close physical intimacy but those of a nervous disposition might find this easier to handle than occupying a compartment with just one other passenger. The stranger in such a compartment might turn out to be a robber, a sexual predator with curious or repulsive preferences, a homicidal maniac, a chain-smoker or a mind-numbingly tedious bore. People felt trapped in these compartments and although of course most journeys were completed without anything untoward happening, in early trains there was no ready way to stop the train or even to alert a member of the crew if something untoward happened. A few travellers therefore sometimes equipped themselves with weapons such as knives and even firearms when they travelled by train. Women travellers often had a hat pin at the ready. It could do a lot of damage.

It was always felt that female passengers were particularly vulnerable to sexual and other forms of assault. For this reason, some compartments were designated 'Ladies Only'. Of course, simply labelling a compartment for the exclusive use of women travellers did not prevent some determined male reprobate from jumping in when the guard's back was turned. He might then subject his victim to some terrifying ordeal, possibly a fate worse than death.

Some prostitutes did business in otherwise empty first-class compartments. Ideally the trains used for such activities were not all-stations stopping trains on busy suburban routes. Skilled prostitutes with able-bodied punters could complete the business in the five minutes it took a train to travel from London Bridge to Cannon Street Station.

Men travelling in a compartment with just one unknown female fellow-passenger might have cause to feel uneasy. Women passengers sometimes maliciously concocted stories that a male fellow-passenger had made indecent comments or suggestions or had molested or sexually assaulted them. If there were no witnesses, the man, even if he was totally innocent, might find that his guilt was taken for granted by the courts and he would find himself having to undertake a lengthy custodial sentence.

Men of the cloth seem to have come through possibly compromising situations benefitting by the fact that their innocence was generally presumed. We will never know exactly what was said or what went on after a young curate entered a compartment containing just a sixteen-year-old girl, this being on a train of the GWR. The girl alleged that he pulled her onto his knee, kissed her passionately and whispered various over-familiar endearments and unseemly suggestions into her ear. The case went to court, the curate denying any wrongdoing on his part. He admitted having started a conversation with the girl during which he had suggested that he might be able to obtain a job for her playing the organ in his parish church. He also admitted having boasted that it was a magnificent organ. Could this innocent comment have been misconstrued? The court thought that he had uttered it in good faith, and he was able to return to his parish with his reputation unsullied.

In 1864, a gentleman was sitting happily in the compartment of a L&SWR train travelling between Surbiton and Woking. He was somewhat startled when he found himself staring into a woman's face a few inches from his but on the outside of the rapidly moving train. She was standing on the footboard of the carriage and clinging on for dear life. With some difficulty he managed to haul her to safety and fortunately some people by the side of the line had also seen her predicament and alerted the guard who brought the train to a swift halt. It appeared that a Mr Nash had earlier entered a compartment containing two women travellers, one of whom was the woman clinging to the outside of the carriage. Her name was Mary Moody. Nash had attempted, with a marked lack of finesse, to chat the other woman up but she had alighted at Surbiton. Mary decided to follow but her reactions were not quick enough and before she could gather up her things, the train began to pull away from the platform. She found herself alone with Nash who, after trying to talk to her embraced her and then attempted an indecent assault. Mary had little choice, as she saw it, but to try to evade his clutches and escape by the daring and dangerous means of the compartment door and carriage footboard of the moving train. Nash was arrested when the train came to a halt and received a custodial sentence.

Assault was not always intentional. A man who had been attacked by footpads near Willesden Junction Station had scared them off when he took out a pistol and fired over their heads. He was so elated by this robust defence of his person and property that a few days later he related the event to a stranger on a train. Warming to his theme, he got rather carried away and suddenly decided to show the stranger how he had dealt with the would-be robbers. He whipped out his pistol and fired it. His aim was not as true as it should have been because instead of the bullet passing over the traveller's head, it made a neat parting in his hair!

THE MURDER OF THOMAS BRIGGS

The country was shocked and horrified by what was thought to be the first murder on a railway train. This happened at the perhaps surprisingly late date of 1864. Thomas Briggs was an aldermanic figure, the epitome of Victorian middle-class respectability. A widower of 69, he was tall, silver-haired, dapper, distinguished-looking and very fit for his age. He was the chief clerk of a banking house in the City. When travelling he always wore a distinctive tall silk hat. He also sported an expensive-looking gold chain stretched across his capacious midriff, the chain being attached to a fine gold watch. He also carried a stout walking stick.

On 9 July, a Saturday, he left the office around half-past four to travel to Peckham for dinner with a niece on whom he doted. It was still light when he left Peckham to catch a horse bus back to King William Street in the City. He then strode briskly to Fenchurch Street Station where he entered a first-class compartment on a train of the NLR. He was alone when the train puffed out of Fenchurch Street at 9.50 to start on its roundabout route via Shadwell, Stepney and Bow to his destination at Hackney. Much of the route ran on low viaducts providing a bird's eye view of the rooftops of inner-city working-class housing interspersed with the myriad small industrial premises then so characteristic of this part of London's East End. Hackney, however, where Briggs lived, was a cut above, boasting a respectable gentility.

The NLR had just over 13 miles of its own line, but its trains also ran on over 50 miles of line belonging to other companies. The NLR had an importance out of all proportion to its size because its small network linked the main lines coming into London from the north and west with the City and the docks in the east. The company's first terminus was a shared one at Fenchurch Street, but it later opened a fine station of its own at Broad Street. It may have been a small company, but it was a proud one. It possessed a fleet of diminutive

Franz Muller hanged in 1854 for a murder on the North London Railway. Did he have an accomplice?

but powerful 4-4-0 tank engines. Its four-wheeled carriages were quite luxurious by the standards of the time.

It was a warm evening and almost totally dark. A weak light in the ceiling provided poor illumination. Briggs had eaten well. He had worked all day. He dozed fitfully. At Bow he exchanged pleasantries through the open carriage window with an acquaintance called Lee who later averred there were two other passengers in the compartment. Lee remembered being mildly surprised to see Briggs travelling at such a late hour. He was also surprised by the appearance of the other two occupants of the carriage. They had not, in his opinion, looked like first-class travellers. Later, when cross-examined in court, he admitted he had had a drink or two in a local pub.

The train pulled out of Bow, being due at the next stopping place, Victoria Park, Hackney Wick, in a few minutes. The next compartment to that occupied by Briggs was also first class and was occupied by a draper called Withall and a female traveller. They were not together. As the train was approaching Victoria Park, Withall described hearing a sudden and weird howling noise, reminiscent, he said, of a dog in distress. His unknown female companion made a remark to the same effect. In another compartment close by, a female passenger had the unpleasant experience of being spattered with drops of blood that came in through the open window. She said she heard no untoward noises.

When the train arrived at Victoria Park, two young men-about-town, Henry Verney and Sydney Jones, joined the train and they stepped into the compartment in which Briggs had started his journey. It was empty but, although it was poorly lit, they immediately realised that a lot of blood was scattered around the compartment. Several personal items could be made out. They included a black leather bag and a walking stick. Under the seat lay a black beaver hat, so squashed that it looked as if someone had stood on it. Thoroughly alarmed, they got the attention of the guard who directed them to another compartment. He realised that the compartment had very recently witnessed foul play. He locked it and gave instructions for a telegraph message to be sent to the superintendent at Chalk Farm, the station where the train terminated. There the carriage was uncoupled and shunted into a siding to await examination by the police.

Meanwhile the driver of a train proceeding in the opposite direction had seen a dark object lying close to the track. He brought his train to a halt and he, the fireman and the guard descended to track level to investigate. The object was the body of a man, battered and bloodied but still alive, although only just. A doctor was soon on the scene. His initial impression was that the injuries on the left of the man's head had probably been sustained by his fall from a train. However, two violent blows had fractured his skull. Briggs, for it was he, died late the next evening. He never regained consciousness.

This horrible murder stirred up a hornets' nest of sensationalist headlines and scaremongering articles in the newspapers. 'Murder on the Iron Way' was true and comparatively moderate. Perhaps more typical was the newspaper which thundered, 'Who is safe? If we may be murdered thus, we may be slain in our pew at church, or assassinated at our dinner table'.

This first railway murder emphasised how vulnerable passengers in compartments could be to the depredations of malefactors. They dared not leap from the train while it was in motion. They had no way of stopping the train. It was not easy to attract the attention of the guard or the men on the footplate. Without a side-corridor in the carriage, it was difficult to gain the attention of travellers in other compartments. What could other travellers do even if they had been alerted to possible trouble nearby? Two passengers travelling in the same compartment but who were strangers would now spend the journey eyeing each other up suspiciously, making sure all valuables were out of sight. The manufacturers of coshes, then more generally known as life-preservers, had their workers slaving away on overtime in order to keep up with demand.

A murder enquiry was launched. It came up with frustratingly few leads while the newspapers clamoured for a quick result. Clues pointed to a young German man called Franz Muller, living in digs in the East End. He had boarded a ship in the London Docks, bound for New York and a new start in life. Two detectives set off for New York in a faster vessel and were waiting for Muller when he arrived there. When he was searched, Briggs's gold watch was found as was his hat to which Muller had made some modifications. He was extradited, brought back to England and his trial began at the Old Bailey began on 27 October. Muller looked small, even frail and certainly not the man to launch a murderous attack on Briggs who, despite being much older, was larger, stronger and fit for his age. It seemed likely that Muller had had an accomplice but who was he and why did Muller insist that he had been on his own? The case attracted enormous public interest and not a little xenophobia. The evidence was largely circumstantial, but the jury took only fifteen minutes to reach their verdict. The execution was set for eight in the morning of 14 November. The location was outside the hated Newgate Prison.

The crowds that gathered at hangings were always boisterous and badly behaved, but the impending death of Muller seems to have attracted the most bestial and wretched of London's population, to a total of about 50,000, all baying for blood and avid for the entertainment to be had from watching a man in his death agonies. The executioner was William Calcraft who, despite a long career in the terminatory business, had never been much of a craftsman. He was unpopular not only with his victims, which was entirely understandable, but also with aficionados who knew a good hanging when they saw one.

As *The Times* reported, the crowd went quiet only as Calcraft was doing his grisly work and Muller's life was ebbing away. Then there was an awed hush. For the rest of the time, there was 'loud laughing, oaths, fighting, obscene conduct and still more filthy language'. So horrible was the behaviour of the crowd at Muller's execution that the event undoubtedly contributed greatly to the developing feeling that executions should be carried out privately behind prison walls. Indeed, it was only about four years later that the last public hanging took place in Britain, again outside Newgate.

It has entered the annals of folklore that Muller was goaded into making a last-minute admission of guilt by the pastor attending him. Whether or not this is true, it is unlikely that any modern court would have passed such a verdict with the forensic and other investigative techniques now known.

As mentioned above, Muller had altered the hat he had stolen from Briggs into a kind of cut-down topper and these became fashionable among young-men-about-town in London. 'Muller Hats' enjoyed several years as fashion items.

On a positive note, some good came from the murder of Thomas Briggs because methods of communication between passengers and what would now be called 'traincrew' began slowly to come into use across the railway system. These went under the generic name of 'communication cord' and when activated they warned the engine driver to stop the train as soon as it was safe to do so. However, it was many years before such apparatus became mandatory. At least one observer commented that a communication cord would not have saved the life of Briggs. The first blow would probably have rendered him unable to summon assistance. The L&SWR put small openings rather like portholes in the dividing partition between compartments and these at least offered some opportunity for frightened passengers to attract attention. These were often used by 'peeping toms' to observe the antics of courting couples in the adjacent compartment.

In the words of the counsel for the prosecution:

> The crime…is almost unparalleled in this country. It is a crime which strikes at the lives of millions. It is a crime which affects the life of every man who travels upon the great iron ways of this country…a crime of a character to arouse in the human breast an almost instinctive spirit of vengeance.

The first railway murder may have been a long time in coming but when it did, it managed to chill and horrify the entire nation.

AN UNSOLVED MURDER ON THE LONDON & SOUTH WESTERN RAILWAY

The public find murders fascinating. They find unsolved murders even more fascinating. One such murder took place on a suburban train of the L&SWR on its way from Hounslow to Waterloo. The year was 1897.

Elizabeth Camp was an attractive, intelligent working-class woman aged 33. She was the manageress of a busy pub in the Walworth district of South London.

Although this was her day off, she was very busy. In the morning, she went to Hammersmith to visit her younger sister and then travelled on to Hounslow for tea with her elder sister. Elizabeth was due to get married and she had been shopping for various items connected with the forthcoming nuptials. Having spent time with her sister, of whom she was very fond, she was feeling pleasantly content when she returned to Hounslow Station to catch the 7.42 to Waterloo. She had even managed a quick drink in a pub with her sister and a man euphemistically described as a 'friend of the family'. Her fiancé, Edward Barry, was due to meet her at Waterloo and they intended to visit a music-hall. Elizabeth was somewhat encumbered by parcels and packages containing the articles she had bought as she selected an empty second-class compartment. Unfortunately, she was never to leave that compartment alive.

Edward was a good-looking, steady man but a bit of a worrier who tended to mother-hen his loved one. He got to Waterloo in plenty of time to meet Elizabeth's train which was due to arrive at 8.23. He was disconcerted when the train arrived, and he was unable to pick her out of the throng of passengers coming through the ticket barrier. It was most unlike her not to be where she said she was going to be.

Inevitably he soon got himself in a bit of a flap. Had she actually been on the train, but had they somehow managed not to see each other? Was she at this moment wandering around the huge station looking for him? What time was the next train from Hounslow due? Edward fussed here and he fussed there, getting more agitated by the minute. He returned to the barrier and noticed a knot of agitated-looking railway workers around an open compartment door of the train from Hounslow. His growing sense of anxiety and foreboding grew when he saw two grim-faced uniformed railway police officers making their way briskly to the carriage.

The practice at Waterloo was for cleaners to service the train before it left for another foray into London's south-western suburbia. Elizabeth's body had been discovered by a cleaner as he opened the compartment door. Her head and torso were largely under the seat and her legs were spread widely on the floor. A growing pool of blood was oozing from the corpse. With scant regard for possible evidence at the scene, the body was lifted out onto the platform. The dead woman had clearly been the victim of an exceptionally brutal attack in which she had been beaten to death and her skull had been stove in. There was blood everywhere and even to an unpractised eye, it was clear that the victim had not gone to her death without having made a desperate fight back.

The body was removed to the mortuary at St Thomas's Hospital. With his heart in his mouth, Edward followed. When he got there, he explained who he was, and he had to identify the battered corpse. The worst-case scenario he could ever have anticipated lay in front of his horrified eyes.

The police scoured the compartment for clues. Apart from clearly having witnessed a struggle to the death, the only item that provided any possible evidence was a bone cuff link on the floor. No trace of Elizabeth's train ticket was found but then the purse which she habitually carried could not be found either. If the motive was robbery, why had one or two jewellery items of minor value not been taken? Why should a would-be robber pick on a fit-looking youngish working-class woman who was well-dressed but clearly not particularly well off? Surely a better-off but more vulnerable victim could have been found by the unknown assailant if he had only exercised some degree of patience?

The salaciously minded quickly homed in on the idea that the motive of the attacker was sex. Cheap, sensational and melodramatic fiction of the Victorian period found a rich seam in the horrible happenings that might befall innocent maidens at the hands of male malefactors travelling in enclosed railway compartments. Any male over the age of puberty was a potential sex-fiend stalking railway stations in order to locate and molest vulnerable women before subjecting them to an appalling fate. Elizabeth had not been sexually assaulted and the frequency of the station stops hardly allowed time for a successful assault on a woman as fit and strong as Elizabeth had been. However, a horribly violent murder had clearly taken place. What was the motive of the murderer? Who, indeed, was the murderer?

The police investigation quickly concluded that since Elizabeth's blood was still warm when her corpse was delivered to St Thomas's, she had almost certainly been killed towards the end of her journey from Hounslow and that her attacker had therefore probably left the train at one of the last three stops before Waterloo. These stations were not particularly busy at that time of the evening. Questioning the staff who had been on duty about anyone seen with blood-stained clothing or acting in any way suspiciously produced no useful results. However, when the side of the line between Putney and Wandsworth was searched, a heavy porcelain pestle was found. It had blood and human hair adhering to it. The hair was identified as belonging to Elizabeth Camp. The police now had the murder weapon. Appeals for anyone to come forward who recognised it drew a total blank. Next an appeal was issued for anyone who had been travelling on the 7.42 from Hounslow who might have seen or heard anything to come forward. This did not produce any useful information either.

Gradually, the furore over Elizabeth's murder died down as the papers found new horrors to gorge on. Police enquiries continued but were scaled down. It was revealed that Elizabeth had once been engaged to a barman called Brown and that the relationship had ended very acrimoniously. Apparently, Elizabeth had lent him money, some of which he had not repaid. Anonymous threatening letters had been sent to Elizabeth which the police thought had been written by Brown. Owing her money and apparently still smarting with resentment at the way he thought he had been treated, he had a motive for the murder. He turned out to have a cast-iron alibi.

There is much painstaking sweat and often little glory in routine police work. As enquiries continued, the police established that Elizabeth had a side-line as a moneylender. Such people are generally disliked. Edward had told the police that Elizabeth frequently carried a considerable amount of money on her person. Could her murderer have been someone who knew this and had waited for an opportunity to rob her when she was alone? Many people owed her money. Could it have been one of her creditors? One of them turned out to be the 'friend of the family' who had joined Elizabeth and her sister for a drink at Hounslow before she had left to return to Waterloo. His name was Stone. He had left Elizabeth and her sister before they went to the station, claiming to have some business elsewhere but since he knew which train Elizabeth was catching, the police wondered whether he had entered the train unseen, alighted at an intermediate station and then, intent on murdering the woman to whom he owed money, joined Elizabeth in her compartment. He had the motive and the opportunity. However, the means were problematical. Was he in the habit of carrying a heavy pestle around with him? Or had he secreted it about his person because he knew that Elizabeth would be visiting Hounslow that day and returning to London on a lightly used train?

Stone became the prime suspect, and the police grilled him thoroughly. Reluctantly, they had to let him go because, they said, there was insufficient evidence to obtain a conviction.

The murder of Elizabeth Camp on the 7.42 from Hounslow to Waterloo remains unsolved to this day.

AN APPOINTMENT WITH THE HANGMAN AT NEWGATE

Louisa Masset lived in Stoke Newington, N16. She was half-French, half-English and 33 years of age when she hit the headlines in 1899. She lived with her married sister and her husband and was the unmarried mother of a small boy called Manfred. She had left France because of the stigma attached to the mothers of illegitimate children. She was a governess and teacher of piano. The child's natural father paid for Manfred to be cared for by a foster-mother in Tottenham. Louisa saw him regularly. She very much had a mind of her own, being no respecter of conventional mores and when a young Frenchman of 19 called Eudor moved in next door, she was soon engaged in a steamy sexual relationship with him.

Unexpectedly, in October 1899, Manfred's father contacted Louisa requesting that he took on the job of looking after the boy. This seemed a good idea and Louisa arranged to meet Manfred's foster-mother and pick the boy up. Before she did so, she put a brick into a bag which she then carried with her when she met him and took him to London Bridge Station. The date was 27 October. Later, a witness came forward to say that she had seen them together during the afternoon in the buffet at the station and that the little boy had seemed very distressed. The same witness saw Louisa again around six in the evening. She was alone. It transpired that she had gone off with Eudor for a dirty weekend at Brighton.

It seems that between the first and second occasions she was seen at London Bridge, she had doubled back to north London. In the late afternoon, two women found the naked body of a small boy in the waiting room at Dalston Junction station on the NLR. It was immediately obvious to the police that he had been battered with a brick which was close by – in two pieces – and then suffocated. Press statements were issued. A murder hunt was launched.

On 30 October, Helen (the foster-mother) received a letter from Louisa telling her that Manfred was now in France and safe and sound but missing her awfully. By now all London was buzzing with speculation about the murdered infant. Helen was horrified that the description of the body matched that of Manfred, and she went to the police. She provided an official identification. Meanwhile a bundle of little boy's clothes had been found at Brighton Station and Helen confirmed that they belonged to Manfred. Louisa was traced, arrested and charged with the murder. She stood trial at the Old Bailey and was found guilty. She was hanged at Newgate on 9 January 1900 after confessing to the murder but without providing a plausible reason for the horrible crime. Louisa Masset was the first person to be hanged in Britain in the twentieth century.

CAUGHT BY THE TELEGRAPH

In early 1845, the case of a murderer who used the railway in attempting to leave the scene of his crime and to evade detection, hit the headlines. It also attracted attention because it was the first case in which the electric telegraph, developed to help safety and communication on the railways, proved highly effective in the apprehension of a suspected criminal on the run.

In 1839, William Fothergill-Cooke and Charles Wheatstone convinced the directors of the GWR to install a modified version of their electric telegraph system on the main line out of London as far as Hanwell. It was successful and in 1842 it was extended to Slough. All manner of messages could now be transmitted quickly to assist the safe and efficient running of the line. Soon other companies were adopting the Cooke and Wheatstone system, and it was to become almost universal across Britain's burgeoning railway system.

John Tawell was a success – or so it seemed. He was intelligent, resourceful, persuasive and personable. His business interests were successful enough to provide him with a lifestyle of some luxury. He was also a devout member of his local Quaker community. However, Tawell had both a murky past and a murky present. When scarcely out of his teens, he had been sentenced to transportation for forgery. His conduct in the Australian penal colony had been exemplary and he had returned to England as a 'ticket-of-leave' man, essentially being licensed for good behaviour. He had learned from his experience. He did not fancy a return to the Antipodes but knew he could be plausible, and he fancied enriching himself, preferably without resorting to indictable crime. He went down one of the well-worn paths of the conman. He insinuated himself into the affections of a rich widow, a Quaker like himself, and after they married, he gained access to her large bank account. He quickly discovered that he had a penchant for extra-marital affairs. His charm and preparedness to throw his money around made for rich pickings, sexually and financially.

One of these affairs was with Sarah Hart, who was a former servant of his. He set her up in a cottage in Slough discreetly out of the public eye but convenient enough for him to visit her regularly. He fathered a couple of children with Sarah for whom he accepted total financial responsibility. He always made sure that she had what he thought was enough money not only for all the basics but also for a more-than-comfortable life. Sarah, like other kept women, enjoyed spending her keeper's money but something was missing. This was the opportunity to socialise and move around freely. Ostracism in fact went with her way of life. Things began to change when Tawell retired from business, which meant a significant fall in his income and in what he was prepared to give Sarah. Tensions now began to enter the relationship. She resented having less money to spend without anything to compensate her for her reduced circumstances. He, for his part, grew increasingly fed up with her constant complaints. Their relationship quickly went from tranquil to tempestuous.

If Tawell had ever actually been in love with Sarah, he was now definitely out of love. She had become a burden and so he resolved to kill her. He made his preparations with some care. On 1 January 1845 he bought some prussic acid at a chemist's shop in the City of London and then cashed a cheque on one of his bank accounts although he knew he did not have the funds to support it. He called in at a City coffee house where he was known, to ascertain what time it closed in the evening. He then headed for Paddington and caught the 4pm local train to Slough. He arrived at Sarah's cottage about 5pm. It seems that the couple started off the evening in friendly enough fashion because Sarah made two visits to a nearby pub to buy some bottles of stout. Later the mood between the couple deteriorated and neighbours heard them arguing. Shouts turned to female screams of pain and Tawell was then seen making his way from the cottage clearly in a state of extreme agitation. Another witness saw him heading for the station. A neighbour had tried to comfort Sarah and a doctor had been summoned. Sarah died just as he arrived. A local priest was also called and, quickly assessing the situation, he set off in his pony and trap for the station just as fast as he could go. It seemed likely that Tawell had caught a train back to Paddington. The priest persuaded the staff to telegraph to Paddington requesting that Tawell be arrested on arrival. The police were indeed waiting but instead of arresting him, they followed him to his lodgings.

Tawell was arrested the next day. He initially denied having been in Slough the previous evening or even of knowing anyone who lived there. Rather patronisingly he told them that his social status put him above suspicion. They must have enjoyed disabusing him of this notion when they charged him with murder.

The trial began on 12 March at Aylesbury and it excited enormous interest. The evidence suggested that Tawell had somehow managed to place prussic acid in the stout that Sarah was drinking and thereby causing her death when she swallowed it. On the third day, the jury retired to consider their verdict and returned quickly with the bald statement 'guilty'. Although this was not entirely unexpected, the verdict was met with oohs and aahs and it seems that Tawell, as has been the case with other male murderers, had elicited the adoration of some of the women in the public gallery who wept openly and loudly when the sentence of death was pronounced on their hero.

On 28 March, Tawell was hanged at Aylesbury. The case is famous less, perhaps, for the nature of the murder than for the fact that Tawell was the first murderer to be apprehended by the authorities using the highspeed form of communication which had just become available courtesy of Cooke and Wheatstone's electric telegraph. Since the GWR played something of a pioneering role so far as the electric telegraph is concerned, it is worth musing on the notion that if Tawell had used another railway to make his way to and from his dastardly deed, he might have got away with it.

TERRORISM ON THE RAILWAYS

The Irish Question has been a running sore in British political life for centuries. It could be argued that the British ruling class historically considered Ireland to be little more than a colony to be controlled and exploited for the benefit of the 'mother country'. Issues around the development of its economy, the ownership of its land and the toxic fall-out resulting from the clash of religious persuasions ensured that Ireland was at the forefront of the political agenda for much of the nineteenth century. Irish MPs sat in Westminster at a time when Irish nationalism was growing inexorably. By the 1870s, Home Rule was coming to dominate British politics. Irish nationalists became increasingly militant and vociferous. Their frustration meant that some, inevitably, turned away from the ballot box and towards the bomb.

A serious phase of terrorist activity broke out in 1883. In London the first evidence of this was a large explosion outside government offices in March of that year. Police investigations revealed a terrorist cell based in the prestigious Charing Cross Hotel belonging to the SER. On the evening of 30 October, two bombs went off on the underground within a few minutes of each other, fortunately without loss of life. The first was on a train near Praed Street (later Paddington) and it showered passengers with broken window glass. Five people needed hospital treatment. Shortly afterwards, a bomb exploded on a train between Charing Cross and Westminster. The lights went out and large amounts of black smoke gave the impression that the incident was more serious than it was. There were no major casualties.

In January 1884, information was received that one or more bombs were going to be detonated at St Pancras. For several days the Midland main line as far north as Leicester was subjected to large-scale close security but nothing untoward occurred. If disruption and diversion of resources had been intended, they were achieved. A couple of weeks later, five containers of explosives were found in Primrose Hill Tunnel on the L&NWR line out of Euston. They lacked fuses and detonators, and it was unclear how they got there and for what purpose they were intended.

A large explosion at the LB&SCR side of Victoria on 26 February 1884 caused much damage and was followed by a fire, but with few casualties. Searches were made at other stations, bombs being found at Charing Cross and Paddington and, a week later, at Ludgate Hill Station. These devices offered the police various clues. Numbers of Irish Americans were arrested and convicted.

A lull in terrorist activity followed until 2 January 1885 when a bomb exploded on the Metropolitan Railway near Gower Street (later Euston Square Station). It was a device by the side of the line, and it detonated at 9.14 when an Aldgate to Hammersmith train was passing. There was a loud and frightening explosion, the lights went out, but casualties were again, thankfully, few. Police investigations led to the arrest, conviction and imprisonment of two men thought to be the ringleaders of the bomb cell. They received life sentences and with their enforced retirement, the bombing campaign ceased.

THE REDPATH FRAUDS

The railway world was rocked in 1856 by the revelations of massive fraud by an employee of the GNR. One of the Company's employees by the name of Leopold Redpath defrauded the company of almost £250,000 – a stupendous figure for the time. An interesting aspect of the case was the extreme simplicity of the methods Redpath employed and the fact that his repeated misappropriation would have been evident to anyone conversant with the basic elements of bookkeeping. The frauds, which started in the summer of 1848, were not discovered until October 1856.

Several companies were projecting railways between London and York. A battle royal had been taking place in committee rooms of parliament and doubtless in smoke-filled back rooms elsewhere in what proved to be an unsuccessful attempt to prevent the GNR receiving legal sanction for the line it proposed to build via Peterborough and Newark. This was the background to the peculation that brought him notoriety.

Redpath was a man of humble origins who we first hear of as a clerk with the Peninsula & Orient Company. Not content with that, he became a wine merchant, but his business failed, and he became bankrupt in 1840. Bouncing back, he then obtained employment with another shipping company who dismissed him for embezzlement. Never a man to allow the grass to grow under his feet, he obtained work as a clerk in the share registration departments of first the Brighton & Chichester and then the London & Brighton Railway Companies. In 1846 he joined the GNR which seemed very much a company on the up. His starting salary was the modest one of £130 a year but he must have impressed his employers because this had risen to £250 by 1854 when he became Chief Clerk to the Registrar. He had some front because he had moved into a luxurious home in Regent's Park, the rent of which was an annual £400. He also rented his own box at the opera and was seen as a public figure of some probity becoming, for example, a governor of Christ's Hospital School. He employed several servants and bought a country retreat in Surrey. This lifestyle could not possibly be sustained on his official salary, but nobody seemed either to have realised this anomaly or seen fit to ask questions.

That he was able to get away with fraudulent activity for so long is something for which his employers must take some blame. Had they bothered to probe into his previous employment history, they would have learned of his bankruptcy, not a recommendation for a man handling large amounts of other people's money. They would also have discovered that he had left at least one previous job 'under a cloud' as the Victorians euphemistically put it. His boss at the share registration department was W.H. Clark, a solicitor who knew little of the practicalities of this business and was only too happy to let his seemingly diligent assistant get on with the job. In 1854, the GNR decided that some retrenchment was needed at head office, and they decided to dispense with Clark's services. Before he left, he had even recommended Redpath to be his replacement, stating that he had basically been running the whole show anyway. Redpath took Clark's job, admittedly on a lower salary. This must have appealed to the notoriously mean Great Northern Board!

Redpath now had total official control of the stock and share registers which he had unofficially monopolised for the previous eight years. On occasions when the clerks of the department had queried some of the entries in the register, Clark had referred them on to Redpath who had assured them that he would immediately and scrupulously inquire into any seeming discrepancies – and then left it that.

What Redpath had been doing was simplicity itself. He created stock, either by inserting an extra figure on stock transfers to make '250' into '1250' or by forging a few names and transferring non-existent stock. All this 'stock' was sold by Redpath through brokers to ordinary investors. Redpath made himself £250,000 and the GNR was paying dividends half-yearly on a total of issued stock which began to exceed the capital it represented. It took until February 1854 for discrepancies to be brought to the attention of the Board, who promptly put Redpath in charge of the investigation! With the net closing in on him, he still found every means of bluffing and procrastinating until in October 1856 he realised that he had run out of options and the truth came out. An enquiry was immediately instituted into the GNR's accounting, auditing and stock registration arrangements.

Not surprisingly, the GNR's shareholders were outraged, and it did not help that when rumours had circulated a couple of months earlier about possible irregularities, the Company Chairman had assured shareholders that he had absolute confidence in the honesty and expertise of all the Company's officers. As it was, the shareholders had to be told that they would not be receiving a dividend because the whole net revenue for the half-year was required to meet the losses sustained by the fraudulent activity.

Redpath was arrested while enjoying a hearty breakfast and appeared at the Old Bailey in January 1857. His guilt was beyond doubt. He was sentenced to transportation and his assets confiscated. The case aroused huge interest not least because of Redpath's public behaviour. Although he had an expensive and showy lifestyle, it seemed totally incongruous that he gave much of his dishonest gains to charities.

These events dented confidence not only in the GNR but in the financial operations of railway companies in general at a time when they had been slowly recovering after the end of the boom years of the 'Railway Mania' in the 1840s. Questions were asked about the competence of senior railway managers, the methods of recruitment they used and the manner with which they supervised their underlings involved with financial matters. Clearly a total overhaul of their practices was urgently required. One outcome was the emergence in the business world of the professional accountant instead of the part-time auditor.

Chapter 8
MISCELLANEA 1

ADDISON ROAD – A FORGOTTEN LONDON STATION

The promoters of the GWR were faced with the problem of finding a site for their London terminus. Several alternatives were considered, only to be abandoned because of strenuous opposition by local interests. It was finally decided that that the line should make a short deviation to join the L&BR near Willesden before entering and sharing the Euston terminus. On this agreed basis, the Great Western obtained its parliamentary authority on 31 August 1835. However, relations with the L&BR which had never been cordial, broke down altogether. The GWR therefore was forced to find another terminus and then obtain new legal powers. Eventually the decision was made to build a line from Acton to a station in the Paddington area.

On 21 June 1836 the Birmingham, Bristol & Thames Junction Railway obtained powers to build a line, three miles long, from Willesden to the basin of the Kensington Canal near what was to become Addison Road Station. This line was crossed by the GWR on the level, close to Wormwood Scrubs. Although GWR trains were to have priority, this was a hair-raising arrangement. A bridge was later substituted for the flat crossing but only after an accident in 1855. Difficulty was experienced in raising the money to complete the line and it was not until 1843 that construction work resumed. By this time, the name of the Company had been changed to the West London Railway (WLR).

On 27 May 1844, the WLR began operations from a junction with the L&BR near the present Willesden Junction to the canal basin at Kensington. Although the main purpose of this line was the carriage of freight, passenger services were operated, and the Kensington district was provided with its first station. In March 1846 the L&BR and the GWR jointly leased the WLR. The GWR had made a junction with its line from the Paddington area at a point close to Wormwood Scrubs which came to be known as Mitre Bridge. In 1854, the successor to the L&B, the L&NWR, joined the GWR to take over day-to-day control of the WLR.

Early passenger carryings were underwhelming largely because the station then named 'Kensington' was some considerable distance west of the main settlement of Kensington, which was growing rapidly at the time. The takings were so poor that trains were withdrawn before the end of 1844. They were restored on 2 June 1862 when it looked as if they would become much more viable with the anticipated opening of the West London Extension Railway to Clapham Junction in 1863. The extension made an end-on junction with the WLR some distance south-east of Addison Road Station. The service commenced on 2 March 1863. The extension came under the auspices not only of the L&NWR and GWR but also the LB&SCR and the L&SWR. All the partners saw that this link across the Thames could play a vital role in plans to extend their services and promote new business possibilities.

In anticipation of the West London Line and its extension becoming an important strategic through route, the station was moved to a new site nearby. This was altogether a more imposing affair, built very much in the style of the L&NWR with two through lines, two main platforms and double bays to cater for local traffic. The new station was fully commissioned in 1869. In 1868 the station was renamed Kensington Addison Road. This was after a nearby thoroughfare and to distinguish it from the station to the east on the Metropolitan Line then called Kensington (High Street) and later renamed High Street Kensington.

The bays at Addison Road station came into their own when two new links were created. The first was opened on 1 July 1864. It left the WLR at Uxbridge Road Junction and joined the Hammersmith & City Line at Latimer Road Junction which allowed for through running to Paddington. The second new link, then something of an anticlimax, left the WLR at Earl's Court Junction just south of Addison Road. It opened in 1869 and curved round to join the Metropolitan District Railway eastbound tracks towards Earl's Court. It was 1872 before this saw regular services.

The West London and West London Extension provided a western bypass of central London and proved to be an extremely useful, if somewhat unknown, part of the London railway network. Both were provided with many connections at each end, these allowing complex freight workings between the routes and yards of the various companies based north and south of the Thames. A wide variety of freight trains travelling to a diverse collection of destinations and headed by a truly catholic range of steam locomotives passed through Addison Road.

'Train spotters', as opposed to people who simply enjoyed watching trains, were a comparatively rare species until the much later days of Ian Allan's enterprise in the middle of the twentieth century. Then his little ABC books giving lists of locomotives drew spotters, in their tens of thousands, to join the craze for number-taking. For some this evolved into a lifelong and absorbing interest in railways. Addison Road, or Kensington Olympia in its later guise, would have provided rich pickings. However, the station probably did not appeal to most spotters because while it was busy with a rich variety of locomotives, most of them were not the more glamorous express locomotives with names, which most spotters were intent on tracking down.

The heterogeneous nature of the freight trains passing Addison Road was matched by the passenger trains using the station. Among destinations that could be reached directly by local trains (although not necessarily all contemporaneously) were Southall, Uxbridge, Waterloo, Clapham Junction, Ludgate Hill, Hounslow, London Bridge, Broad Street, Mansion House, Victoria, Baker Street, Richmond, Euston, Cannon Street, Henley-on-Thames and Croydon.

Among these services were the so-called Outer and Middle Circles, in both cases a misnomer in that they were not continuous. The first, operated by the L&NWR, commenced 1 February 1872 and ran from Broad Street to Mansion House by a roundabout route through Hampstead, Willesden Junction, Addison Road and Earl's Court. The second, commencing on 1 August 1872 and operated by the GWR, connected Bishopsgate and Aldgate via Baker Street, Paddington, Addison Road and Earl's Court.

Addison Road was also graced by numerous long-distance cross-country services largely from towns in the North-west, South Yorkshire and the Midlands destined for places on the south coast such as Hastings, Eastbourne and Brighton. Many of these trains ran only on summer Saturdays but they brought a touch of the exotic in terms of the locomotives that might be hauling. They mostly changed engines at Addison Road, adding to the activity around the station. Perhaps the best-known of them was the 'Sunny South Special' which first ran on 1 March 1905. It ran throughout the year. This train consisted of sections from Manchester, Liverpool and Birmingham and it ran through to Brighton and Eastbourne. The LB&SCR and Bradshaw's Guide referred to the train as the 'Sunny South Special' but, for whatever reason, the L&NWR refused official recognition of what had started as a nickname.

Electrifying short-haul urban and suburban passenger services made considerable sense and the first electric trains to serve Addison Road commenced on 5 November 1906. These initially ran to and from Latimer Road where passengers could change onto Hammersmith & City Line trains to Paddington and the City. They terminated in the bay platforms at the north end of Addison Road Station which became known as the "Metropolitan Bay' because the Hammersmith & City was partly owned by the Metropolitan. Soon the trains were extended to the City itself. The L&NWR was the next to provide Addison Road with an electric service, this being from Willesden Junction to Earl's Court. This service started in 1912. On 1 May 1914 another L&NWR service began to operate between Willesden Junction and Earl's Court.

Earl's Court and Olympia exhibition halls opened in the 1880s adjacent to Addison Road Station and staged numerous events which drew large crowds, many of whom passed through the station. Some events were popular enough to require the running of extra trains.

When the station had opened there had been much open land nearby which was marshy but when this had been drained and brought under control, large amounts of domestic and commercial building took place from the mid-Victorian period. However, despite the area around Addison Road disappearing under bricks and mortar, the station never generated large amounts of its own originating passenger traffic. It was always busier as a passenger interchange, and it also handled very large amounts of parcels and milk traffic It is still busy but not, alas, with all the different kinds of traffic once seen there.

RAILWAYS TO THE GREAT EXHIBITION

The idea of the Great Exhibition can perhaps be credited to Henry Cole who was what would nowadays be described as a 'mover and shaker'. He had a senior position at the Public Record Office, and he became Chairman of the Society of Arts. He had influence which contributed in 1850 to a Royal Commission being established to raise the necessary funding. Major public figures sat on this Commission which was presided over by Prince Albert. When it was clear that a large amount of money was becoming available, a site had to be found and after some deliberation, Hyde Park was controversially decided upon, *The Times* being extremely hostile. It gloomily forecast that the Park would become 'a bivouac of all vagabonds. Kensington and Belgravia would be uninhabitable and the Season would be ruined'.

A competition was held for the design of the building to house the exhibition and over 230 entries were rejected before one submitted by Joseph Paxton was accepted. It was a greatly enlarged version of the conservatory he had designed at Chatsworth House in Derbyshire. It embraced all the latest technological innovations in the production of glass, the use of cast iron for structural purposes and prefabrication, its components being made elsewhere and assembled on site. It had 2,300 cast-iron girders and 900,000 square feet of glass. It was a striking building and its glittering appearance after rain when the sun came out quickly gained it the affectionate nickname of 'The Crystal Palace'.

The Exhibition was the wonder of its day. It was intended to be an international trade fair with countries from across the world providing exhibits of the goods and services that they wanted to market. The hidden agenda was that this was Britain's trade fair, and a very large part of the exhibition was given over to showcasing the fact that she was, at this time, the unquestionable international leader in industrial and commercial activity and wanted to sell even more of her goods abroad. Indeed, Britain was the dominant exhibitor as befitted her position at that time of 'The Workshop of the World'. Nevertheless, the Exhibition was a genuine international affair.

The Exhibition was undoubtedly a great success. The average daily attendance was over 40,000. Queen Victoria made eight visits before the official opening and went thirty-four times afterwards. Charles Dickens, on the other hand, only went twice. One visitor was a woman of 84 who had walked from Cornwall. She apparently enjoyed the show but, having seen it, set off immediately back home. There were 19,000 exhibits classified under Raw Materials; Machinery and Mechanical Inventions; Manufactures; and Sculpture and Plastic Arts. No such grand display had ever been assembled before. It became the fashion for British visitors to scoff at many of the overseas contributions.

However, the quality of many of those particularly from France, Germany and the USA should have alerted them to the fact the days of Britain's worldwide superiority were numbered, as potential rivals were playing catch-up. This was early evidence of Britain's tendency to fatal complacency.

There was an ethical drive behind the Exhibition. Prince Albert was one of its most enthusiastic supporters. He was an extremely earnest man who sincerely believed that such enterprises would encourage amity among the nations of the world. This laudable but rather naïve notion stood alongside another view from those who wanted the Exhibition to be seen as a 'Festival of Labour' or even as a 'Festival of the Workingman'. This might sound demotic, but words change in meaning or emphasis. 'Labour' in the context of 1851 referred equally to the working efforts not only of the proletariat, the 'horny handed sons of toil' but to the leaders of industry. Both, it was averred, were honourable because they were not idle. It could be argued that the Exhibition revealed the deep divisions in Victorian society. One critic of the Exhibition dismissed it as 'plunder, wrung from the people of all lands, by their conquerors, the men of blood, privilege and capital'. Medals were awarded for what judges deemed to be particularly meritorious entries. In almost every case such medals were awarded not to the workers whose labours had actually produced the exhibits but to the entrepreneurs who stood to gain most by their sale. It was, after all, a trade fair.

Some of the success of the Great Exhibition must undoubtedly be ascribed to the railways which were developing into a genuinely national network and were the only travel medium that could have moved so many people to London as cheaply and efficiently. Thomas Cook, already prospering as what we would now call a 'travel agent', arranged the transport for 165,000 of them. As the *Illustrated London News* pointed out on 21 September 1850:

> Already the working classes in Manchester, Liverpool, Sheffield, Birmingham, the Potteries, and the great iron districts between Glasgow and Airdrie, as well as other places, have commenced laying by their weekly pence to form a fund for visiting the Great Exhibition of 1851 … Were it not for cheap excursion trains, this great source of amusement and instruction would have been unattainable by hard-working poverty [sic)], and the Exhibition would have lost one of its great attractions.

It was perhaps to be expected of the times that many of the Victorian bourgeoisie looked favourably on the Exhibition as an example of 'rational recreation'. It would provide an instructive, educative and mind-broadening experience. It is therefore easy to see how the process of getting so many people to London frequently started with local subscription clubs set up by committees largely of middle-class people. The subscribers agreed to pay a small, fixed amount on a weekly basis and the club when it had accumulated enough money would negotiate with the local railway company or with agents who would make the necessary travel and hospital arrangements. The most successful of these agents was Thomas Cook, who already had experience of organising railway excursions. He worked with extraordinary energy organising good value deals with the Midland Railway as well as lodgings for those wanting to stop over in London. While Cook undoubtedly was looking to make money, this particular business may also have appealed to him because alcohol consumption was banned at the Exhibition, and he was a fervent exponent of abstention.

It is not easy for us in the twenty-first century to appreciate the excitement, awe and delicious fear that the Exhibition must have evoked in so many of its visitors. It is probable that most of them, even those living in the Home Counties, would never have visited London before. This was even more true of those living in the far-flung parts of the realm. Most people had little reason in their lives for leaving their home districts unless it was to migrate in search of work. Travel before the railways was difficult, dangerous and expensive. The idea of travelling for education or recreational purposes was simply not an option for ordinary people. Although during the 1830s and 1840s the railways had begun running special trains aimed at what we might call the 'leisure market', most people remained very much tied to their immediate surroundings. The opportunity to travel to London and visit the Exhibition and perhaps stay a night or two in the Metropolis would have presented them with the greatest adventure of their lives. Despite this, some people seem to have been almost nonchalant about the experience. A workman from Huddersfield left his home in the evening of 22 July paying 5s for his third-class return fare. He took a pack of sandwiches and 1s, which was the entrance fee for the next day's admission to the Exhibition. He enjoyed viewing the show, ate his sandwiches, drank from a water fountain, caught the return train and was back at work in Huddersfield within forty hours – all for a total expenditure of 6s! The price of a railway excursion ticket from Leeds to London and back was 15s first class. The only possible blight on such apparent bargains was the overnight accommodation on offer in London, which was frequently the subject of much complaint, most particularly for those only able to afford the cheaper end of the market.

Without the railways, people living any distance from London could not possibly have visited London and the Exhibition in the numbers they did. By 1851 there was already an intensive network of railway lines except in rural Wales and Scotland, Northumberland and Devon and Cornwall. Railways enabled the Great Exhibition to be the first event that attracted people from right across the nation to travel to London. The Great Exhibition and the role played by the railways in contributing to its success were landmarks in widening the ways in which people spent their leisure time and they alerted them to the great benefits that could come from travelling for pleasure.

A FEW RAILWAY ACCIDENTS

The feverish entrepreneurial enterprise which created Britain's railway system in the period from 1830 to 1914 was powered by the desire for profit. Any form of government regulation was anathema to the political economy of the time. The railway companies fought tooth and nail against official intervention in their affairs, including the compulsory imposition of statutory measures concerning safety. Railways were faster, heavier and could carry more passengers or larger cargoes than any previous form of transport. Safety measures cost money and cut into potential profits which, of course, was why the companies so doggedly opposed them.

In the public interest it was inevitable that governments would have to exercise some level of control over railway operations. Early operations involved trains moving at what were then unprecedented speeds, often without any effective braking or signalling systems. As late as the 1870s and 1880s, the figures for deaths and injuries to railway passengers and workers alike make grim reading. Rolling stock was flimsy, oil-lit passenger accommodation especially vulnerable to fire. Railway operating staff often worked such long hours that their vigilance was severely impaired. In fairness, it was not unknown in the early days for passengers to attempt to ride on carriage roofs, join moving trains or leap out of trains to recover a hat or retrieve a parcel dropped. Familiarity with this new form of communication largely eliminated such human misjudgements over time.

London was perhaps fortunate in that it avoided the more serious accidents that blighted the railways of the provinces all too often. On the evening of 28 June 1857 at Lewisham, a train halted at signals was run into forcibly by a following train. It was packed with Londoners who had been enjoying a late afternoon and evening out by the Thames at Gravesend and were returning to town. The total inadequacy of the signalling arrangements was to blame but it was also obvious that the company concerned, the SER, had no effective procedures in place to deal with an emergency of this sort. The situation was not helped by the well-meaning but incompetent efforts to help of survivors and people from the locality. Crowds of somewhat ghoulish onlookers obstructed efforts to reach the dead and injured. Eleven people died at the scene and sixty-three were injured. As usual at the time, senior officials of the company rushed to blame their employees for their neglect. The subsequent official enquiry exonerated the railway employees involved.

At Tottenham on the Eastern Counties Railway (ECR) on 20 February 1860, the locomotive of a crowded Cambridge to London train sheared off the track, damaged part of the station buildings and then piled up with most of the carriages shattered to smithereens. Seven people died but many more sustained serious injuries. The official enquiry found that the tyre of one of the engine's driving wheels had broken off. It had been an accident waiting to happen, the blame being put on the company because of its faulty inspection practices. The report also commented on the extremely flimsy construction of the carriages. The ECR denied any responsibility. It stated that the accident happened because of circumstances beyond its control.

The NLR was a small but extremely busy railway. It had an intensive timetable of regularly scheduled passenger services. Goods trains had to be slotted in where and when possible and there could be even more pressure when special passenger excursions were run. On 2 September 1861, five special excursions were operated to Kew from where they were due to return between eight and nine thirty in the evening. It seems quite extraordinary that the actual time these trains left Kew was down to the local stationmaster. He had no way of communicating with colleagues along the line that he had decided to despatch one of these trains before 20.00. Regulation of railway operations were so slack at this time that no one in authority knew that this excursion had left Kew earlier than expected. Between Kentish Town and Camden, a ballast train was being shunted into a siding when it was hit by the train from Kew which had appeared unexpectedly. This happened on an elevated stretch of line and the locomotive and several carriages plummeted into nearby fields and caught fire. More than 300 passengers were injured but, miraculously, only 16 were killed. The company moved swiftly to place the blame the signalman who had decided to shunt the ballast train off the main line. In the subsequent enquiry, it emerged that he was only 19 years of age, was partially deaf and regularly worked a 15-hour day for 14s a week. This and a number of other accidents were stoking public anger about the inefficient and dangerous nature of so many railway operations. Demands were intensifying for the government to introduce properly supervised regulation despite strenuous opposition from almost every railway company.

On 28 November 1870, eight people died in an accident on the L&NWR at Harrow. A fast-moving double-headed express from Euston to Liverpool hit a rake of coal wagons which had broken away from a train being shunted into a siding. The officer of the Royal Engineer called upon to investigate the accident and make a report noted that just in that one year, 1870, no fewer than thirty-four accidents had been reported on the lines of this company. Twenty-four had involved collisions in stations.

The L&NWR was under the spotlight again when, on 18 April 1892, a Bank Holiday, there was a serious incident at Hampstead Heath Station. Curiously, it did not directly involve a train. Hampstead Heath had long been the resort of Londoners on high days and holidays. On this particular occasion, an estimated 100,000 people had flocked to the Heath to enjoy themselves. By the late afternoon, crowds were heading to the station to catch trains home. A staircase gave access to the platform, the main facilities of which were at street level. At about 18.00, the stairs were becoming overcrowded when a child tripped and dozens of others behind lost their footing. Unfortunately, at the bottom of the stairs was a stoutly built ticket collector's cabin. Bodies began to pile up against this immovable object. Eight people died in the resulting crush. The coroner's court returned a verdict of accidental death.

The company was publicly castigated for locating the ticket collector's cabin in such a position that it partly blocked the bottom of the stairway and posed a serious hazard when the station was having to deal with large numbers of passengers.

By 1900 the railways found themselves having to implement a mass of legal requirements which tackled the issues arising from poor managerial organisation and inadequate safety systems. The Board of Trade had had to persuade, and when that proved insufficient, force railway companies to adopt basic safety mechanisms. These included interlocking signalling, the use of the block system to ensure moving trains maintained safe distances from each other and continuous brakes that applied to every carriage on trains carrying passengers. It must be said that many railway companies had to be dragged kicking and screaming into the twentieth century. Although no railway system can ever be made entirely safe, railway users and railway employees had government intervention in the private companies to thank for the vast amount of rail-borne traffic which moved safely around London and elsewhere. By 1900, railway accidents had become rare enough to make newspaper headlines when they did occur.

THE EARLY DAYS OF RAILWAY BOOKSTALLS

Given the impact of railways, it would be easy to suppose that early railway travellers, being so enthralled by the experience of train travel, would spend the journey gazing with rapt fascination at the wealth of sights that passed their eyes. Not so. From the earliest days of railways there seems to have been a largely unspoken assumption that passengers travelling by train would find the process boring and that something would be needed to relieve the tedium of the experience; some diversion to make the journey at least tolerable. One diversion from boredom is eating; another is immersion in printed matter. Nature abhors a vacuum. The railway bookstall was soon to make its appearance although not before vendors had appeared on the platforms of the Liverpool and Manchester Railway's terminus stations selling newspapers and railway guides. This practice had certainly begun by 1839.

Soon it was found that a permanent fixture enabled a much wider range of goods to be displayed and made available for sale. The bookstall was about to arrive, being the successor to the mobile vendor and his descendant who had been a vendor with a simple little folding table displaying a limited selection of wares. Some early bookstalls were staffed by former railway employees who had suffered injury in their employment and had had to leave the service. On other occasions, widows of former employees who had been fatally injured while on duty ran such stalls.

Some early railway companies therefore displayed a degree of social conscience in letting out retail space to such people. However, it was not long before entrepreneurs began to find that retail outlets on stations could be a profitable venture while the railway companies realised that rents for more substantial retail operations could generate useful income. The first in London and probably the first such enterprise in the UK was the bookstall set up by William Marshall at Fenchurch Street Station in 1841. This stall represented a diversification for Marshall who already supplied newspapers wholesale to the GWR.

Alas for innocence! An indignant article appeared in *The Times* on 9 August 1851 in which the writer held forth in high dudgeon about bookstalls in general and especially those at the major London termini. While he had no problem with the sale of newspapers on these stalls, he fulminated about what he disparagingly referred to as 'French novels' hobnobbing on the shelves with beer bottles and various kinds of luridly coloured sweetmeats. It aroused his ire that the proprietors were pandering to the most vulgar of tastes, peddling titillating and morally decadent printed matter and encouraging the consumption of alcoholic beverages. This article was quite moderate in tone compared with other contemporary outbursts which described bookstalls as little better than brothels because they attracted all kinds of human detritus such as pickpockets, beggars, prostitutes, idlers and drifters. Those who owned the stalls were disreputable creatures only too happy to pander to their clients' basest instincts. One complainant described those working in bookstalls as 'dissolute ne'er-do-wells'!

These observers who so greatly enjoyed venting their self-righteous spleens must have done research on which to base their conclusions. Presumably this involved them loitering with studied nonchalance around these bookstalls while making note of the displays and the comings and goings of the punters with prurient relish. It was ever thus with the chattering classes. Enough of a fuss was made, however, for a Parliamentary Select Committee to be set up with the purpose of considering ways of monitoring and controlling the kind of reading material sold on railway bookstalls.

H.W.Smith started as a wholesale newsagent in 1792 and, when the railways arrived, began distributing London newspapers and periodicals to the provinces. His grandson was concerned about the somewhat tarnished reputation of early bookstalls and wanted to provide travellers with rather more wholesome reading material. In 1848 he successfully tendered for the exclusive right to provide stalls selling newspapers and periodicals on the stations of the LNWR in return for a yearly rent of £1,500. Thus, was born the 'WH Smith & Son' empire of reputable bookstalls. A refinement quickly added was the provision of small circulating libraries in some of his bookstalls.

Our self-righteous *Times* correspondent did his best to find what he called 'trash' on the WH Smith bookstall on Euston Station but had to admit to failure. By this time, Smith's rather prudish bowdlerisation of the literature his stalls sold had earned him the nickname 'Old Morality' but he had few worries as his business grew and flourished. Soon Henry Walton Smith's bookstalls were providing a service to the public on railways as diverse as the L&SWR, the Lancashire & Yorkshire and the North British. In 1863 Smith bought out the smaller chain of bookstalls owned by Horace Marshall, son of the pioneering William Marshall. WH Smith bookstalls became a feature of all the large London stations and even of many minor suburban surface and underground stations in London and its hinterland. His domination of bookstall provision did not go unchallenged, particularly after 1900 but the company remained pre-eminent in the business in England at least.

Grumblings about the vacuity, if no longer about the salaciousness at worst, or the sheer lack of literary merit of the literature sold on station bookstalls, continued for many years. In 1855 the novelist Anthony Trollope, whose employment involved travelling extensively on the railway, joined in the criticism by describing the novels he found on station bookstalls as the very worst of their kind. However, these self-appointed arbiters of public taste could not get around the fact that large numbers of travellers eagerly grabbed the chance to while away a train journey by losing themselves in fiction of dubious literary merit, but which was escapist, sensationalist or of the type described in those days as 'lewd'. Nowadays such material would be regarded as no more than titillating. The phrase 'railway literature' was a pejorative one that came to be used by those who were, or pretended to be, above such things, although the querulous complaints made by some of them suggested considerable familiarity with their contents. The word 'yellowback' was also used pejoratively for these types of publication from the predominant colour of the wrappers produced by one company specialising in books of this sort. 'Yellowback' evolved to become a general term applying to cheap reprints, irrespective of the nature of their contents.

Several publishers produced cheap, often paper-covered editions of their titles for sale in the bookstall trade. Routledge, for example, had a series called 'The Railway Library'. When this venture ended after fifty years, it had produced no fewer than 1,300 titles. It is likely that railway bookstalls overall were one of several agencies in the Victorian period which brought reading to an increasingly wide audience against a background of rising literacy. The publisher John Murray, anxious to counter the opprobrium aimed at early bookstalls and their literary offerings, was to the fore in producing literature specifically for the bookstalls of a kind to counter the varied criticisms. These were described as providing 'sound and enterprising information and innocent amusement'. The WH Smith bookstalls, for example, sold vast numbers of cheap editions of the 'Waverley' novels written by Sir Walter Scott. So, it came about that the earnest traveller could edify his journey by studying *Specimens of the Table-talk of Samuel Taylor Coleridge* or, if that palled, *Jesse's Gleanings on Natural History.* Matthew Arnold, the Victorian poet and cultural critic, noted healthy sales of popular scientific works from bookstalls and was gratified that some were being bought by railway servants clearly bent on self-improvement. There was evidently a marked and growing demand for a wide range of reading matter. The availability of cheap books from station bookstalls contributed to the broadening of knowledge and understanding which should be a concomitant of widened reading and a mark of a civilised society.

Chapter 9

SOME LONDON BRANCH LINES

EPPING TO ONGAR

The ECR opened a line from Stratford, through Woodford, to Loughton on 22 August 1856. Parliamentary authority was given for an eleven-mile extension from Loughton through Epping to Ongar in 1859. This line was known as the Epping Railway. Construction was delayed by a lack of funds. Further powers were then obtained in 1860 to construct a further 14 route miles to Great Dunmow. The Epping Railway was absorbed by the ECR in 1862 shortly before the ECR and various other companies were subsumed into the GER. The new owners proceeded to build the section from Loughton to Ongar which opened in April 1865. This was deep in Essex countryside and the GER probably wisely decided to obtain parliamentary powers to abandon the building of the proposed line beyond Ongar to Great Dunmow. Suburban development began as far as Loughton and, more sparsely, on towards Epping, guaranteeing acceptable levels of passenger traffic. Beyond Epping en route to Ongar, the surroundings of the railway remained predominantly rural and traffic was consequently light.

This backwater of the GER is interesting because housing development saw traffic levels build up to the extent that in the 1930s London Transport became interested in taking over the route to Epping and Ongar and extending the Central Line tube eastwards from Liverpool Street through Stratford to Leyton where it would join the tracks of what by then had become the Epping Branch of the London & North Eastern Railway. The line came under London Transport auspices and was electrified to Epping by September 1949. The 6 miles to Ongar remained steam-worked by British Railways until 1957 when the somewhat odd decision was made to electrify what was still basically an obscure rural branch. Here was a definite counter to the generalisation that electrification automatically led to housing development. The Ongar section remained stubbornly rural, one of several similar examples which contradict the generalisation that speculative housing development always followed the opening of new lines and stations in London's periphery. The service to Ongar was withdrawn in the 1990s, having become a notorious loss maker. For lovers of the odd, it provided the spectacle of tube trains travelling along single track through pleasant rural scenery calling at lonely and very ill-frequented stations equipped with all the accoutrements associated with the London Underground such as the immortal roundel.

NORTH WOOLWICH

Stratford in the early nineteenth century was a small settlement close to where the London to Colchester Road forded the River Lea. It had a tradition of industrial activity which over the years had included gunpowder-making, calico-printing, distilling and timber-milling. It grew rapidly in the 1840s and became a railway settlement where the ECR and its successor, the Great Eastern, established a railway hub which included a station, a complex network of lines, an engineering works and goods yards.

Stratford stood on higher ground than the area to the south which lay in the flood plain of the Thames and was composed largely of unoccupied flat marshland albeit with some market gardening. Its desolation began to be broken down in 1846 when a railway line was opened south from Stratford to a point near the confluence of the Thames and the River Lea. This line was initially thought of as a financially unwise venture and was nicknamed 'Bidder's Folly' after the contractor associated with the venture. However, it soon proved to be an unexpected success when its initial terminal point, which became known as 'Thames Wharf', became the location of an ironworks and shipbuilding complex. This in turn attracted other development including housing and became known as Canning Town.

In 1847 the line was extended eastwards, to carry passengers and freight, to a bleak and sequestered spot called North Woolwich where a ferry plied to and from the sizeable town of Woolwich, at this time not served by rail. In 1851 the ECR, which worked the line, opened a pleasure ground initially known as the Royal Pavilion Gardens. This quickly attracted many visitors both from London's East End and coming across from Woolwich on the ferry and the traffic generated helped to offset a decline caused when a direct railway was opened between London and Woolwich. A compact but quite impressive station was opened at North Woolwich in 1854 replacing the earlier terminus. The desolate marshland and waste were about to undergo a remarkable transformation. Ships were becoming bigger and trade was growing rapidly. More and larger docks were needed, fully enclosed and secure as opposed to the riverside wharves which had characterised the old Pool of London. Already new dock facilities had been built downstream from the Pool such as the Millwall and West India Docks opened in the early nineteenth century. A consortium of businessmen including Bidder realised that the marshland south of Stratford known as Plaistow Marshes was ideal for the building of even larger docks and set about constructing what became known as the Royal Victoria Dock, opened in 1855. This prodigious scheme involved diverting the line from Stratford to North

Woolwich east some distance from Thames Wharf Junction before turning south and then east again to North Woolwich. The original line came to be known rather curiously as the Silvertown Tramway which served large numbers of wharves and industrial premises close to the Thames.

It was boom time in the Plaistow Marshes as industry was growing attracted into the area with its railways and its increasing capacity for handling large ships and their cargoes. In 1880 another dock, even larger than the Royal Victoria, was opened. This was the Royal Albert Dock which was connected by a channel to the Royal Victoria Dock. A swing bridge was provided across this channel for trains proceeding to and from Stratford and North Woolwich. Later, a tunnel was built at this point, used mainly by passenger trains while the swing bridge remained open for those trains that would have difficulties with the gradients into and out of the tunnel.

With further lines built to serve the massive Beckton Gasworks and the Port of London Authority Railway, to Gallions, opened in 1881, the southern part of the marshes now had an intensive railway network. This latter line was used mostly for passenger trains to the pier and hotel at Gallions which could serve ocean-going vessels. Connections at Stratford and beyond allowed access to the main line network and traffic built up to the extent that the section from Tidal Basin to Stratford Market was quadrupled. Several major railway companies found it worthwhile establishing freight depots adjoining the route, using running powers over the line. Small locomotives tended to be used for the freight services in the area and main line locomotives were rarely seen on the lines to North Woolwich.

Passenger services over the line were particularly busy at peak times carrying huge numbers of workers to and from their places of employment on both sides of the river. Many crossed the Thames to and from Woolwich using what in 1889 became the Woolwich Free Ferry, or the foot tunnel. In 1858, a connection was made at Abbey Mills near Plaistow enabling trains to use the LT&SR's metals to run to and from Fenchurch Street in the City. Other passenger services ran to Stratford, Liverpool Street and to Palace Gates, this via a route of extraordinary complexity. The passenger services were suffering from tram, bus and District Line competition even before 1914.

HIGH BARNET AND FINCHLEY

The Edgware, Highgate & London was a small but ambitious company which had plans to build lines into the hilly and attractive countryside of Hertfordshire and Middlesex, often referred to as the 'Northern Heights'. The first of these, 9 miles long, ran from a junction with the GNR at what was then Seven Sisters Road, now Finsbury Park, through Highgate and Finchley to Edgware. This opened on 22 August 1867 by which time the company had been absorbed by the Great Northern.

Initial expectation of traffic was shown by the fact that the line, as built, was single-track but as business grew by 1870, so the track was doubled as far as Finchley, now Finchley Central. A branch from Finchley to High Barnet, with double track, was opened on 1 April 1872. Usage built up rapidly to the extent that the High Barnet line became the main route and Edgware was served by a shuttle to and from Finchley. Traffic grew impressively, causing serious congestion on the approaches to King's Cross. To help relieve the situation, an agreement was made with the NLR for it to operate trains from its London terminus at Broad Street to High Barnet via a recently opened connection from Canonbury to Finsbury Park.

High Barnet station stood in an elevated position and steam trains had to work hard to get there. From Finsbury Park to Highgate, severe gradients of between 1 in 60 and 1 in 77 were encountered, followed by 1 in 95 and 1 in 110 to High Barnet. It was these gradients and the build-up of traffic which led London Transport in 1935 to propose to extend its Northern Line from its terminus then called Highgate, but now Archway, to join what was now the L&NER's line from Finsbury Park. It was intended to electrify the line, use Tube rolling stock and run trains through to Edgware and High Barnet.

NUNHEAD TO GREENWICH PARK

This line received parliamentary sanction on 28 July 1863. Although it was only 2½ miles long, in July 1864 powers were obtained for four connecting spurs. Three of these were at Lewisham which would have provided a junction with the North Kent Line of the SER and with the SER's line from London to Tonbridge via Sevenoaks, then under construction. The fourth spur would have allowed the LC&DR using running powers to gain access to Woolwich and the SER, again with running powers, to reach Crystal Palace. This short line could therefore have provided crucial links in South London's developing network. However, the links were never built and the legal powers authorising them were allowed to lapse.

The LC&DR was always a financially challenged company and, because of one of its periodic cash flow crises, it was not until 18 September 1871 that the section from Nunhead to Blackheath Hill, just short of 2 miles, was completed. Continuing financial problems meant that it was not until 1 October 1888 that the LC&DR began to start running trains into its station on the north-west side of Greenwich Park.

Traffic never developed to the rather optimistic levels that had initially been entertained. It did not help that passengers to and from Greenwich Park usually had to change trains at Nunhead. Trains on the SER offered a more direct and faster service. Trams and early motor buses leached away most of what little traffic offered. The line should probably never have been built and was the result of desperate inter-company rivalry rather than sound business reasoning. The LC&DR was avid to gain access to what it thought would be the lucrative traffic offered by Greenwich. Services were suspended on 1 January 1917 ostensibly as a wartime economy measure. This was a handy excuse to get rid of a facility that was never likely to pay, and it came as no surprise when, after the Great War ended, the closure of the section from Lewisham Road was made permanent.

THE SOUTH LONDON LINE
It might seem to be stretching the branch line concept somewhat to include the South London Line here. It was also deeply urban and for much of its route ran alongside or shared tracks with other routes. For all that, it was something of a backwater but of historical importance as the first section to be electrified of the extremely complex surface network of what later became the Southern Railway.

The South London Line was built by the LB&SCR and pursues something like a semi-circular route through London's inner suburbs from London Bridge to Victoria. The first section from London Bridge to Loughborough Park (later East Brixton) was opened to traffic on 13 August 1866 and the rest on 1 May 1867.

From London Bridge to Peckham Rye the South London shared tracks with the LB&SCR's line thence to Sutton which opened on 1 October 1868. From Peckham Rye to Wandsworth Road the line ran alongside the LC&DR's route to Loughborough Junction and Victoria. Between Peckham Rye and East Brixton, the LB&SCR had to construct all four tracks for the use of both companies. From Wandsworth Road, the LC&DR owned all the tracks.

Usage was slow to build up. Obviously, there were few through passengers as the trains wended their circuitous way from London Bridge to Victoria or *vice versa*. The introduction of electric trams and later of motorbuses robbed the line of much short-distance travel and so the LB&SCR resolved to take on the competition by electrifying the route. The decision was taken to electrify it on the overhead system with single-phase alternating current at 6,600 volts. The electric trains began to run on 1 December 1909 and led to a remarkable increase in passenger use. Three-and-a-half million passengers were carried in 1908, a figure which rose to eight million in 1910. The line was converted to 660 volts dc third rail by the Southern Railway in 1928.

THE BRENTFORD BRANCH
The line to Brentford was unusual among branches in the Greater London area for being built not with some suburban passenger traffic in mind but as a means for the GWR to gain access to the Thames and the London docks. Before the 1850s, goods to and from the docks had to be carted in cumbersome fashion through the streets of the capital. With the use of river craft like lighters and barges, the GWR would be able to ship cargo straight to the London docks by water. At this time the GWR was still wholly committed

to the broad gauge, but this was already isolating them and there seemed no prospect of their building a line of their own or co-operating with another company for a mixed-gauge approach through or around London to reach the docks. A line to Brentford from Southall on the GWR main line to the west, while perhaps not the ideal solution, was perhaps the best pragmatic option available. Had the GWR been seriously interested in attracting passenger traffic, they might have created a junction near Southall allowing through trains from Paddington. Instead, the junction faced west.

The branch was legally authorised on 14 August 1855 for the Great Western & Brentford (Thames Junction) Railway, in effect a cat's-paw of the GWR. Arrangements were quickly made for the GWR to lease the line and it was absorbed by the GWR in 1872. It was 4 miles long and provided with broad gauge double track. A dock was built at Brentford and goods workings started on 18 July 1859. Previously the GWR used a depot between Southall and Hayes to transfer goods and coal to barges on the Grand Junction (later Grand Union Canal). There were several locks on the canal, and it suffered from the disadvantages indigenous to canals such as periodic shortages of water or ice making it impassable. Navigation of the Thames would allow much larger vessels to be utilized and enable useful economies to be made. The Brentford Branch was a scaled-down version of an earlier ambitious proposal by the GWR to build a line from Southall to Brentford and then to follow the course of the Thames to a terminus at Millbank.

Those who study Britain's railways since privatization often ponder ruefully over the number of bodies that need to be involved when decisions are being made. Just to show that there is nothing new, for the Brentford Branch such bodies included the Lords of the Admiralty, Her Majesty's Commissioners of Woods, Forests & Land Revenues, the Corporation of the City of London and the Conservators of the River Thames.

A GWR Class '517' with its auto-trailer at Trumpers Crossing Halte on the Southall to Brentford Branch. The word 'Halte' was a short-lived fashion. The GWR, always seeking to generate income, opened many similar facilities of this cheap and simple sort. (Courtesy of John Scott Morgan)

A unique feature of this line was to be seen just south-east of Southall close to Hanwell Asylum. At a spot called Windmill Lane, a road and what was then called the Grand Junction Canal crossed the railway at the same point. The road crossed the canal on a bridge of orthodox design and the canal was carried over the railway at an acute angle in a cast-iron trough, over 8ft deep. The canal aqueduct is supported on a central brick pier placed between the two railway tracks. This complex structure is known locally as the 'Three Bridges'. I.K. Brunel was the engineer for the Brentford Branch and this bridge may be one of the lesser-known items of Brunel memorabilia. It has stood the test of time.

Another curiosity of the branch was that because passenger traffic was so light, it was accommodated on one track and the goods line was provided with mixed-gauge track. In effect, the branch consisted of two single tracks and this odd arrangement, which commenced on 1 October 1861, continued until March 1876 when it was superseded by normal double line working. The broad-gauge track was removed at the same time.

Passenger services, which were lightly used, commenced on 1 May 1860. Steam railcars running at half-hourly intervals were introduced in May 1904, but they experienced keen competition from tramcars as the district the line passed through became increasingly built-up. For journeys to and from London they could not compete with the L&SWR line from Waterloo to Hounslow and points west. They were withdrawn as a temporary economy in 1915 and restored in 1920 only for passenger services to be finally ended in 1942.

This was a line for oddities because the one intermediate passenger stopping place before Brentford rejoiced in the name 'Trumpers Crossing Halt for South Hanwell and Osterley Park'. This was a grandiose name for a very small wayside facility. That may have been odd but, additionally, for a while the GWR rather whimsically styled the word 'Halt' as 'Halte'. The use of 'Trumpers' in the name may have been mischievous because Trumper was a local landowner who had vehemently opposed the building of the line.

Brentford became something of an industrial enclave in outer south-west suburban London. The docks and wharves were extensive, and the presence of inland port facilities attracted a variety of industrial premises. In the twenty-first century there have been moves to reintroduce passenger services on the Brentford Branch.

THE STAINES BRANCH

Staines is an ancient settlement which became a significant staging point in the halcyon days of the coaching industry. With coaching's decline, it went into the partial doldrums. It gained its first railway connections on 22 August 1848 when the Windsor, Staines & South Western Railway began public operations. This was a creature of the L&SWR and therefore no friend of the GWR. In 1873, parliamentary approval was gained for the Staines & West Drayton Railway (SWDR) which was strongly under the influence of the GWR. A junction with the L&SWR's Windsor line was proposed but not actually constructed until 1940. It was a symptom of the antipathy between the GWR and the L&SWR that the latter objected to this junction which the GWR had hoped would allow it access with the necessary running powers to the Staines station of the L&SWR. The latter Company was also deeply suspicious that the GWR, in seeking to make use of its metals at Staines, was engaged in a nefarious manoeuvre to find ways of gaining access to the South Coast. This was not a mere conspiracy theory. The GWR had indeed been in discussions with the L&NWR which was keen to create a through route to the south, avoiding London. The possibility of using the line from West Drayton to Staines and extending it to Leatherhead where connections could be made with the LB&SCR and the SER was among the options being considered. Wrangling between the GWR and the L&SWR was one of the reasons why completion of the line was delayed for an inordinate time.

In 1882, agreement was reached whereby the GWR would work the line while the SWDR would attempt to obtain powers to build a separate station at Staines to make the line entirely independent of the hated L&SWR. A site for this not particularly conveniently situated station was eventually found although not without further acrimonious wrangling, some of which was due to the dire financial position of the SWDR. It was all a rather sad story by the time the section from West Drayton to Colnbrook was opened on 9 August 1884. It somehow typified the semi-farcical nature of the SWDR's activities that just as its directors were congratulating themselves on having the line complete and ready for opening, one of its bridges collapsed close to where it crossed the L&SWR and much to that company's glee. At long last the line was declared open throughout on 2 November 1885, but the SWDR was so bereft of ready cash that the usual festivities accompanying such an event were dispensed with. The SWDR was fully absorbed by the GWR in 1900.

The terminus of the branch was later known as Staines West from 1949 and could only be described as quirky. The main station building was a sizeable house formerly belonging to the manager of a nearby mustard mill. The lower floor of this building was adapted for railway use while, very oddly, the staircase to the upper, private rooms rose from the booking hall. The single platform stood on land where the garden had previously been located. The option of using part of an existing house was cheaper for the financially challenged SWDR than building a complete new station. The branch closed to passengers on 29 March 1965.

LINES TO THE CRYSTAL PALACE AND THE 'ALLY PALLY'
Londoners and others did not want 'their' Crystal Palace in Hyde Park to be dismantled once the Great Exhibition was over. Few buildings seem to have elicited so much affection so quickly. However, the terms under which it had been erected in a

The High Level station at Crystal Palace was built by the London, Chatham & Dover Railway in the expectation of heavy leisure traffic to the Crystal Palace when it was rebuilt on its new site in South London. A large station capable of handling huge crowds was built but, a bit like the relocated Crystal Palace itself, it never quite lived up to expectations.

Royal Park required its swift removal. It was carefully dismantled – its prefabricated structure being helpful in this respect – and stored. Sir Joseph Paxton created the Crystal Palace Company and then set about raising the finance to buy the building and re-erect it on a new site. The chosen site was 200 acres of parkland with many mature trees at Sydenham Hill. It was a quiet rural spot with commanding views over London. The idea was to build what would probably nowadays be described as a multiplex leisure 'experience'. In the 1850s, reflecting different values, it was designed to be a centre of recreation, culture and education.

The new Crystal Palace building was considerably larger and grander than its predecessor which had stood in Hyde Park. Huge amounts of money were spent to furnish the interior with items chosen to depict the art and architecture of the great civilisations of the past. Exotic plants were obtained for the grounds and a superb collection of palms which had to be kept in tropical conditions within the main building. There were many permanent exhibits concerned with natural history

A charming painting by Camille Pissarro showing a train climbing through London's southern suburbs on the South Eastern & Chatham's route to Crystal Palace.

Just to the west of London is Wharncliffe Viaduct on the main line of the Great Western Railway originally from Paddington to Bristol. It is thought that this is featured in Turner's famous painting *Rain, Steam and Speed*, although others believe that Turner used the bridge over the Thames near Maidenhead.

and anthropology. The gardens were to be on a grand scale comparable with the best in Europe. Shows and exhibitions were to be staged in the grounds and in the galleries of the huge building. It cost £1.3 million to get the new enterprise up and running. Two tall water towers at either end of the building provided the supply for the innumerable fountains and the humidity necessary in the parts of the building full of palms and other tropical exotica. These were designed by none other than I.K. Brunel and were just about the only items still standing after the disastrous fire that destroyed the building in 1936.

In the grounds, many life-size models of prehistoric creatures proved to be a never-ending source of fascination. They are still there and are one of the most tangible pieces of remaining evidence of this remarkable venture. The new Crystal Palace opened in an atmosphere of great jubilation on 10 June 1854.

High hopes were entertained that the Crystal Palace with its permanent exhibits, its changing exhibitions and its galaxy of attractions to cater for all tastes would prove to be a venue drawing in people not only from Greater London but also from much of the south-east of England and even elsewhere. From the start it had been envisaged that railways would provide the means of mass transport for the crowds that would be needed if the venture was to be a financial success. Paxton had worked very closely with the LB&SCR. The Crystal Palace was close to stations at Sydenham and Penge on the LB&SCR's route from London Bridge to Brighton, but it was decided to maximise access to the new attraction by building a spur line from this route to a new station situated close to the Palace from which passengers would be able to walk under cover straight to the building. Passenger services began running into the station (later Crystal Palace Low Level) on the day the building was officially opened. The LB&SCR directors were not disappointed by the Crystal Palace's ability to pull crowds. On one day in 1859, trains conveyed 112,000 people to the Palace of whom 70,000 had travelled via the line out of London Bridge. Another line, the West End of London & Crystal Palace Railway, not at first operated by the LB&SCR but having good relationships with it, approached Crystal Palace from London via Balham, Streatham and Gypsy Hill. It was soon extended south and east to Norwood Junction and what was then New Bromley (now Shortlands).

To serve the Palace and shift the crowds, the LB&SCR built a very substantial station with a covered way of iron and glass up to the south end of the building. A siding was provided for the Crystal Palace Company and over the years many very strange items intended for exhibition purposes were loaded and unloaded at this point. Discounted tickets for travel and entry were available and through tickets were issued by other companies including the L&NWR which enjoyed running powers to the LB&SCR's Crystal Palace Station.

The LC&DR quickly decided that it wanted a serious slice of the action at the Crystal Palace and via a client company, the Crystal Palace & South London Junction

Railway, it completed a branch line in August 1865 from the Peckham Rye area through Honor Oak and Upper Sydenham to what eventually became known as Crystal Palace High Level and Upper Norwood. Through trains from Victoria had to clamber up gradients as steep as 1 in 60 to reach the terminus. Just before reaching Crystal Palace, the line passed through Paxton's Tunnel which was close to a fine house in which Paxton himself lived for several years. The last few miles of the line passed through a hilly, wooded district peppered with the villas of the affluent and which was never likely to likely to offer much originating traffic in the early days or indeed even up to the time of its closure in 1954 when of course recreational traffic to the Crystal Palace had long since ended.

The LC&DR built a station at the end of the line which was so splendid that it immediately consigned even the existing very well-appointed LB&SCR station to a definite second place. It had a trainshed of glass, iron and brick which cost over £100,000 and neatly complemented the Palace itself. The whole place was extensive enough to have served as a terminus station in a major provincial city. Generous amenities were provided for passengers and those with first-class tickets even had their own dedicated access to the Palace. The whole building was designed to be able to handle vast crowds, up to 7,000 or 8,000 an hour, and to do so in great style.

Clearly both the LB&SCR and the LC&DR invested a great deal of money in these lines and stations, but did they provide the hoped-for financial rewards? Londoners were extremely proud and fond of their re-sited Crystal Palace but that doesn't necessarily mean that they flocked to it in great numbers, or at least in the numbers hoped for. In 1866, a fire destroyed the north transept, and it was indicative of the Crystal Palace Company's already rather forlorn hopes that it was never rebuilt. The Sabbatarian movement kept up the pressure to prevent Sunday opening which meant that the Palace was largely unable to open on precisely on the day when it could have expected the best crowds of the week. Admittedly, the Crystal Palace became famous for its magnificent fireworks displays staged by Messrs Brock & Co but many who watched them did so from afar and without paying to enter the grounds. By the 1890s, the glitter had abandoned the Crystal Palace, and the Company was becoming increasingly insolvent. In 1913, a public subscription had to be raised in order to save the Crystal Palace. The Palace and its two accompanying stations were proving to be a white elephant. This was ironic because the Great Exhibition in the original Crystal Palace had demonstrated so forcibly to the world how the railways could provide the means for vast numbers of people to travel easily and cheaply.

We cannot leave the Crystal Palace without mentioning another fabled railway which ran in its grounds. In 1864, an experimental 'pneumatic' railway was built. It was effectively a development of Brunel's unsuccessful atmospheric railway in south Devon. Brunel himself had been dead for five years. A passenger carriage ran on a broad gauge track for 600yds through a tunnel, quickly and silently, linking the two stations and the Palace itself. A return fare of 6d, expensive at the time, proved no deterrent to those who wanted to sample this novel form of propulsion. A single carriage running on broad gauge rails took passengers on the journey of less than a minute. The success of this small-scale operation encouraged proposals for what would have been London's first tube railway. It would have run from Whitehall to Waterloo under the Thames and work began but was abandoned in the financial crisis of 1866. It is said that the stub of this tunnel is still in place.

Fashion is capricious and in time the 'pneumatic railway' was closed but before long a myth developed that the carriage remained within the bricked-up tunnel and contained a grisly cargo of long-forgotten skeletal passengers. Traces of this tunnel could be seen for many years and in the early 1990s an edition of the *New Civil Engineer* carried an article with photographs taken many years previously inside the tunnel. No abandoned carriage containing equally abandoned skeletons was to be seen. According to the article, no trace of the tunnel now survives.

Another oddity at the Crystal Palace was the *Chemin de Fer Glissant* which Francophones will instantly translate as something like 'Gliding Railway'. This was a carriage or carriages running, without wheels, on iron girders and propelled by a combination of compressed air and high-pressure water. This, it was claimed, would be an ideal solution for inner-city road congestion because it would be an elevated railway and far cheaper to build and operate than conventional railways. Trains would run quietly, smoothly, swiftly and safely. This somewhat Heath Robinson-like contraption was built and operated at exhibitions in Paris and Edinburgh before opening to the public at Crystal Palace Park on a temporary basis in March 1891. This system was no mere whimsy, and an attempt was made to interest authorities responsible for urban transport systems. However, there were numerous technical problems which would have required much time and money to address. The potential customers, perhaps wisely, shied away from seriously considering the 'Gliding Railway' as a possible solution to the issues they were facing.

The early success of the Crystal Palace probably ensured that north Londoners would want a pleasure dome of their own. In 1862 a consortium of businessmen bought a site in what was then hilly open country between Hornsey and New Southgate. A park was opened on 23 July 1863. On a particular eminence, they built the Alexandra Palace (named for the Princess of Wales) using much material recycled from the building housing the International Exhibition which had been held at Kensington in 1862. The relocation and erection of this building experienced many problems and, although it was completed in 1866, cash-flow difficulties meant that it could not be brought into use until 1872. It was formally opened in May 1873 and sixteen days later was razed to the ground by fire. This could be considered bad luck but the owners, encouraged by early visitor numbers, decided to start rebuilding immediately, despite the Palace not having been insured. The building reopened in 1875. Meanwhile, since there had been little residential development between Highgate and the Palace and the trickle of voyeurs wanting to view the burnt out remains had died out, the trains, which had been running virtually empty, were withdrawn from 31 July 1873.

Even before the Palace itself had opened its doors, interest was being shown in building a railway to a location expected to attract huge crowds especially on high days and holidays. In 1864, the Edgware, Highgate & London Railway (EH&LR) obtained legal powers to build a branch from its proposed Highgate station to a terminus at Muswell Hill close to the new park. A further act in 1866 authorised the EH&LR to extend into the park to a point close to and just below the north-western façade of the Palace. At the same time an approach to the Alexandra Palace from the east by the GER was sanctioned. Various other schemes to build railways to the Palace were mooted but came to nothing.

The EH&LR line from Highgate opened to coincide with the original opening of the Palace itself on 24 May 1873. The line was worked by the GNR from the start. Although very large numbers had used the line to reach the Crystal Palace and the park in the early days, it seemed as if something of a jinx hung over the place. Despite a wide range of attractions including concert halls, reading rooms, theatres, music festivals, flower, fruit and dog shows, a circus, a racecourse, archery and cricket grounds, foot and penny-farthing races, a Japanese garden and a boating lake, initial popularity was not sustained. Attempts to match the hugely popular firework displays that took place at the Crystal Palace failed to catch on.

A new Palace, somewhat larger, rose from the ashes and when it opened on 1 May 1875 a full service was restored including trains of the NLR running to and from Broad Street. It somehow typified the luck of the line that on the first bank holiday after the reopening, 94,000 people visited the Park and the Palace and most of them came by rail. This should have been a cause for self-congratulation but there was a derailment in Copenhagen Tunnel outside King's Cross and returning trains were blocked all the way back to the Palace. Many passengers simply alighted from wherever the trains had stopped and walked for the rest of their journey. Some others spent the night in the trains. It was a public relations disaster.

It did not help the Muswell Hill Estate Company as owners of the grounds, or the GNR, that from 1876 the Palace closed through the winter. In terms of numbers carried, the Palace, the Park and the branch looked reasonably successful, but numbers were insufficient to make them a paying proposition. A change of ownership did not manage to turn round the 'Ally Pally's' fortunes and it tended only to be well-used on bank holidays and warm summer Sundays. Attempts to sell off parts of the Park for residential purposes were not particularly successful because the original legislation authorising the project had put restrictions on how much of it could be sold for that purpose.

The Alexandra Palace was in danger of becoming a white elephant. Periods of closure, sometimes of several years' duration, obviously affected demand on the branch line and it, too, underwent periods of being largely comatose. For much of the time trains ran only to Muswell Hill rather than the station at the Palace itself. In 1898, confident that substantial suburban development would at last be taking place, the GNR reopened the line to the terminus. This did not have any great effect and in 1900 the Palace and the Park were sold to the local authority. Some of the land was sold off for building purposes. The long-hoped for residential development then began taking place and much new middle-class housing appeared around Muswell Hill. An intermediate station was opened at Cranley Gardens to serve the mushrooming suburbs. No sooner was the GNR able to record encouraging rising levels of passenger usage than more convenient electric trams and motor buses began to extract traffic.

The subsequent history of the branch was just about as chequered as its past. It was a story of being run down and then revived with brave new hopes only for these again to be dashed. The branch from Highgate was included in plans for electrification as part of the Underground system and much preparatory work was carried out. The final passenger trains ran in 1954. Had the line become part of the Underground, it would probably have become viable, and it is likely that it would have been running today as part of the Northern Line.

The GER had also set its sights on the bountiful traffic that it hoped would be generated by a line built to serve Alexandra Palace but only started to move after flirtatious approaches from the Muswell Hill Estate Company who obviously wanted to encourage any venture that would maximise railway access. In 1866, a GER branch line was authorised from what was going to be the Seven Sisters station on the GER's proposed branch to Enfield Town. Associated with this project was a loop line curving round north of the Palace and joining up with the line to Highgate and Finsbury Park of what became the GNR. This would have encountered serious engineering challenges because of the hilly nature of the terrain in this part of the Northern Heights. Nothing came of this latter proposal and the GER, in serious financial straits, obtained powers in 1871 to abandon its projected line to the vicinity of the Palace.

So far this seems rather like a rerun of the dismal saga of the GNR's approaches to the Ally Pally. However, in 1874 the GER took up the challenge again and received legal sanction for a branch line from Seven Sisters to a station somewhat misleadingly named 'Palace Gates'. It was a long uphill walk to gain access and the entrance to the Palace could not be seen from the station. The generous accommodation and facilities for handling large numbers of passengers at Palace Gates station suggested that substantial leisure traffic was anticipated. The station was built as a through station but never functioned as one. This branch came into full use on 7 October 1878 with intermediate stations at Green Lanes & Noel Park and West Green.

We have followed the rather sorry story of the Ally Pally's few ups and frequent downs and certainly both railway companies' hopes of abundant traffic to and from the Palace and Park were usually only met during particularly good weather or when special events were being staged. However, much speculative housing for moderately well-paid working people was built close to much of the Palace Gates line and considerable commuter traffic built up to and from Liverpool Street. In 1887, a through service from Palace Gates to North Woolwich was inaugurated and this became widely used by workers at the docks and the various railway installations at Stratford.

Like the Great Northern branch, that of the Great Eastern found its traffic being eroded by competition from handier electric trams and motor buses and changing work patterns as some of the older sources of employment declined in importance. Neither station had ever offered a particularly quick or convenient service into central London.

Both branches lost their passenger services in the years after the Second World War, it perhaps being surprising that they lasted as long as they did. Although suffering another severe conflagration in 1980, the Ally Pally survived to be rebuilt once more and continues to make its lowering presence felt over this part of north London. The world moves on. Its branch line railways are now part of history, but the suburban main line station previously known as Wood Green & Alexandra Park was renamed Alexandra Palace on 17 May 1982.

The Crystal Palace and the Alexandra Palace may have had mixed fortunes, but they gave generations of Londoners much pleasure.

Chapter 10

MISCELLANEA 2

RAILWAY BRIDGES ACROSS THE THAMES

Investigations by archaeologists suggest that in prehistoric times there may have been a crude bridge across the Thames in the Vauxhall area. The Thames then would have been a considerably wider watercourse, shallow in places and with a much more sluggish flow than today. It ran through a flood plain much of which was marshy, especially on the southern side. The river would have constituted a formidable barrier to those wanting to get from one side to the other, especially when it was in spate. We know that it was fordable as Caesar's army had to cross it in 55 BC but although Westminster and Brentford have been mentioned as the possible location of the ford, the site remains unknown. When in AD 43 the Romans annexed Britain, they built Londinium on an area of higher ground on the north side of the Thames. They proceeded to build a wooden bridge across the river just downstream from the present London Bridge.

Although the fate of this bridge is unknown, at least from the tenth century, it is likely that there was another wooden bridge in the vicinity. It was not until 1209 that a masonry bridge was built, and this was to last over 600 years and to become the stuff both of legend and stirring reality. Later known as 'Old London Bridge', it was the only bridge across the Thames central to the sprawl that was developing into London until Westminster Bridge was completed in 1750. By that time, London Bridge had become grossly congested and an obstruction to efficient commerce between the two sides of the river. That it took so long to build a bridge at Westminster owed much to the power of the Company of Watermen who controlled transportation on and across the river itself and wanted to maintain their dominant position. The Corporation of the City of London was also hostile to any bridges further upstream as it was thought that such bridges would encourage the westward migration of trade and industry.

It is hard for us to envisage the intensive level of activity on the Thames in the eighteenth and nineteenth centuries. In the continuously built-up parts of London there were innumerable stairs or landing places for the picking up and setting down of passengers and, in many cases, horses and wheeled vehicles as well. Additionally, ferries plied their trade across the river. Many people preferred to use the river to move around because it was quicker than using what passed for roads. It was also safer, because those roads, especially around the fringes of London, were the haunt of highwaymen and footpads. In wet weather the roads might be impassable. Steam power was introduced in the early nineteenth century and paddle steamers provided regular and frequent passenger transport along the river. They were much faster than sailing vessels or the ferries rowed by watermen. Steam tugs pulling strings of barges carried all kinds of goods to and fro. Large numbers of sailing barges added to the hive of activity which was the Thames at this time.

More bridges were to follow in the eighteenth and nineteenth centuries and by 1900 the Thames from Richmond to Tower Bridge was traversed by eighteen road bridges, nine railway bridges and two footbridges. Here we will briefly consider the history of the nine railway bridges on this stretch of the river, proceeding downstream from Richmond. They all made contributions to the development of modern London.

RICHMOND RAILWAY BRIDGE

Richmond was prospering by the time its manor house was transformed into a splendid royal palace by the fifteenth century. Many wealthy Londoners moved there to what became a favoured rural area well away from the filth and pestilence of London and Westminster. In the eighteenth century many fine residences were built. Richmond was a fashionable place to live.

Richmond was the location of the first railway bridge to cross the Thames in the London area. It was built in 1848. A few years earlier, steamboats were providing six journeys per day to central London, but their days were numbered because, over such a distance, the railways provided a significantly quicker and safer service. The railway had reached Richmond in 1846 and trains to the London terminus at Nine Elms on the Surrey side of the river took just thirty-two minutes. The service to Richmond proved to be a great success and by 1847 was handling 25,000 passengers a month.

The bridge was opened in 1848 when the L&SWR extended its line through Staines to Windsor. *Punch* magazine did not think much of this venture, calling it 'the London and Datchet Snailway'. The bridge was designed by Joseph Locke, the L&SWR's engineer, and it consisted of three spans of cast iron with piers encased in stone. It was praised by the *Illustrated London News* as a 'handsome structure'. After a similar bridge collapsed in 1891, a replacement was erected consisting of steel and using the old piers and abutments. It looked very similar to the original.

The bridge helped to bring Windsor more closely into the thrall of the metropolis and with quick access to London now available, it encouraged some affluent outer-suburban housing development in the area. River steamer excursions to Windsor now found themselves with a rival, although many Londoners still preferred the steamers with their slower progress through the unfolding scenery, their rough-and-ready camaraderie and, of course, you could drink your way up and down the river on board.

KEW RAILWAY BRIDGE
By the eighteenth century, Kew had become a select residential district and in the mid-century a start was made on creating what became the internationally known Kew Gardens.

In 1869, the L&SWR opened a line from South Acton via Kew Gardens to Richmond. The designer of the necessary bridge across the Thames near Strand-on-the-Green was W.R. Galbraith. He was a prolific civil engineer doing much work for the L&SWR, building tube lines in London and routes in his native Scotland. Among the projects he headed was the Waterloo & City Line, often, not without affection, called 'The Drain'.

It took five years to build and was often referred to as 'Strand Bridge' to differentiate it from the nearby Kew Bridge. The bridge consists of five 35m. spans of wrought iron lattice girders supported on cast-iron columns embellished with decorative capitals. Its riverside abutments are brick with ornamental stone mouldings. Its appearance was criticised when it opened, not least because it looked very intrusive when viewed from the highly favoured Thameside residences of Strand-on-the-Green. Trains of the District Line later shared the tracks over the bridge.

BARNES RAILWAY BRIDGE
Until the early nineteenth century, the village of Barnes was curiously remote, probably because it could only be approached by the river or across the Common. This began to change in the 1840s as roads were opened, particularly from the Hammersmith direction.

The railway bridge was brought into use in 1849 on a line of the L&SWR from Barnes to Chiswick, Brentford and Hounslow. It was another of Joseph Locke's creations. Although an observer of the first train to cross described the bridge as 'light and elegant', it is widely regarded, even with some affection, as ugly but the several additions it has had over the years have not enhanced its appearance. Those parts of the bridge composed of cast iron were replaced by wrought iron in 1895.

In 1849 the completion of the bridge was delayed for a month because a cottage in Back Lane, Barnes, due to be demolished for the construction of the railway, was occupied by an expectant mother who, it was decided, could not be moved. The *Illustrated London News* predicted that the line across the bridge would benefit the market gardeners of the district by enabling them to get their produce quickly and cheaply to Covent Garden and other markets in the Metropolis.

Although the Oxford and Cambridge Boat Race is no longer such a prominent event in the annual sports calendar as it once was, Barnes Railway Bridge is famed for being a landmark close to the finishing post. The Race, which is from Putney to Mortlake, has been staged almost continuously from 1845. A pedestrian footpath over the bridge provided a grandstand view of the final stage of the Race. The L&SWR, never averse to exploiting an unexpected source of revenue, charged the substantial sum of 15s to those spectators who wanted to take advantage of the view of the Race from the bridge. Special excursion trains were run by the Company to move the hordes who wished to view the Race but not all could afford to buy a place on the bridge.

PUTNEY RAILWAY BRIDGE

In medieval times, Putney was a fishing and farming community. In the seventeenth and eighteenth century it became a favoured residential area for wealthy London merchants and members of the court who built themselves large mansions often surrounded by extensive estates. In 1801 Putney's population was about 2,400; by 1914 there had been a tenfold increase and Putney had become a largely middle-class suburb. With the opening of the L&SWR line to Richmond in 1846, District Railway trains to and from Wimbledon and the City and some L&SWR trains to and from Waterloo serving East Putney from in 1889, there was greatly increased accessibility to and from Central London. Putney became ripe for housing development. A consequence was demolition of most of the large houses and the building of what we would characterise as a typical Victorian and Edwardian middle-class suburb.

Complaints had been raised about earlier railway bridges across the Thames and the Act of 1881 which authorised the Putney Bridge required it to be of an 'ornamental character'. The bridge was designed by William Jacomb of the L&SWR, although completed by others, and consisted of wrought-iron lattice-girder spans on columns filled with concrete. Locals referred to Putney Railway Bridge as 'the Iron Bridge'. A pedestrian pathway is attached to the downstream side of the bridge.

BATTERSEA RAILWAY BRIDGE

This bridge was built in 1863 by the West London Extension Railway, a non-operating company jointly owned by the GWR, L&NWR, L&SWR and LB&SCR. In its early years it was unusual in that it was provided with mixed-gauge rails, combining standard with the broad-gauge track of the GWR. There were five river spans of wrought iron, supported by granite piers with six brick arches on each bank.

The bridge provided a link between the systems north and south of the Thames, bypassing the congested central parts of London. However, in the nineteenth century, passenger services across the bridge never really caught on and it was only in the twentieth century that the bridge or at least the services running over it, both passenger and freight, really came into their own. For some years, one of the passenger services across the bridge was a fascinating one operating between Paddington and Victoria and providing the visual treat of, for example, a locomotive and train of the LB&SCR gracing the GWR redoubt of Paddington. The labyrinth of lines connecting with the West London and West London Extension Railways made the line over the bridge particularly suitable for freight trains transferring loads between the various companies and their sidings and marshalling yards both north and south of the river. Even before the First World War, the line was also being used by enterprising holiday trains running mostly between the industrial districts of the Midlands, the North-West and seaside resorts in Kent and Sussex which were promoted as providing the best guarantees of sunshine in Britain's capricious climate.

The bridge was and remains one of London's lesser-known railway crossings of the Thames, maybe because no major roads cross the river in its vicinity. It is sometimes referred to as 'Cremorne Bridge' after the nearby well-known Cremorne Pleasure Gardens in Chelsea which attracted large crowds from 1832 to 1877. The site on which the gardens stood has largely been redeveloped.

GROSVENOR RAILWAY BRIDGE

Also known as the Victoria Bridge, the Grosvenor Railway Bridge was the first railway bridge to be built across the Thames in what might loosely be described as 'Central London'. The proposed bridge received parliamentary authorisation in July 1858 and the bridge opened in June 1859. It was built by the LB&SCR and shared the distinction, with Battersea Railway Bridge, of mixed-gauge track since GWR trains also ran over it. At first only two tracks were carried by the five wrought-iron arches but after the LC&DR also obtained authority to operate into Victoria, a second bridge was built alongside the first. It opened in 1866 and with its five additional tracks made the Grosvenor Bridge the widest in the world at the time. Traffic continued to build up and in 1907 a third bridge was added. Grosvenor Railway Bridge was now 54.2m wide and carried ten sets of rails. They were intensively used.

The origins of the bridge and of Victoria Station which, of course, it serves, was with the West End and Crystal Palace Railway. This had been created to exploit what it was thought would be the huge demand for people wanting to travel to Sydenham to visit the Crystal Palace after it had been taken down and relocated. A site at Sydenham Hill was found for it and rebuilding began in 1852. The new Crystal Palace was considerably bigger than the original and was designed to be the centrepiece of a massive facility wanting not only to provide pleasure but also to have an educational function and cultural function. Sydenham Hill was then a rural spot but with magnificent views towards London and the majestic new Crystal Palace was erected to make maximum use of the location. The initial London terminus of the West End & Crystal Palace Railway was opened in 1858. It was named 'Pimlico' which was rather odd because Pimlico was a district on the opposite, northern side of the Thames. This station was inconveniently sited, and it made eminent sense to cross the river and build a new station closer to Central London. The line into Victoria made some use of the bed of the disused Grosvenor Canal. This had originally been constructed in 1725 by the Chelsea Waterworks Company.

The bridge was designed by the eminent engineer John Fowler. He was to gain great fame as the partner of Benjamin Baker in the building of the Forth Bridge in Scotland.

HUNGERFORD RAILWAY BRIDGE

The pre-history of this bridge was somewhat chequered. In 1682 Sir Edward Hungerford built a fruit and vegetable market in the grounds of his family house which had burned down in 1669. He modestly named the market after himself. The market did not prosper, and it was rebuilt in 1833 adding meat and fish to what was already on offer. In 1851 a bazaar and art gallery were added, only for the place to be burned down in 1854. In 1860 the site was chosen for the location of Charing Cross railway station. Perhaps it was not before time because some unkind person described Hungerford Market as 'little better than a monster dust-heap'.

A bridge already existed in the vicinity, called 'Hungerford Bridge'. This was an elegant suspension footbridge designed by Brunel. It opened in 1845, the hope being that it would make access from the South Bank easier and encourage more customers for the market. This was not particularly successful because on the South Bank the bridge gave access to an area of appalling slums. Brunel was rather offhand about the contract to build the bridge as he already had many other irons in the fire that he probably thought were more prestigious. However, he did a good job and the bridge perhaps had rather more merit than he thought, because it was one of the longest suspension bridges in the world at the time and quickly became very well-used, especially after Waterloo Station opened in 1848.

In 1859, an Act authorised the Charing Cross Railway Company to build a line from London Bridge station across the Thames and into a new station at Charing Cross, handy for Trafalgar Square and the West End. The company bought the market and the bridge and John Hawkshaw, engineer to the SER, was engaged to design the new railway bridge. With an eye to economy, he retained Brunel's brick piers but added four new cast-iron piers. The new bridge was described as 'functional', rather than beautiful. One critic described it as an 'eyesore'. It was a wrought-iron lattice-girder bridge, 414m long and 15.24m wide with space for four tracks. There were footways on either side with a toll payable for access. Provision was made for landing stages for steamboats.

BLACKFRIARS RAILWAY BRIDGE

The L&CDR was an ambitious but impecunious company that wanted to gain a foothold on the north bank of the Thames. It was anxious to be the first railway company based south of the river to build a station in the City, and hence to be in a favoured position to exploit the potentially lucrative traffic likely to be generated by getting there first. The plan was to link up with the Metropolitan Railway at

Farringdon which offered the attractive possibility of tapping into north to south cross-river traffic.

Parliamentary authority was obtained in 1860 and Joseph Cubitt was appointed to build the bridge and, by happy coincidence, the adjacent road bridge. The bridge was designed to carry four tracks and it had five wrought-iron girder spans. Each of the piers had three cast-iron cylinders which were sunk into the river, filled with concrete and faced with stone. From each pier rose iron columns with ornate capitals which supported the superstructure. The abutments were of brick faced with Portland stone from the recently demolished old Westminster Bridge. The L&CDR's coat of arms was displayed and these, brightly painted, can still be seen today although the original bridge which they adorned has been demolished. The bridge was opened on 21 December 1864 and two stations, Blackfriars Bridge and Ludgate Hill, were opened by the L&CDR, the latter in 1865. Through connections with the Metropolitan Railway were completed in 1866 making the line across the bridge potentially a very useful link.

As might have been expected, traffic developed and to increase its capacity, a second bridge was built alongside. It was often called 'St Paul's Railway Bridge'. It was designed by Sir John Wolfe-Barry and Henry Marc Brunel, second son of Isambard Kingdom Brunel. This bridge opened on 10 May 1886.

CANNON STREET RAILWAY BRIDGE

There was no love lost between the SER and the L&CDR and the former was displeased when the latter began to build its terminus at Blackfriars, giving it a vital foothold in the City. Determined to get one over on its hated rival, the SER decided to make a terminus of their own and upstage their rivals by locating it even nearer the centre of the City. The SER received parliamentary sanction in June 1861 to extend a line across the Thames and build a station conveniently located for the Bank of England. Cannon Street Station opened on 1 September 1866. The cost of building the bridge and the Station stretched the SER's resources to such an extent that it decided not to proceed itself with the building of a hotel. A large and opulent hotel was built as a frontage to the street but not owned at that time by the railway company.

John Hawkshaw was the engineer, and he built a station which looked extremely impressive from the south bank and from the river. It had an overall roof and two lofty towers at the country end topped by features not unlike the steeples of Wren's churches nearby. The bridge initially accommodated nine tracks and consisted of five spans of wrought-iron plate girders supported by four cast-iron columns. On either side of the tracks there were footways, one for railway employees, the other for the public on payment of a halfpenny toll. This was abolished along with all other tolls on London's bridges, in 1877. Piqued by losing the right to levy a toll, the SER decided to close the public footway.

With the intention of maximising potential traffic, the SER ran most of its trains proceeding beyond London Bridge first into Cannon Street and then reversed them back over the river and, via a north-to-west spur, into Charing Cross. This manoeuvre, although seeming rather fussy, attracted many passengers wanting to travel to and from the West End and the City until the District Railway provided a direct service roughly parallel with the north bank of the Thames. Eventually trains crossing the bridge and undergoing his rigmarole were withdrawn but not before they had gained some notoriety because the first-class compartments, which were provided with blinds, were used by prostitutes to provide a 'quickie' for paying customers in the few minutes that it took a train to run from Cannon Street to Charing Cross.

Initially the bridge was called the 'Alexandra Bridge' commemorating the Danish princess who the Prince of Wales had married just before work began on the Cannon Street project. This name dropped out of favour and to all and sundry it became the 'Cannon Street Railway Bridge'.

The railway bridges across the Thames contributed much to the creation of the complex and extensive transport infrastructure necessary for the development of the Metropolis in the nineteenth and early twentieth century. They were functional rather than being designed with aesthetics in mind but, at least in their original form, they probably did not deserve the kind of opprobrium poured on Blackfriars Railway Bridge by the art critic and social theorist John Ruskin, 'The entire invention of the designer seems to have exhausted itself in exaggerating to an enormous size a weak form of iron nut, and in conveying the information upon it, in large letters, that it belongs to the London, Chatham & Dover Railway.'

SHERLOCK HOLMES AND LONDON'S RAILWAYS

The investigations of Arthur Conan Doyle's Sherlock Holmes take him around London but also out of the metropolis and he makes considerable use of the railway system. It is hard to escape the impression that Conan Doyle was something of an enthusiast for railways and railway travel. He seemed to have his favourite stations and lines. Perhaps he liked the West Country because Paddington (for the GWR) and Waterloo (L&SWR) feature more frequently than other termini and his stories loftily eschew any journeys from St Pancras (Midland Railway) even when a trip to the hills of Derbyshire is being undertaken. This is odd because he often tells Watson to 'look it up in *Bradshaw*', this being an authoritative monthly publication with comprehensive coverage of the timetables of Britain's railway companies, even if an IQ of prodigious proportions was needed in order to extract the required information from a nightmarish mass of confusing footnotes and symbols. Some of the routes used for journeys made by Holmes look at first sight to have either been impossible, difficult or inconvenient. On closer examination, however, it appears that Conan Doyle probably knew his *Bradshaw* well and that leaving, say Victoria, for a journey into Surrey and then returning to Waterloo was in fact perfectly feasible, if not necessarily by the best or most obvious route. Not all Holmes' peregrinations make any kind of sense. Why, for example, should he and Watson join a train of the L&CDR at Victoria when their immediate destination is Newhaven on the LB&SCR? They alighted at Canterbury and would have faced several changes in order to reach Newhaven. Or was it all a decoy to avoid the clutches of Professor Moriarty, Holmes' nemesis? Other London termini that Holmes used are London Bridge, Charing Cross, Liverpool Street and King's Cross. In *The Adventure of the Abbey Grange* Holmes and Watson take a cab through what Doyle lyrically describes as 'the opalescent London reek' to Charing Cross where they have tea in the refreshment room before joining their train.

Holmes excels himself in the adventure of *The Norwood Builder*. He and Watson are sitting in their chambers in Baker Street one morning bemoaning the lack of the kind of piquant cases on which Holmes has been able to exercise his talents in the past. Suddenly a frantic-looking young man bursts into their room and announces, "I am the unhappy John Hector McFarlane." If he thought that the mere mention of his name would evoke instant recognition, McFarlane was disappointed. Holmes looked him up and down and then said, 'You mentioned your name as if I should recognise it, but I assure you that, beyond the obvious facts that you are a bachelor, a solicitor, a Freemason, and an asthmatic, I know nothing whatever about you.' McFarlane is accused of murder over a will, and he enlists Holmes' support in order to prove his innocence. Holmes quickly brings his rapier-like intellect to bear on the problem. He examines the will and then pronounces:

> It was written in a train: the good writing represents stations, the bad writing movement, and the very bad writing passing over points. A scientific expert would pronounce at once that this was drawn up on a suburban line, since nowhere save in the immediate vicinity of a great city could there be so quick a succession of points. Granting that his whole journey was occupied in drawing up the will, then the train was an express, only stopping once between Norwood and London Bridge.

Holmes was right, of course, and he went on to provide evidence of McFarlane's innocence.

The Bruce-Partington Plans was written in 1908 but set on a day of dense London fog in November 1895. The body of a young man, a government employee at Woolwich Arsenal, is found by the side of the Metropolitan Line close to Aldgate. He did not appear to have been robbed and in his pocket were papers giving details of a highly secret naval submarine. How had the young man, whose name was Cadogan West, come to be found dead by the railway and what was someone so junior doing with such sensitive items on his person, items to which he would not have had official access? The Metropolitan Railway was built on the 'cut-and-cover' principle and the location where the body was found was in the open air and on a curve just after the junction where a branch diverged for Aldgate East and Whitechapel. Holmes deduces that the body was placed on the top of a carriage of an Inner Circle Line train where it was open to the elements, and it regularly stopped for signals. He found such a location near Gloucester Road station. Cadogan West's body then fell off its precarious perch as the train jerked while passing over the junction points at Aldgate. The rest of the case was simplicity itself.

Holmes studiously avoided travelling on the Underground while moving around London, preferring horse-drawn cabs. These may have allowed Conan Doyle to give more of a sense of the character and atmosphere of the capital, something he clearly revelled in. On the other hand, while cabs may have been more convenient for door-to-door journeys, where they paralleled the lines of the growing underground railway network, they are likely to have been considerably slower. Sometimes speed was of the essence when he was on his missions. Was there a reason for Holmes' aversion to travelling on the Underground?

LONDON'S VICTORIAN RAILWAYS IN ART

Although London, because of the size and relative affluence of its population, had always been a significant manufacturing centre, the establishment of Britain's staple heavy industries, dependent on coal and steam power, was largely around the coal-producing districts elsewhere. Most of Britain's early railways were also to be found around those districts – after all, they were created primarily for the transport of coal and other bulky and heavy minerals.

Publishers offered commercial prints of variable quality depicting such major early lines as the Stockton & Darlington, opened in 1825 and the Liverpool & Manchester in 1830. London's early railway development lagged behind, as mentioned elsewhere. However, the building of the first main line railway into London was recorded visually with a degree of detailed accuracy that had never been done before and has rarely been achieved since. It was the work of John Cooke Bourne, an artist and lithographer. In 1836 he took to watching work progressing on the building of the L&BR into and out of Euston. He became so fascinated by the operations involved that he decided to produce a careful visual record of this civil engineering prodigy. Bourne was an extremely competent draughtsman with a superb understanding of line and form. He made many sketches of the work in the London area, including the construction of the Euston Arch and the Arch as completed and having won a powerful patron, he went on to have folios of tinted lithographs published of the continuing work through Camden and eventually all the way to Birmingham. Bourne's work is realistic and

Well-heeled passengers hailing cabs at Victoria. This station dealt with large numbers of passengers travelling to and from the Continent.

An elegant lady waits for her train and is surrounded by her luggage.
By Camille Pissarro, the location of this delightful picture is, amazingly,
Willesden Junction!

meticulous and provides vital historical evidence of the methods employed in the construction of this pioneering line. It also did a useful public relations job for the new-fangled railways whose disruption of and intrusion into both town and country was provoking considerable hostility at the time. It may have produced hostility, but it also generated great interest and Bourne did very well in terms of sales.

J.M.W. Turner was one of Britain's most prolific and successful painters. His *Rain, Steam and Speed* of 1844 is included here because at least the train he shows was heading for Paddington and passing through London's periphery. The painting is generally regarded as a classic. Turner provides an impression of a broad-gauge steam-hauled train hurrying through a storm and passing over a bridge. In real life, it is the very shallow-arched bridge over the Thames just east of Maidenhead and Turner took several trips on trains to get the right details for his composition. He stuck his head out of the window, sketching away, getting soaked in the process and almost certainly annoying his fellow-passengers who may not have appreciated the artistic genius at work in their midst. A boat drifts aimlessly on the river and a road bridge can be seen veering off to the left as if its purpose is being superseded by the new high-speed form of communication. Turner was fascinated by the harnessing of steam as a means of power and the painting shows a perhaps grudging and slightly fearful admiration for the exciting new spectacle of a steam train at speed.

A somewhat neglected aspect of the art of the Victorian period is genre or figurative painting which depicts episodes from everyday life. From the point of view of social and cultural history, these works can be a source of valuable evidence. Some of them deal with scenes on railway stations and two of the best-known ones depict King's Cross and Paddington. *Going North, King's Cross Station* was produced in 1893 by George Earl. It depicts a crowded scene on the platform at King's Cross with a large party getting ready to join a train going up the East Coast Main Line to Scotland. It is August and the smart and clearly well-heeled travellers are gathering to go northwards for the grouse-shooting season. Their luggage, their guns and their dogs are shown in realistic detail. This painting is one of a pair. The other is titled *Coming South, Perth Station*. It is now September, and the party are about to board the train back to London. Various stags' antlers, animal furs and hampers probably containing salmon are testimony to the party's successful depredations on the wildlife of Scotland. It was a wonder there was any fauna left if this haul was anything to go by.

W.P. Frith specialised in genre paintings of crowd scenes. His *The Railway Station* of 1862 is perhaps the best-known of all railway paintings and it contains an almost overwhelming amount of detail. It shows a departure platform at Paddington with passengers, luggage, servants and all, preparing for their journey. A small group of poor people can be seen on the left, hurrying in their anxiety to catch the train. In the centre, Frith depicts some typical middle-class people, including his own family, and a bridal party. Their relative wealth means that they are used to trains and they are calm and unhurried. Towards the right of the picture two real-life detectives are arresting a well-dressed man, almost certainly a white-collar criminal, before he had the chance to escape on the train. There is a comprehensive medley of other characters including a foreigner engaged in a dispute with a cabbie about his fare, a lady making a fuss about her baggage, a calm-looking station superintendent bent on making order out of chaos and a sportsman clearly departing on a fishing trip. In all Frith depicts eighty-six people including himself. The public loved the painting. The critics were less effusive. Despite all the action taking place in *The Railway Station*, Frith's painting is somewhat stuffy, and it provoked some lesser artists into producing parodies of it.

James Tissot was a French painter who fled Paris after the fall of the Commune in 1871 and stayed in Britain until 1882. He produced many paintings of fashionable society but also found inspiration for depictions of the Thames and other scenes around London. *Waiting for the Train* shows a well-dressed and clearly well-to-do young woman standing on a platform surrounded by her baggage awaiting the arrival of her train. The location is totally unrecognisable today. She is standing on the main line platforms at a rural-looking Willesden Junction. Another delightful work by Tissot is titled *The Arrival Platform at Victoria Station*.

Camille Pisarro was a French Impressionist painter who spent some time in Britain and painted *The Station* in 1871. It depicts a train of the LC&DR leaving Lordship Lane Station on what proved ultimately to be the unsuccessful line to Crystal Palace High Level.

John O'Connor was an Irish painter who met with some success in London and left us with one particularly memorable painting, *St Pancras Hotel and Station from Pentonville Road*. The foreground is a lively depiction of the workaday Pentonville Road descending the east side of the valley of the River Fleet. It is sunset on what has been a fine day. Dominating the scene is the misty, almost ethereal outline of Scott's Midland Grand Hotel fronting Barlow's magnificent trainshed. The domination by the hotel of its mundane surroundings is absolute and yet there is also a sense of it being a vast mock-Gothic folly.

The louring impact of the railways on their viaducts over the working-class districts through which they passed is brilliantly conveyed in one of the drawings in Gustav Doré's famous collection *London: A Pilgrimage*, published in 1872 and produced in conjunction with Blanchard Jerrold. It is titled *Over London – By Rail*. In the distance a steam train crosses a tall viaduct while belching out copious amounts of smoke and, doubtless, soot. Huddled in the shadow of the viaduct are monotonous rows of mean proletarian dwellings whose backyards are teeming with a cowed yet somehow dignified humanity. Sullen light hangs over the crowded scene – all is grey and grimy. It is realistic stuff – the depiction of the hard under-belly of nineteenth century capitalism and industrial exploitation. Doré's London was a place on which the sun never shone. Doré was primarily a book illustrator, and he produced many depictions on the London underground railways of the time which were realistic rather than heroic or elegiac.

George Cruikshank was a complex character perhaps best-known for his caricature work in which he was clearly influenced by earlier great exponents of the art such as Gillray. His work frequently has a moral purpose especially when he is attacking 'The Demon Drink'. He seems to have had little sympathy for the railways as demonstrated in the striking drawing in which the railway is portrayed as a demonic fire-breathing monster bearing down on a helpless family living in its path and who are just about to be either crushed to pieces by it or sucked up into its rapacious maw.

Punch; or the London Charivari, first appeared in July 1841. In its earliest days it was an unashamedly radical champion of the oppressed and a scourge of the established body politic. However, its satirical content proved successful with the Victorian middle classes, confident enough as they were of their position in the world's leading nation to be able to appreciate jokes against themselves. Who paid the piper called the tune and *Punch* later evolved into an upholder of that complex set of notions that can be described as 'Victorian Values'. Be that as it may, those who wrote for and produced the illustrations for *Punch* found in railways an enormously rich seam of material perhaps mostly around the human quirks and foibles that railways and railway travel brought out. In its early days it inveighed against what it considered to be the arrogance and greed of railway companies, their directors and shareholders. Another periodical in which artwork depicting railways in London and elsewhere appeared was *The Illustrated London News.* It first appeared in 1842. It had no satirical or humorous element, being more in the nature of a weekly newspaper but it contained many well-drawn pictorial images which provide valuable evidence of the impact of railways in London and elsewhere.

LIVING BY THE SEA AND WORKING IN LONDON

To those of us fortunate enough not to have to travel far to work, it seems incomprehensible that anyone should volunteer to spend four or more hours a day undertaking an expensive journey in often overcrowded trains for the privilege of being employed in London and living by the sea. Many commuters during the winter do not even see their home surroundings in daylight for perhaps three months or more, except at weekends. Yet almost from the earliest days of railways, there have been commuters prepared to undertake the expense, the drawn-out tedium and the frequent frustration of the daily round trip to work in London.

No sooner had the line from London to Brighton opened in September 1841 than the operator put on a train exclusively for first-class passengers which left Brighton at 08.30 and, calling only at Croydon, reached London Bridge at 10.15. The return working left London Bridge at 15.00 which suggests that those using the service enjoyed 'Directors' hours. The original London & Brighton Company amalgamated with the London & Croydon in 1846 to form the LB&SCR and more trains for businesspeople were instituted. The LB&SCR network spread to embrace other seaside towns such as Worthing, Littlehampton, Bognor, Seaford, Eastbourne, Bexhill and St Leonards and some commuter traffic built up, but it was handicapped because of the relative slowness of the trains serving these places.

There were numerous small towns along the Kent coast and for traffic from many of these the hated rivals, the LC&DR and the SER were cutthroat rivals. The companies were at one time in direct competition at Margate, Ramsgate, Dover and Folkestone, for example, but trains took a long time to get up to the Metropolis and the cost of the tickets and the time involved meant that the early commuters were those who were affluent and senior enough not to need to work normal office hours. What, after amalgamation, became the South Eastern & Chatham Railway carried out various projects in the 1900s in order to speed up and encourage more commuting from various points along the North Kent coast.

Along the Essex Coast, trains operated by the LT&SR started running to Leigh-on-Sea in 1855 and Southend a year later. This development triggered some limited residential development in a previously remote and rural area. A fast train for commuters was put on to and from Fenchurch Street but at this time trains ran via Tilbury and the time taken, even on an 'express' service did not encourage daily travel. Once the more direct route from Pitsea via Upminster to Barking and Fenchurch opened in 1888, the best trains from Southend took less than an hour and commuter traffic began to build up quickly. Southend's residential population grew extremely rapidly. It was a mere 8,000 in 1891 but 70,767 in 1911 by which time the town had become a favoured residential base for affluent City workers. In 1889, the GER opened its own line to Southend from Liverpool Street via Shenfield to tap into the growing market being provided by Southend. The Great Eastern made considerable improvements to services from Clacton, Frinton and Walton-on-the-Naze in 1910 which encouraged more long-distance commuting to and from those towns.

The various electrification schemes of the period since the First World War saw the Southern Railway greatly increase and improve the services for those who wanted to combine seaside living with working in the Metropolis.

CHARLES DICKENS AND CHANGE BROUGHT ABOUT BY THE RAILWAYS

The railways impacted on London in an infinite variety of ways. A major impact was on the physical environment. We know that Charles Dickens was an astute observer of economic and social change at the time that the building of early railways was having a cataclysmic effect on parts of London. Dickens could not but be fascinated by what he saw and in a novel like *Dombey and Son* published 1847-8 he has provided us with a vivid fictionalised piece of living history which helps us to grasp the dynamics and tensions created by the coming of the railways in this exciting and revolutionary era.

Railway developers needed large amounts of land and would obviously always try to buy it as cheaply as possible. In practice this often meant acquiring land already used for market gardening purposes, for small industrial premises frequently employing polluting processes and for slum housing. *Dombey & Sons* gives the reader graphic descriptions of scenes during and after the building of the L&BR as it passed through the district of Camden Town. He chose an imaginary rundown neighbourhood called 'Stagg's Gardens'. This is Stagg's Gardens immediately before the arrival of the railway engineers and builders:

It was a little row of houses, with little squalid patches of ground before them, fenced off with old doors, barrel staves, scraps of tarpaulin, and dead bushes; with bottomless tin kettles and exhausted iron fenders, thrust into the gaps. Here the Stagg's Gardeners trained scarlet beans, kept fowls and rabbits, erected rotten summer houses (one was an old boat), dried clothes and smoked pipes.

Soon the company's engineers were engaged in their depredations and Stagg's Gardens would never be the same again.

There was no such place as Stagg's Gardens. It had vanished from the earth. Where the old rotten summer-houses once had stood, palaces now reared their heads, and granite columns of gigantic girth opened a vista to the railway world beyond. The miserable waste ground, where the refuse matter had been heaped of yore, was swallowed up and gone; and in its frowsy stead were tiers of warehouses, crammed with rich goods and costly merchandise. The old by-streets now swarmed with passengers and vehicles of every kind, the new streets that had stopped disheartened in the mud and wagon-ruts, formed towns within themselves, originating wholesome comforts and conveniences belonging to themselves and never tried nor thought of until they sprung into existence. Bridges that had led to nothing, led to villas, gardens, churches, healthy public walks. The carcasses of house, and beginnings of new thoroughfares, had started off upon the line at steam's own speed, and shot away into the country in a monster train.

Dickens then outlines to his readers some of the more general changes that railways are bringing about but still refracted through what was Stagg's Gardens:

There were railway patterns in its drapers' shops, and railway journals in the windows of its newsmen. There were railway hotels, coffee-houses, lodging houses, boarding-houses; railway plans, maps, views, wrappers, bottles, sandwich-boxes, and timetables; railway hackney-coach and cab-stands; railway omnibuses, railway streets and buildings, railway hangers-on and parasites, and flatterers out of all calculation. There was even railway time observed in clocks as if the sun itself had given in…To and from the heart of this great change, all day and night, throbbing currents rushed and returned incessantly like its life's blood. Crowds of people and mountains of goods, departing and arriving scores upon scores of times in every four-and-twenty hours, producing a fermentation in the place that was always in action. The very houses seemed disposed to pack up and take trip.

These words of Dickens, although written so long ago, still resonate with his fascination and understanding of the revolution that was taking place before his very eyes and in which the railway was such a vital and dominating factor.

VICTORIA STATION IN VICTORIAN DAYS

Victoria Station opened to the public on the morning of 1 October 1860. Unusually for what, even then, was clearly a station of importance, no official ceremony accompanied the occasion. It was also unusual in that the company that owned the station and its approaches operated no trains.

Ever since the dawn of the railway age in London, companies approaching the capital from the south had wanted to obtain a foothold on the north side of the Thames and build a station in the West End. Clearly with this in mind, the LB&SCR built a station called 'Pimlico'. It opened for traffic on 29 March 1858. The name and the location were odd because the station was situated in Battersea on the Surrey side which, then and now, could hardly be described as part of the West End. Pimlico, of course, is a district north of the river. Having said that, the 'Pimlico' station was only seen as a temporary expedient while the question of a bridge across the river was being explored.

On 23 July 1858, the 'Victoria Station and Pimlico Railway Company' received authority to build a station near Victoria Street in the Westminster district as well as a line, necessarily on a bridge, from the existing LB&SCR Pimlico station and across the river. On the approach to the new station, use was going to be made of the course of the Grosvenor Canal. This had been built in 1725 for the Chelsea Waterworks Company in connection with their water supplies. It had been converted in 1824 for commercial purposes while still also providing a facility for the Waterworks Company. The bridge was built quickly, only a year elapsing between the commencement of construction work and the first train using the bridge on 9 June 1860. Traffic built up quickly and a widened bridge was opened in December 1866.

The Victoria station occupied a site of about 14 acres and from very early on was, in effect, two stations because the LC&DR also bought land for a station adjoining that of the LB&SCR. Trains of the GWR and the L&NWR also used Victoria gaining access via the West London and West London Extension Railways. Mixed gauge track was required to accommodate the Great Western trains, but broad-gauge trains only ran from 1863 to 1866. Other 'foreign' companies that operated into Victoria for a period were the Great Northern and Midland Railways.

The two parts of the station, the Brighton and Chatham, were not built as a whole and the station lacked a sense of unity, with most of its facilities duplicated. Major rebuilding was carried out at the turn of the century which considerably improved the station but did not totally eradicate this duality.

The Grosvenor Hotel, built 1860-1 and aimed at the upper end of the hospitality market, was an integral part of the complex although, perhaps strangely, it was not owned by either of the two main railway companies that shared the station.

HOLBORN VIADUCT

In 1866, the LC&DR started running trains across Blackfriars Bridge and through the City to connect with the Metropolitan Railway at Farringdon. In doing this, it provided the first connection through London connecting the railway systems on opposite sides of the Thames. A station named 'Ludgate Hill', was opened to serve to serve the City, but it quickly proved inadequate for the trains operated by the LC&DR, the MR, the GNR and the L&SWR which required its services. Numerous freight trains also used this route.

Ludgate Hill was a markedly feeble station compared with the imposing nearby Cannon Street Station of the hated rival, the SER. The site occupied by Ludgate Hill Station could not be extended and so the LC&DR decided to build a separate station close by and adjacent to Holborn Viaduct itself. This structure was completed in 1869 and bridged the valley of the River Fleet, helping to bring the City and the West End closer. Sixty-three dwellings were demolished for the building of the new station and 825 people were displaced.

The new 'Holborn Viaduct' station was at the end of a spur 241m long off the line to Farringdon. Six platform faces were provided. It opened on 2 March 1874 and among its services were main line trains from the south coast and east Kent which had divided at Herne Hill, one portion proceeding to Victoria for the West End and the other to Holborn Viaduct for the City. These latter tended to be patronised by wealthy City commuters travelling to and from their seaside homes in places like Margate and Ramsgate. The station also handled boat trains for Queenborough and Dover. A few local trains used Holborn Viaduct but to serve trains to and from Farringdon, two platforms were opened on the through line on 1 August 1874 and they were given the name 'Snow Hill' after a nearby street. In 1912 this facility was renamed 'Holborn Viaduct Low Level'.

To provide a dignified frontage to the street, a handsome six-storey hotel was opened in November 1877, although it was not operated by the LC&DR. In 1886 a small 'overspill' station just south of Ludgate Hill was opened and this was initially called 'St Pauls'. Changing traffic patterns reduced demand for the services using Holborn Viaduct and trains through the tunnel to Farringdon and to Moorgate respectively ceased running in 1908 and 1916. With the latter suspension, Holborn Viaduct Low Level closed.

The former deadly rivals, the LC&DR and the SER, came together in a working relationship as the South Eastern & Chatham Railway from January 1899 and Holborn Viaduct found itself increasingly cast in the role of a backwater with brief spurts of activity at rush hours, some parcels traffic and little else. In 1911 a census revealed 5,000 passengers a day using the station compared with 81,000 at Liverpool Street, for example. Holborn Viaduct was sliding into obscurity.

'FOREIGN' GOODS DEPOTS SOUTH OF THE THAMES

The larger railway companies of Victorian England were highly territorial. They devoted much time and effort to consolidating their fiefdoms but also took it upon themselves to engage in imperialistic forays into the territory of rival companies. This meant that there were some companies vying with each other for traffic that was finite in potential. One company might extrude a line into another's area for little better reason than to show that it could do it, even if there was no solid business case for such a line. There were many parts of London where lines were in competition with each other, but it would not be unreasonable to say that some companies were recognised as largely serving the area north of the Thames and others doing their business to the south.

The reality was not always as clear-cut. One of the intriguing features of the complex spaghetti of lines that was London's railway network was the agreement between companies of the 'you scratch my back and I'll scratch yours' sort where, not being in direct competition, they could come to arrangements of mutual benefit.

So it was that trains of the LB&SCR might be seen at the Great Western Railway's Paddington or a train of the GER would appear at the Midland Railway's St Pancras. The terms under which these arrangements were made included the extensive use of running powers and these were carefully laid down in legal terms.

Early railway development created two systems in London, one north of the river and the other south but necessity required links to be made and these were initially to be found in the West London Extension Railway of 1863 and the Metropolitan Railway extension south from Farringdon in 1866. Both of these connections saw a range of passenger services but, for present purposes, it was the goods traffic that crossed from north to south that is of interest, and this was dominated by the carriage of coal. Most of the coal destined for London was transported by the MR, the GNR and the L&NWR and it came largely from pits in the East Midlands and South Yorkshire. It is often forgotten that London in the Victorian era was Britain's major industrial centre and required huge supplies of coal as, of course, did the hearths of

London's homes. The three companies were not only in competition with each other but also taking on the coastal trade conveying coal down the east coast and into the Thames carrying the 'black gold' from pits in Durham and Northumberland. It was in the interest of these companies based north of the river to gain easy access to the market represented by London south of the river. It was therefore also in their interest to make mutually beneficial arrangements with railway companies largely associated with territory south of the river. So it was that goods trains headed by the 'northern' companies could be seem running around places as solidly 'south London' as Clapham Junction, Brixton and Peckham.

In 1864, the GNR provided £300,000 for the impecunious LC&DR to assist it completing its Metropolitan extension. In return it received, among other benefits, the right to establish goods and coal depots south of the river within about fifteen miles of Ludgate Hill. The GNR established a coal depot near Elephant & Castle which was handy for serving the growing housing in the area. By 1873, as many as five dedicated trains were running daily to this depot.

In 1871 the Midland opened a depot of its own not far away at Walworth Road also gaining access over the metals of the Metropolitan and the LC&DR and in 1873 this was being served by no fewer than six trains daily. It is worth mentioning that there were limitations on the length of the trains that could be handled via Farringdon. At Brixton, just over two miles away, the LC&DR built a coal depot which it then leased to the Midland and this began operations in 1876. The Midland had a third depot at Wandsworth Road, opened in 1874, also served by the London, Chatham & Dover.

The L&NWR had a depot at Falcon Lane, opened in 1869 and near Clapham Junction. This was on the West London Extension Railway of which the GWR, the LB&SCR, L&NWR and L&SWR were partners. As London grew outwards, patterns of demand shifted and the L&NWR opened a depot at Knights Hill deep into LB&SCR territory between Tulse Hill and North Dulwich. Another depot was an anomaly because it was a rare example of the Midland and L&NWR working together. It was at Peckham Rye on the metals of the LB&SCR and opened in 1891. Two depots could be found in proximity but on either side of the LC&DR's obscure branch from Nunhead to Greenwich Park, at Brockley Lane. One belonged to the L&NWR, the other to the GNR.

In the early twentieth century, two other 'foreign' companies obtained a foothold south of the Thames. They were the GER opening a depot on the LB&SCR at New Cross in 1904, and the GWR at Battersea. It was opened fully on 1 January 1913. This handled large amounts of general merchandise as well as coal and indeed some of those depots mentioned while largely engaged in the coal trade, did also service quantities of ordinary goods traffic.

We know that there were people who followed railways as an interest and a hobby right from their earliest days. For those enthusiasts who knew a little but not a lot, it must have come as a surprise to see notices in deepest South London announcing the presence of a depot of such 'foreign' companies largely associated with parts of the country far away. Equally eye-catching must have been the sight of a GNR locomotive, for example, in deepest South London.

THE LONDON EXTENSION OF THE GREAT CENTRAL RAILWAY

The Manchester, Sheffield & Lincolnshire Railway (MS&LR) was very definitely a provincial railway with lines stretching from North Wales and South Lancashire into the West Riding of Yorkshire and North Lincolnshire. It conveyed vast amounts of coal. It was a workaday railway. It was mockingly known as 'The Money Sunk and Lost' but it really did quite well.

While it was not true that all of England's railways converged on London, it was the aspiration and the achievement of many of the more prominent ones to establish a foothold in the capital. Clearly a wish to break out of the provincial mould was entertained by the MS&LR, given unfruitful discussions that were held around 1873. These consisted of a dialogue with the Midland Railway, the outcome of which was intended to be the construction of lines that would have given the MS&LR running powers towards London from Rushton in Northamptonshire. Defeated but unbowed, in 1889 the MS&LR obtained powers for an extension from Sheffield, south to Annesley, just north of Nottingham. This was a statement of intent, and it was clear that the company was bent on forging its own independent approach to London. The inspiration for this came from the thrusting ambition of Edward Watkin, a buccaneering railway promoter who already had a finger in numerous

railway pies and had a vision of a high-standard main line from traditional MS&LR territory through the heart of the Midlands to a terminus in London. If this was not ambitious enough itself, Watkin envisaged the possibility of this line linking up with the Metropolitan, East London and South Eastern

Sir Edward Watkin (1819-1901) was one of the most thrusting and rapacious of Victorian railway entrepreneurs. His dream was for a direct line from the North of England through the Midlands, London, Kent and a tunnel under the English Channel directly to a variety of destinations in Europe. He was deeply involved with the Metropolitan, South Eastern and Great Central Railways and therefore a man of great influence in London's railways. (Unattributed picture from Author's own collection)

Railways, in all of which Watkin had major influence, to provide a route through to Dover and, via a tunnel under the Channel, to Paris and perhaps elsewhere on the European Continent. In the face of many doubters, a superbly engineered line was built south from Annesley through Nottingham, Leicester and Rugby to join up with the Metropolitan at Quainton Road in Buckinghamshire, making joint use of its metals to the Harrow area before a short independent section took the line into the terminus in the Marylebone area. The Bill for the 'London Extension' was received on 28 March 1893. Indicative of its aspirations and of what it was about to achieve, the MS&LR renamed itself the 'Great Central Railway' in 1897.

While the London Extension had a ruling gradient of 1 in 176 and was laid out for high speed, the section of the line shared with Metropolitan Railway trains was plagued with sharp curves and severe gradients. The final stretch of the GCR into Marylebone presented many ticklish engineering problems because parts of it penetrated areas containing the homes of the wealthy and the holy of holies in the Lord's Cricket ground of the Marylebone Cricket Club. Tunnels and covered ways were built to placate the residents of influence. Land containing an orphanage was bought. The orphanage was demolished and relocated to Hertfordshire. The land on which it had stood was presented to the MCC as a practice ground in exchange for the inconvenience to which its members of the 'great and good' had been put. Much poor-quality working-class housing had to be demolished and there was some requirement for the GCR to re-house at least some of those displaced. This resulted in the erection of six five-storey tenement blocks, named Wharncliffe Gardens, to provide accommodation for 2,690 people who lost their homes. About 1,700 other people who lost their homes because of the building of the GCR were left to fend for themselves in the finding of new accommodation.

All this had cost the financially challenged GCR a great deal of money and there was no money left over for a grand London terminus. Instead, a rather cute little terminal was built, reminiscent perhaps of a terminus of a secondary line in some provincial cathedral city. Land was acquired for a total of ten platforms but only four were ever needed and the station never 'grew up'. It opened on 15 March 1899 and the first departure left with just four passengers on board. Although traffic did build up, passenger numbers continued to be modest even though the trains were well appointed and comfortable although certainly not particularly fast.

Marylebone had an air of unhurried serenity that was not matched by London's other termini serving long-distance routes. In John Betjeman's immortal words, 'On the street side it looks like a branch public library in a Manchester suburb.' No wonder wags coined the phrase 'Gone Completely' to mock the Great Central!

The frontage of the station was formed of a glazed iron porte cochere stretching across Melcombe Square to provide access to the Hotel Great Central otherwise known as the Great Central Hotel. This opened for business shortly after the station itself opened. It contained 700 bedrooms, had a palm court and, according to some sources and denied by others, a cycle track on the roof. It somehow typified the GCR's impoverished state that while it was obviously closely associated with Marylebone station and the GCR, the hotel was built and run independently.

THE RAILWAY OFFICES OF LONDON

All the main line railway companies that served London not only had their termini but also ran offices in various parts of central London. They were sometimes known as 'booking' or 'forwarding offices'. They brought their businesses nearer to the potential customers and with their offices often located in prominent parts of the capital they reminded the public that they served London even if their actual passenger or goods stations were some distance away. They functioned as booking and enquiry offices for both passenger and goods services and they received parcels which were then forwarded to the companies' main line stations and depots.

These local railway offices were often only the size of small shops with half-a-dozen staff while the largest would have storage space, a loading bay and stables for horses and accommodation for wagons. They tended to be concentrated in the City and the West End where business activity was most intensive, and many were located in former coaching inns. The largest number of these offices were operated by the L&NWR with the Midland and Great Northern close behind in terms of numbers, these all being companies that connected London with places to the north. The Great Western was the first company to make use of these facilities and eventually ran twenty-six offices.

The number of these establishments fell rapidly after the First World War, being rendered surplus to requirements through the growing use of motor transport, telephones and various economic and social changes.

THE RAILWAY CLEARING HOUSE

Before the grouping of Britain's railways after the First World War, the large number of railway companies meant that it became essential to find ways to apportion the appropriate amount of revenue from money received for a passenger journey or the transit of any other kind of consignment where two or more railway companies were involved. It was also necessary to provide a system of classifying for revenue purposes the vast range of different kinds of merchandise which the railway, by law, was required to handle. The main function of the Railway Clearing House was the settling of inter-company accounts, but it came to provide a variety of other useful services. The Railway Clearing House was set up in 1842 at a time of rapid railway development.

It should be remembered that Britain's railways were promoted in a spirit of so-called free enterprise, the origins of the early ones such as the Liverpool & Manchester or the London & Birmingham being to make money for their investors by primarily serving the industrial and commercial interests of the places mentioned. This degree of local initiative and the political economy of the time precluded government intervention to ensure the creation of a national system of railways serving the needs of the country holistically. The consequent proliferation of railway companies meant that there were transhipment problems when traffic needed to be exchanged between the lines of different companies. There developed a vast and increasingly bewildering variety of freight classification and charging structures. A passenger requiring travel from, say, Truro to Tynemouth, might traverse the lines of half a dozen or more companies and be required to rebook several times en route. Some companies refused to allow the rolling stock of other companies to run on their tracks. It was very messy. A means was needed to bring about some semblance of sanity and system.

A clearing house already existed in the banking industry, and it was a banker with railway interests, Carr Glyn, who took a lead in the development of a similar facility for the railways. The start of the Railway Clearing House (RCH) was distinctly modest with a handful of employees based in Drummond Street near Euston Station. Although the services it offered only caught on slowly, by 1913 the RCH occupied a large building also close to Euston and it had 2,500 employees.

The RCH was always a voluntary organisation but by 1870 companies operating nearly 95 per cent of the railway network were using its services. Although there was no statutory authority for its services, most railway companies found it greatly advantageous to avail themselves of its provision. The creation of the nationalised British Railways after the Second World War largely rendered its services redundant.

BROAD STREET STATION

London could justifiably be said to been overprovided with large railway termini. Most of them have survived into the twenty-first century but one which closed in 1986 and is now largely forgotten is Broad Street. This station was ideally placed for the City and in the Edwardian period it handled almost as many trains and passengers as London Bridge or Victoria.

Broad Street is associated with the NLR which originated as the East & West India Docks & Birmingham Junction Railway. This was an important link by which the London & Birmingham (later L&NWR) extruded a line eastwards from Chalk Farm to Poplar and the London docks. Completed in 1851, it carried immense amounts of freight to and from the docks and the manufacturing districts in the provinces. The name of the company was changed to the North London Railway in 1853. The London & North Western invested heavily in the NLR and the two were always closely associated although the NLR was always a lusty infant.

Although it enjoyed a profitable existence as the conduit for all this freight, the NLR was also a passenger railway and the first terminus for its services was at the Fenchurch Street Station of the London & Blackwall Railway which was reached by a very roundabout route through London's inner north-eastern suburbs. Traffic built up to the extent that the facilities at Fenchurch Street became greatly overstretched. To obviate the lengthy and inconvenient distance this facility required, the NLR took the bold step of building a station more convenient for the City in Liverpool Street adjacent to and at a higher level than the GER's Liverpool Street Station, opened in 1874. The building of the branch into Broad Street station (the City Extension) was very costly and a large, grandiose but unprepossessing station was built with the L&NWR sharing the cost since it intended to use a part of the station for its own services. The station had the appearance and all the accoutrements of a main line terminus and indeed was one for a short time. The station opened in 1865. Soon afterwards, NLR trains stopped running into Fenchurch Street.

By 1913 there were nine passenger platforms dealing with at least ten departures hourly with more at peak times. In 1874/5 a connection was made with the GNR which provided access to and from places in Middlesex and parts of Hertfordshire, as distant as Hatfield. Trains from these places began running into Broad Street, giving some relief to the GNR's congested lines into King's Cross. The trains were operated by the NLR with the Great Northern paying a fixed sum per train mile. The long-distance main line services alluded to above were short-lived. They were introduced in 1910 and were an enterprising venture aimed at City businessmen for whom time was money. The 'City to City Express' ran from Wolverhampton and Birmingham and carried a 'lady typewriter' who provided secretarial services en route. These trains were curtailed in the First World War and never resumed.

The L&NWR built an extensive goods station at the side of and below the passenger station at Broad Street and in its heyday this was also extremely busy because there was still much manufacturing industry to be found around this part of London.

Here, in the 1890s, was an imposing terminus in the heart of the City handling heavy traffic and with every appearance of prosperity but by about 1900 there were ominous signs of change. Although the station was convenient for City workers, it was inconvenient for other parts of London, especially the West End. Additionally, the routes to Broad Street were somewhat indirect. Improved services on rival radial lines, especially the District Railway, not only to the City but to the West End, were abstracting traffic from places on London's periphery. An even more potent threat was posed by the spread of electric tramways providing more direct, more frequent and cheaper transport into the fringe of inner London from the suburbs through which the NLR passed. In the years immediately before 1914, motor buses started providing robust competition. In the 1900s further damage was inflicted by the opening of tube stations serving districts such as Camden Town, Kentish Town and Hampstead and providing fast links to parts of central London for access to which there was rising demand. It did not help that the NLR developed an unenviable reputation for the uncomfortable ride provided by its aged passenger rolling stock.

The London & North Western took over the management of the NLR in 1909 at a time when passenger traffic was being lost. It was thought that electrification of the former NLR lines might bring about a transformation of its fortunes and plans were outlined for a third rail system, but this was delayed by the onset of the First World War.

Although Broad Street hung on, increasingly tenuously, into the 1980s, it encapsulated in a particularly intense form the way in which wider economic and social change plus innovations and improvements in urban transport could, in a relatively short time, render established and lucrative railway operations increasingly outdated.

A GHOST OF THE UNDERGROUND

Covent Garden Underground Station opened on 11 April 1907, four months after the start of public services on what was then the Great Northern, Piccadilly & Brompton Railway, later thankfully shortened to the Piccadilly Line. The station is easily distinguishable as one of those designed by Leslie Green and it has his trademark dark red or 'oxblood' tiling on the façade. It lies between Holborn and Leicester Square Stations and is notable because the distance between it and Leicester Square provides the shortest interstation journey on the entire Underground system. Now heaving with tourists, Covent Garden, like so many other London districts, has seen immense changes and at one time it contained a convent from which the area took its name, albeit with a minor change of name.

Between 1832 and 1879, Dr John Cumming was a local clergyman who attracted large congregations because of his hellfire sermons and his apocalyptic predictions that the world was about to end. A great entertainer who may even have believed his own rhetoric, many things attracted his wrath, amongst them being underground railways. In 1860, presumably in relation to the future Metropolitan Railway, he thundered, '… the forthcoming end of the world will be hastened by the construction of railways burrowing into infernal regions and thereby disturbing the Devil.'

Covent Garden had long had associations with the world of the theatre. Close by is the Theatre Royal, which was established in 1660. Others followed. The nearby theatres provide the scenario for one of the best-known ghosts associated with the London Underground, that of the actor whose stage name was William Terriss. Greatly popular, he was a master of the dramatic arts and was extremely dapper, commonly sporting trademark white gloves and cape. His everyday routine included visiting the bakery that used to stand on the site of the existing underground station. Although the station was not built until eight years after his murder, he kept coming back to the site of the dastardly deed and it is clear that although he was appreciated by his audiences, he had enemies who envied him for his success. One such was Richard Archer Prince. His inability to win much work seems to have caused him to become mentally unstable and he became known as 'Mad Archer'.

On 16 December 1897, totally destitute and at his wit's end, Prince stabbed Terriss, inflicting mortal injuries outside the Adephi Theatre where the latter was currently appearing. Charged with murder, the jury found him guilty but unfit to plead and he was consigned to Broadmoor.

Price was despatched to the high security hospital but there are those who say that the ghost of the murdered Terriss decided to stick around in the district he knew so well. An apparition has been reported on numerous occasions in the theatre, accompanied by strange noises, lights going on and off inexplicably and disembodied footsteps. At the station, site of his favourite bakery, several staff over the years claim to have witnessed similarly inexplicable phenomena, often after the station has closed for the night.

Chapter 11

LONDON'S RAILWAYS IN THE EDWARDIAN ERA

A feature of nineteenth century London was the extension of the continuously built-up area outwards which meant the growth of suburbs with the resident population of the inner area declining and an increasing delineation of residential areas based on the income of the residents. Demand for public transport increased because of this and a significant fall in prices from the 1870s to the 1890s meant a rise in real wages with people wanting and being able to pay for the services of an expanded public transport system. Commuting increased and so did 'off-peak travel' as consumers sought out a huge range of new retail outlets especially in the West End. Gradual reductions in the working week combined with spare cash also meant that people travelled to enjoy the increasing leisure facilities becoming available, many of them highly capitalised. It is easy to overlook the fact that London was Britain's leading industrial district as well as its largest conurbation and, as such, exerted a huge influence on economic activity in the provinces. Industrial and domestic consumers provided an almost insatiable demand for coal, for example, and companies like the Midland, the Great Northern and the Great Eastern in conjunction with the Great Northern, and the Great Western to a lesser extent, devoted massive resources to satisfying this demand. On occasions, loaded coal trains stood nose to tail on the approaches to London waiting for access to marshalling yards for sorting and distribution purposes.

Nine major railway companies served London, three of which were leading national players. They were the GWR, the MR and the L&NWR who between them controlled over 35 per cent of the national railway network. None of these companies could really be described as 'London railways'. The Midland resolutely maintained its headquarters at Derby and all three did the bulk of their business in the provinces. However, the business potential of London was a crucial factor in their activity and their premier express passenger services as well as many of their other activities were oriented towards serving London such was its national economic and social domination. The three shared a certain disdain for the provision of suburban services which meant that Paddington, St Pancras and Euston may have had impressive long-distance services but not the sheer numbers of trains, mostly short haul, that were a feature of stations such as Liverpool Street, Waterloo, London Bridge and Victoria.

The six other main line companies were all considerably smaller while still being significant operators and they were: the GER; L&SWR; Great Northern; Great Central, the South Eastern & Chatham and the LB&SCR. The GER operated intensive suburban services and longer-distance facilities to various locations in Essex, Hertfordshire, Cambridgeshire and East Anglia. The L&SWR ran to Portsmouth, Southampton and counties like Wiltshire, Dorset, Devon and Cornwall. The GNR served Lincolnshire, the east Midlands and South and West Yorkshire while the GCR, the latecomer, was primarily a company operating in a belt from south Lancashire through parts of the West Riding and across to north Humberside. It only became involved with London when at the late date of 1899 it opened its extension from Sheffield through Nottingham and Leicester to Marylebone. The South Eastern & Chatham had most of its network in Kent and the LB&SCR operated largely in Sussex. These two companies were rivals in some parts of the south-east and in competition for cross-channel business.

A few other companies could justifiably be described as London railway companies. First there were those we think of as 'underground' operators. These were the Metropolitan which was a curious concern almost having pretensions to be a main line company and extruding tendrils out into distant and deeply rural parts of Buckinghamshire. The Metropolitan District shared the working of the Circle Line with the Metropolitan and like it had rolling stock built to main line structure gauge. Where its trains ran underground, they did so mostly on the 'cut-and-cover' principle. The London Electric Railways operated deep level tubes which later evolved into the familiar Northern, Bakerloo and Piccadilly Lines. Other deep level operators were the City & South London which later became the City Branch of the Northern Line, and the Central London Railway. The two other companies were the North London which was a subsidiary of the L&NWR and the LT&SR. The former had a small but busy and rather curiously-shaped network around north and north-west London. The LT&SR did what it said on the tin and never seems to have had pretensions to do anything more. It was taken over by the Midland Railway in 1912. In Broad Street and Fenchurch Street respectively, these two latter companies had stations which were among the more obscure of London termini while handling quantities of passengers many city stations in the provinces could only dream about. When it came to passenger comfort and facilities at least on its long-distance trains, the Midland set a standard which others tried to emulate but had not really succeeded by this time. Short-haul passenger accommodation provided by most companies varied from the austere to the downright awful. The close-coupled sets of carriages employed by the NLR and the GER, for example, packed their woebegone and long-suffering passengers in like the contents of sardine cans. These carriages lacked heating and much in the way of lighting and were based on the compartment principle.

In raw figures, the Midland, the Great Western, the Metropolitan District and the Metropolitan in that order handled the largest number of passengers but comparing the figures of the two main line companies with the two London-based ones is hardly appropriate given the very different nature of their passenger-carrying operations. In the movement of freight, the GWR, the L&NWR and the MR dominated. Again, figures by themselves do not necessarily provide very useful insights. The NLR carried extremely heavy freight traffic because it acted as a conduit for traffic to and from the London docks. These trains were operated by other companies over North London metals and the tonnage statistics are credited to them rather than the NLR itself. This tonnage greatly exceeded that which the NLR generated on its own right which was not inconsiderable. Even lines like the Metropolitan, later to be inextricably linked with passenger traffic, doing so much to open up 'Metroland',

There is nothing new about chaos on stations and overcrowded trains. This is the Christmas rush in the early days of Bishopsgate Station. Victorian travellers seem overburdened with luggage. This station was replaced by Liverpool Street in 1875.

carried healthy freight traffic. Coal was carried to gas works and for domestic use while much of the building material used for suburban housebuilding went by rail and there was even dairy produce from the Vale of Aylesbury.

The British railway network reached its apogee in the 1900s by which time it was beginning to experience serious competition in large urban areas especially from electric trams and, from 1910 in London, the flimsy-looking but highly successful 'B-Type' motor bus. In the Metropolis there were isolated closures of inner-city stations during that decade, a process which speeded up markedly during the First World War when 'temporary' closures, ostensibly because of staff shortages, often ended up becoming permanent. London by 1914 had a railway network of baffling complexity but one which has never really stabilised.

London was served by all four of the major businesses into which the large number of previous smaller companies were consolidated in 1923. This 'Big Four' faced a set of serious, even threatening, challenges in the years that followed, but it did so drained of resources because of the war effort. In their operational activity, equipment, management practices and general ethos the railways were still largely in the thrall of the Victorian past. It was an uncomfortable necessity to face up to the

A Drummond 'T14' Class 4-6-0 heading through the outskirts of London on an express for the West of England. These locomotives introduced in 1911 were impressive-looking machines and were nicknamed 'Paddleboxes'. They underwent modifications but they never lived up to their imposing appearance. (Courtesy of John Scott Morgan)

Railways were often the target of humour in the nineteenth century. Not all of it was as good-natured as this cartoon titled 'Reading between the Lines'.

London saw immense public works taking place in the Victorian period. This is suggested in this rather inaccurate cross-section with Charing Cross Station in the background above the District and Metropolitan underground lines, part of Bazalgette's radical new system of sewers, and the Embankment. Railways contributed greatly to London becoming a modern civilised place in which to live, at least for many of its inhabitants.

fact that so much that was familiar needed to be jettisoned and so much that was new had to be absorbed and become common practice.

How the railways of London faced up to the demands posed by the inter-war years and the following decades, is a fascinating story ably told in a number of excellent studies.

BIBLIOGRAPHY

Badsey-Ellis, A., *The Birth of the Tubes*, Capital Transport, 2019

Barker, F. & Hyde, R., *London as it might have been*, John Murray, 1982

Barker, T.C. & Robbins, M., *A History of London Transport, Vol. 1*, George Allen & Unwin, 1975

Betjeman, J. & Gay, J., *London's Historic Railway Stations*, John Murray, 1972

Biddle, G., *Victorian Stations, Railway Stations of England & Wales 1830-1923*, David & Charles, 1973

Binney, M. & Pearce, D., *Railway Architecture*, Bloomsbury, 1979

Brandon, D. & Brooke, A., *Blood on the Tracks, A History of Railway Crime*, The History Press, 2010

Brindle, S., *Paddington Station. Its History & Architecture*, English Heritage, 2004

Brown, J., *London Railway Atlas*, Ist edition, Ian Allan, 2006

Carter, E., *An Historical Geography of the Railways of the British Isles*, Cassell, 1959

Clayton, A., *Subterranean City, Beneath the Streets of London*, Historical Publications, 2000

Course, E., *London's Railways*, Batsford, 1962

Croome, D.F. & Jackson, A.A. *Rails through the Clay*, 2nd edition, Capital Transport, 1990

Day, J.R. & Reed, J., *The Story of London's Underground*, Capital Transport, 2005

De Mare, E., *The London Doré Saw*, Allan Lane, 1973

Douglas, H., *The Underground Story*, Robert Hale, 1963

Dyos, H.J. & Wolff, M., *The Victorian City. Images and Realities, Vol 2*, RKP, 1973

Ellis, C. Hamilton, *Railway Art*, Ash & Grant, 1977

Evans, A.H.B. & Gough, J.V. (Eds), *The Impact of the Railway on Society in Britain*, Ashgate, 2000

Freeman, M., *Railways in the Victorian Imagination*, Yale University Press, 1999

Gray, A., *Crime on the Line*, Atlantic Publishers, 2000

Green, O., *London's Underground. The Story of the Tube*, Frances Lincoln, 2023

Halliday, S., *Making the Metropolis. 1815-1914, Creators of Victoria's London*, Breedon, 2003

Halliday, S., *Underground to Everywhere, London Underground's Railway in the History of The Capital*, Sutton Publishing, 2001

Hodge, P., *The Steam and the Gaslight. Travelling by Train in late Victorian London*, Melrose. 2010

Jackson, A.A., *London's Local Railways*, 2nd edition, Capital Transport, 1999

Jackson, A.A., *London's Termini*, 2nd edition, David & Charles, 1985

Jones, G Steadman, *Outcast London. A Study in the Relationship between Classes in Victorian Society.* Peregrine, 1984.

Kellett, J.R., *Railways & Victorian Cities,* RKP, 1969

Klapper, C., *London's Lost Railways,* RKP, 1976

Lascelles, T.S., *The City and South London Railway,* Oakwood, 1987

Leboff, D., *The Underground Stations of Leslie Green,* Capital Transport. 2002

Olsen, D.J., *The Growth of Victorian London,* Batsford, 1976

Piper, D., *Artists' London,* OUP, 1982

Porter, R., *London. A Social History,* Ist edition, Hamish Hamilton, 1994

Richards, J. & McKenzie, J., *The Railway Station. A Social History,* OUP, 1986

Scholey, K., *London's Great Railway Century 1850-1950.* The History Press, 2012

Sheppard, F., *The History of London. London 1808-1870: The Infernal Wen,* Secker & Warburg, 1971

Sidney, S., *Rides on Railways,* (Ed. B.Trinder), Phillimore, 1973

Simmons, J., *St Pancras Station,* George Allen & Unwin, 1968

Simmons, J., *The Railway in Town & Country 1830-1914,* David & Charles, 1986

Simmons, J., *The Victorian Railway,* Thames & Hudson, 1991

Smith, G.R., *Old Euston,* Country Life, 1938

Smullen, I., *Taken for a Ride. A Distressing Account of the Misfortunes and Misbehaviour of the Early British Railway Travel,* Herbert Jenkins,1968

Taylor, S., *The Moving Metropolis. A History of London's Transport since 1800,* Lawrence King, 2001

Thomas, R.H.G., *London's First Railway: The London & Greenwich,* Batsford, 1972

Trench, R. & Hillman, E., *London under London. A Subterranean Guide,* John Murray, 1985

Weightman, G. & Humphries, S., *The Making of Modern London, 1815-1914,* London, 1983

White, H.P., *A Regional History of the Railways of Great Britain. Vol 3: Greater London,* 3rd edition, David & Charles, 1987

White, J., *London in the Nineteenth Century,* Ebury, 2007

Wolmar, C., *The Subterranean Railway. How the London Underground was built and how it changed the City forever,* Atlantic Books, 2004

SAMPLE WEBSITES

https://www.thehistoryoflondon.co.uk

http://mikesrailwayhistory.railfan.net

http://www.nlrhs.org.uk

https://historyhouse.co.uk

https://tfl.gov.uk

https://www.networkrail.co.uk

https://www.british-history.ac.uk

https://londonlist.com

https://www.londonrailwayrecord

INDEX